Puerto Ricans at the Dawn of the New Millennium

Edited by Edwin Meléndez and Carlos Vargas-Ramos

D0255303

CENTRO de Estudios Puertorriqueños

HUNTER **CU NY** The City University of New York

Copyright © 2014 by Center for Puerto Rican Studies. All rights reserved.
No part of this publication may be reproduced, distributed, or transmitted in any form or by any means, including photocopying, recording, or other electronic or mechanical methods, without the prior written permission of the publisher, except in the case of brief quotations embodied in critical reviews and certain other noncommercial uses permitted by copyright law.

Library of Congress Cataloging-in-Publication Data

Puerto Ricans at the dawn of the new millennium / edited by Edwin Meléndez and Carlos Vargas-Ramos.
    pages cm
  Summary: "This work collects the most current data on social, economic, and civic conditions of the Puerto Rican population in the United States available from governmental sources, mostly from the U.S. Census Bureau. It presents a picture of endurance and resiliency in the midst of declining opportunities"—Provided by publisher.
  Includes bibliographical references and index.
  ISBN 978-1-878483-88-1 (paperback : acid-free paper) — ISBN: 978-1-878483-89-8 (ebook)
  1. Puerto Ricans—United States—Social conditions—Statistics. 2. Puerto Ricans—United States—Economic conditions—Statistics. 3. Puerto Ricans—United States—Politics and government±Statistics. I. Meléndez, Edwin. II. Vargas-Ramos, Carlos.

E184.P85P825 2013
305.868'7295073—dc23

                        2013037540

Published by
Center for Puerto Rican Studies
Hunter College, CUNY
695 Park Avenue, E-1429
New York, NY 10065
centrops@hunter.cuny.edu
http://centropr.hunter.cuny.edu

Cover art: Néstor Otero.
Art Direction: Kenneth Kaiser
Printed in the United States of America on acid-free paper.

TABLE OF CONTENTS

INTRODUCTION

PUERTO RICANS AT THE DAWN OF THE NEW MILLENNIUM

EDWIN MELÉNDEZ and CARLOS VARGAS-RAMOS

The demographic and socioeconomic profile of Puerto Ricans at this early point in the New Millennium is dramatically different from what it was just a decade ago. To begin with, consider the fact that equal numbers of Puerto Ricans, 3.8 million, lived stateside and on the island in 2003.[1] However, by 2012, the most recent year for which data are available, there are 4,970,604 Puerto Ricans living stateside and 3,515,844 million Puerto Ricans residing on the island, representing a population swing of nearly 1.5 million over nearly a decade.

Such a population swing constitutes a migration wave to rival the magnitude of what is known in the literature as the "Great Migration" of Puerto Ricans to the United States during the 1950s. Fueled by the collapse of the Puerto Rican economy and the inability of the political establishment to stabilize the fiscal crisis and reduce crime and violence, an extraordinary wave of migration from Puerto Rico to the United States has changed the landscape. If these patterns continue, by the end of the decade it is probable that two-thirds of Puerto Ricans will reside stateside.

Even as stateside Puerto Ricans became more numerous than those living on the island, a significant change in population settlement and dispersion has also transpired. The Puerto Rican population has grown in almost every state and region of the United States. Puerto Ricans now make up 9.4 percent of the total Hispanic population, and 1.6 percent of the country's total population. These changes warrant both our understanding of this transformation and the forging of fresh approaches and collective responses to the new challenges posed by these patterns.

Consider for instance that in the last decade over a million stateside Puerto Ricans migrated across state lines. This extraordinary rate of mobility is higher than the rate for the population of the United States as a whole or for any other major ethnic group. More stunning is the fact that this pattern of migratory behavior is fueled by movement among those born in the United States, not by island-born or recent migrants as one might speculate based on prior historical patterns. In fact, seven out of ten Puerto Ricans moving to another state during the last decade were born in the United States.

Consider also that the South, as a region, and Central Florida, in particular, are the main destinations of interstate movers and recent migrants. Though by now the reader of this essay is probably familiar with this trend, what is most significant and least known is the likelihood that in just a few years, more Puerto Ricans will live in Florida than in the state of New York, the historical entry port and traditional enclave of Puerto Ricans. Similarly, it is apparent that before long, the fast-growing Puerto Rican population in the South, West, and Midwest will outnumber Puerto Ricans in the Northeast.[2] When (not if) this event happens, it will mark a significant shift in the history of Puerto Ricans in the United States.

What explains such dramatic population swings? Related to these patterns of population movement and resettlement is the disproportionate impact of the Great Recession on Puerto Ricans on both the continent and the island. To ascertain the impact of the recession on stateside Puerto Ricans, Centro conducted a national survey[3] that included a sample of close to twelve hundred respondents, about 500 of whom were Puerto Rican. This proprietary data was combined with available public data from the American Community Survey (ACS) to construct a detailed profile of how the Puerto Rican community coped with the impact of the recession and how their responses compared with those of other racial or ethnic groups including non-Hispanic whites, non-Hispanic blacks and other Latinos. The findings from this study are revealing and begin to explain the observed migratory and interstate mobility patterns of stateside Puerto Ricans.

The Puerto Rican story is one of resiliency. This is a community that despite facing difficult challenges in finding employment and staving-off poverty has been especially proactive in taking steps to overcome dire circumstances. The narrative that emerges from our research is very different from that of past decades, which sought to explain economic disadvantage by so-called underclass behavior, lack of attachment to the labor markets, or the detrimental effects of migration. Our findings also challenge the portrayal of Puerto Ricans as lacking socioeconomic advancement compared with other "immigrant" groups.

Several years after the Great Recession officially ended, the effects are still palpable to the jobless and the poor and to those whose incomes have stagnated or who have taken lower-paying jobs. Yet the majority of Puerto Ricans have recovered faster and fared better in the aggregate than other ethnic groups. Puerto Ricans' resiliency is demonstrated by their seeking jobs wherever these were available, by taking training to improve skills and employability, by changing careers and occupations to accommodate employment demand, and in general, by deploying more strategies for improving competitiveness in the job market than other ethnic groups. As a result, though the earnings for full-time, year-round Puerto Rican workers remained basically stagnant between 2007 (the last business cycle peak year) and 2011, their relative standing improved compared with average earnings of workers in the United States or non-Hispanic white workers. Puerto Rican women have shown the most significant gains in earnings during this period, in both absolute and relative terms.

Yet a sizable portion of the Puerto Rican community is still caught in the trough of the recession like many others. Puerto Ricans continue to be overrepresented in the low-wage labor market and among the poor, lag behind in educational attainment, and have greater need for childcare in order to participate in the labor force than other groups. For this segment of the population resiliency is insufficient in the midst of declining opportunity. Despite tangible advances in electing representatives to state and local office and in having well-established community and professional leadership, these gains have not been translated into substantial improvement for those suffering adverse social circumstances.

In this volume, Centro researchers explain recent trends in socioeconomic conditions among stateside Puerto Ricans and their implications for the future. We have organized the volume into three sections covering the following topics: Population Movements and New Settlements; Education and Economic Opportunity after the Great Recession; and Old Problems, New Challenges. In this introduction, we use these headings to provide a general context for the discussion.

Population Movements and New Settlements

The 1950s are considered the period of the Great Migration, given that about half a million Puerto Ricans migrated to the United States (Vázquez Calzada 1988). However, it is likely that a much higher number of Puerto Ricans migrated to the United States in the 2000s.[4] For the first time under the jurisdiction of the United States, Puerto Rico experienced a net decline in population. Today, population figures show that 57 percent of Puerto Ricans reside in the states and only 43 percent on the island. This population surge from the island to the United States has had significant consequences for stateside Puerto Ricans.

Migration to and from the United States is an enduring element in the daily life of Puerto Ricans. Data from ACS and the Puerto Rico Community Survey (PRCS), available since 2001 and 2006, respectively, provide the opportunity to ascertain the social and economic characteristics of migrants moving to and from the island. With this data, it is now possible to create a detailed profile of recent migrants, exploring the factors that contribute to the decision to migrate and ascertaining their meaning for both stateside and island Puerto Ricans.

In the chapter titled "Puerto Rican Migration and the Brain Drain Dilemma," Kurt Birson presents a detailed profile of recent migrants. In general, the data indicate that recent migrants to the United States "tended to be younger, neither more or less educated, were more attached to the labor force, and consisted of more blue-collar workers compared to their counterparts that they had left behind." These findings are interesting because they challenge the prevalent view presented in the popular media in Puerto Rico of a "brain drain" of more educated and skilled workers from the island. Although the relatively small sample size precludes the analysis of detailed occupational categories, the data indicate that more educated and skilled workers in the "Management, Business, Science, Arts" category constitute 23 percent of migrants from the island to the United States, while they represent 30 percent of the labor force in Puerto Rico. Although women in this occupational category constitute 29 percent of female migrants, in parity with their island distribution, men in this category are grossly underrepresented in the migration outflow at 17 percent.

The educational attainment of migrants is consistent with the occupational pattern. Among those twenty-five years of age or older, individuals with bachelor's or graduate degrees were slightly underrepresented among migrants when compared with Puerto Rico's labor force. Those with graduate degrees represented 5 percent of migrants in comparison with 6 percent of Puerto Rico's labor force, while those with bachelor's degrees represented 15 percent of the flow versus 16 percent of the island's labor force.

It is also important to consider the data on the labor-force attachment of migrants. Despite high unemployment and a low labor-force participation rate in Puerto Rico, one year after arriving in the United States, Puerto Rican migrants showed a remarkable attachment to the labor force. Fifty-six percent of the migrants from the island were in the labor force, with 40 percent employed and 25 percent unemployed. These findings regarding the characteristics of recent migrants portray, to a large degree, an exodus that is representative of the island population and migrants who are mostly in search of employment and economic opportunity.

One of the most important findings reported in this volume is that between 2000 and 2011, a total of 1.2 million Puerto Ricans, equivalent to a quarter of the Puerto Rican mainland population, crossed from one state into another.[5] The continued dispersion of the Puerto Rican population throughout the country has come to characterize a new period in the history of Puerto Ricans in the United States. While the majority of Puerto Ricans are still concentrated in the Northeast, their concentration continues to increase in the South. New York is still the state with the most Puerto Ricans, with more than one million, but Florida is closely behind with nearly 850,000, and poised to take the lead by 2020. In the chapter titled "A Brief Look at Internal Migration of Puerto Ricans in the United States: 2001–2011," Centro researcher Juan García-Ellín analyzes the composition and main points of origin and destinations of these migratory flows. To our knowledge, this is the first time that data from over a decade of observations have been combined in an effort to analyze the internal migration of stateside Puerto Ricans. Who moves? Where do they go? Are they men or women, young or old, born in the United States or on the island, more or less educated?

García-Ellín finds that migration to the South and Northeast accounted for most of the population flow, with Florida receiving the greatest number of migrants. The South received about half of the total flow of internal migration (599,359), and Florida received about half of the flow to the South (283,045). For the most part, New York is the largest sending state to Florida, but also sends migrants to the neighboring states of New Jersey, Connecticut, and Pennsylvania. Florida receives migrants from these eastern states as well as Illinois. Overall, these migrants are slightly more educated than the stateside Puerto Rican population as a whole, with overrepresentation among those with some college education (32.3% of the flow compared with 27.6% of the population) and underrepresented among the least educated (20.8% of the flow have less than a high school degree compared with 26.6% of the population).

In "Puerto Ricans in Florida," Centro researcher Patricia Silver offers a unique case study of the contemporary stateside Puerto Rican experience. New Puerto Rican settlements in Florida are concentrated in the central region, while the smaller and older settlements are in Miami and South Florida. The origin of these communities can be traced to military service, land sales, and the opening of the Disney World complex in the early 1970s. Although the educational profile of Puerto Ricans in these areas is not different from those in other parts of the country, Florida's Puerto Rican households enjoy a slightly higher median income and lower poverty rates. In Central Florida, there is an even distribution of Puerto Ricans who were born in the United States and on the island. Even as Puerto Ricans in Florida have made some modest gains in political representation, they were energized by the 2012 Presidential election in which they voted in record numbers.

In another chapter entitled "New Puerto Rican Diasporas in the Southern United States," Silver dissects the magnitude of the flows and characteristics of migrants to the seven southern states that had over 10,000 Puerto Ricans in 2000 and that grew by over 10,000 Puerto Ricans from 2000 to 2010. Over the last decade, Florida has seen the largest growth in population with a gain of 365,000 to reach almost 850,000 as reported by the 2010 Census. The remaining settlements in the South are smaller in comparison. The second-largest settlement is in Texas, with about 131,000 in 2010. In the southern states with the largest population growth, Puerto Ricans generally have a better educational profile than stateside Puerto Ricans as a whole, although there are important differences between states. While in Florida and South Carolina, those with a bachelor's degree and above are about equally represented as they are among Puerto Ricans nationally, Puerto Ricans in Virginia have a sizable advantage in this category as well as among those with graduate and professional degrees. There also tends to be a smaller gap in median household income between Puerto Ricans and non-Hispanic whites in the southern states.

The Puerto Rican population in the South has experienced different socioeconomic dynamics from what has been reported in the literature about earlier settlements, and Silver concludes with suggestions for further research on Puerto Ricans in the the South. In contrast to early migrants to New York and settlements in other northern cities, contemporary migration to the South is relatively more scattered with lower concentrations of Puerto Ricans. The majority of Latinos in the region are of Mexican descent (or Cuban in Miami), and racial dynamics are tainted by the history of Jim Crow segregation. Furthermore, the mix of Puerto Ricans born and raised in the United States and recent arrivals from the island induces a different cultural experience. These racial and inter-ethnic dynamics offer a new complexity that is yet to be fully understood.

One of the critical questions posed by this surge in the number of Puerto Ricans moving to various areas across the country is whether or not increased population dispersion has led to greater social isolation. Centro researcher Carlos Vargas-Ramos uses the most common social science indicators to address the question, "Are Puerto Ricans More Segregated?" Using decennial census data, he found that the segregation of Puerto Ricans from non-Hispanic whites decreased markedly between 2000 and 2010 as measured by the dissimilarity index.[6] In 2000, nearly half (45%) of Puerto Ricans lived in the 26 counties identified as having high levels of segregation (i.e., with dissimilarity scores higher than .60). By 2010, this number dropped to about a third of Puerto Ricans who lived in the 20 counties identified as having high levels of segregation. In similar fashion, Puerto Ricans are mingling with other ethnic groups as they increasingly reside in areas that are also populated by blacks and non–Puerto Rican Latinos.

Education and Economic Opportunity After the Great Recession

According to the National Bureau of Economic Research, the recession that began in December of 2007 lasted until June of 2009. Yet, years after the Great Recession technically ended, many workers and working-class families are still experiencing its effects. In the chapter titled "Puerto Rican Economic Resiliency after the Great Recession," Kurt Birson and Edwin Meléndez use a unique survey conducted in 2012–2013 and one-year estimates of Census Bureau data from the ACS for 2007 through 2011 to analyze the impact of the recession and the strategies that workers have implemented to cope with economic adversity. In particular, they examine the longterm effects of the recession on the stateside Puerto Rican community compared with its effects on the major racial and ethnic groups within the United States—non-Hispanic whites, non-Hispanic blacks, and Latinos.

Puerto Ricans experienced the highest increase in unemployment in the labor force of the United States during the recession, from 6.1 percent in 2007 to 9.8 percent in 2011. Among the unemployed, the percentage of those who were undergoing longterm unemployment rose dramatically, from 30.7 percent in 2007 to 46.4 percent in 2011. Of course, the erosion of employment during the recession had an effect on poverty rates for Puerto Ricans. Two years after the recovery started, Puerto Rican poverty rates for all individuals remained three percentage points higher than in 2007, reaching 27.4 percent in 2011. For Puerto Rican children under 18 years of age, the poverty rate of 35.5 percent was among the highest of all other groups and twice that of non-Hispanic whites.

Despite the worsening employment indicators across the board for Puerto Ricans, mean earnings for full-time, year-round workers stayed about the same on average ($42,390 in 2007 compared with $42,351 in 2011); they actually improved 4 percent for Puerto Rican women, rising to $38,591 by 2011. Similarly, the overall ratio of .80 of Puerto Rican workers' earnings in 2011 to non-Hispanic whites' earnings was higher than the ratios for non-Hispanic blacks (.76) and for Latinos overall (.59). The earnings ratio improved slightly for Puerto Rican men over pre-recession levels, from 74.2 percent to 74.4 percent, but improved four percentage points from 83.8 percent to 88.0 percent for Puerto Rican women. This relative increase in the earnings ratios of Puerto Rican women compared with non-Hispanic white women was the result of a slight gain during the period for Puerto Rican women and a slight loss for non-Hispanic white women.

The data from the "Puerto Ricans and the Impact of the Recession" study suggest that Puerto Rican workers implemented a variety of strategies to improve their competitiveness in labor markets. Among the employed, they reported moving to find a job (26%), taking training for new skills (25%) or job hunting (17%), taking a job in a new field (24%), visiting career centers (13%), and using the Internet for job searching (36%) at a higher rate than all other ethnic groups. Furthermore, the evidence from various chapters in this volume documents the high internal mobility and migration from the island, which is primarily driven by efforts to gain employment.

These findings on the labor-market standing of Puerto Ricans two years after the recession ended are indicative of two different scenarios within the stateside Puerto Rican community. One group of workers suffered higher unemployment, often for long periods, while at the same time workers who remained employed year-round were not affected palpably by the recession and may have even experienced improvement in their labor-market standing. In general, a more proactive behavior in skills development and adaptability to tighter job markets led to better outcomes for workers coping with the recession.

One of the most significant paradigmatic changes in approaches to alleviating poverty over the last decades has come from the community development movement. The so-called asset-building approach proposes that the failure of anti-poverty strategies has been partly rooted in its focus on income rather than on asset development. Advocates of an asset-building approach claim that a focus on savings, investments in post-secondary education and training, and creating a nest egg for retirement, along with other strategies and programs that enable people with limited financial resources to accumulate longterm, productive assets, will have a greater impact on poverty alleviation.

In a novel study on the wealth gap among Latinos, using data from the Consumer Expenditure Survey for 2008, Birson, Borges-Méndez and Ampaabeng, found that two-thirds of Puerto Ricans are wealth poor and have the highest proportion of "negative wealth" (i.e., debt) or no assets relative to other Latino subgroups. These scholars found that in 2007:

> Puerto Ricans had the lowest mean net wealth of all Latino and non-Latino groups, standing at approximately $14,822. Mexicans had the highest mean net wealth among Latinos at $39,120. Non-Latinos had the highest mean net wealth at $91,191. (2014: 166)

Any approach to asset building within the Puerto Rican and overall Latino population has to start with the dramatic wealth gap that exists relative to non-Hispanic whites. At the heart of the problem is the fact that Puerto Ricans have the lowest mean assessed value for housing assets, the most important component of wealth, which accounts for 86 percent of all assets for the population as a whole. Housing assets for Puerto Ricans are primarily affected by extreme spatial segregation in low-value housing areas and very low incomes that impede conventional financing, especially in the Northeast where Puerto Ricans are still concentrated. Although home ownership and equity are critical when explaining wealth differences, the gap is the same for all types of assets, such as savings, cars, business ownership, retirement, stocks, bonds and other financial investments.

How workers fare in job markets and in accumulating wealth to cope with economic fluctuations are closely related to educational attainment, an area in which Puerto Ricans have made steady gains over the last decade. Between 2000 and 2011, the proportion of high school graduates increased 12 percentage points to .75, and the rate of completion for a bachelor's degree gained almost four percentage points to reach .16. Yet, paradoxically, disparities in relation to other groups have remained constant. Even more puzzling, disparities for Puerto Ricans residing in New York City and gender disparities are substantially higher across the educational attainment ladder. Enrollment in college or graduate school among Puerto Ricans and Latinos overall is about 10 percentage points lower than it is among non-Hispanic whites in New York State and in the country as a whole. The disparity is 16 percentage points in New York City, with 20.5 percent enrollment rates for Puerto Ricans compared with 36.4 percent for non-Hispanic whites.

In the chapter titled "Rebuilding the Puerto Rican Education Pipeline for a Multilingual and Multicultural Future," Centro researcher Luis Reyes presents an educational profile of Puerto Ricans in New York City, discusses the limitations of the civil rights framework embedded in current transitional bilingual education programs, and proposes a reform agenda that is culturally and linguistically appropriate for Puerto Rican and other Latino children. An education reform agenda that will benefit Puerto Rican children includes the recognition of bilingualism and the native language of children as a foundation for learning and school readiness, the engagement of parents and community organizations in school governance and partnerships, and the adoption of a rigorous curriculum.

Youth not at school or work are commonly referred to as "disconnected youth" in the academic literature and popular media. Research on disconnected youth portrays a population that is largely African American, male, and low-income. However, Puerto Ricans have as high an incidence of not being at work or school as African Americans and a higher rate than other Latinos. In the chapter titled "School, Work and the Transition of Puerto Rican Youth to Adulthood," Edwin Meléndez, M. Anne Visser, and Kurt Birson present a statistical profile of Puerto Rican youth ages 16 to 24, and discuss policies to benefit them.

Puerto Ricans have a rate of non-participation in school or work of 23 percent, similar to that of non-Hispanic blacks but almost double the rate of non-Hispanic whites and four points higher than the overall rate of 19 percent for Latinos. The rates of being not at school or work increase with age for all groups, but Puerto Ricans have the highest rates within each of the age cohorts. The proportion of Puerto Ricans who attend school and do not work is fairly similar to that of Latinos and non-Hispanic whites, suggesting that there is a core group among Puerto Rican youth who follow the idealized pattern of transitioning from high school into college enrollment or employment training. The chances of being out of work and school by age 24 are one in six for non-Hispanic whites, but one in three for Puerto Rican youth. The majority of youth ages 22 to 24 are entering the work force, yet a significant number of young Puerto Ricans reach this stage completely disconnected from school or work.

In sum, disparities in school enrollment and employment among Puerto Rican youth begin early, when entering high school, and grow throughout the transition to post-secondary education. These disparities, the authors suggest, are intricately related to educational attainment, and confirm a general finding in the literature that "disconnected youth" have less education than their counterparts (Bloom et al. 2010; Fernandes and Gabe 2009). The evidence presented in the chapter indicates that work and education are closely related in the transition to adulthood for many young people. The authors suggest that pathways programs combining education and workforce development could be especially beneficial to Puerto Rican youth (Visser and Meléndez 2011).

In a recent study, Centro researchers identified pathways programs preparing students for careers in growing fields—health services, green jobs, education, and social work—that are linked to degree-granting higher education institutions (De Jesús 2011; Mercado 2011; Torres-Vélez 2011). The findings from these studies call for greater integration of Puerto Rican community-based organizations into school and work youth programs. The challenge is for community leaders to engage employers and industry leaders in addressing the needs of Puerto Rican and other Latino youth.

Old Problems, New Challenges
It is evident that migration patterns are fueling significant population changes for stateside Puerto Ricans. In this volume, we take a closer look at the interdependence of the island's economy and migration. Over the years, Puerto Ricans in general and the government of Puerto Rico in particular have regarded migration as an escape valve for growing unemployment. In the early

1950s, when policies were developed to support the massive export of workers, migration was portrayed as having an additional benefit: return migrants, with enhanced skills and experience in growing industries and occupations, would spur the island's economic development. In essence, migration reduced unemployment and served as a training ground for workers.

Today economic circumstances have changed. Schools are closing for lack of students, new residential buildings are empty, commercial spaces remain vacant for years, pension funds are defunded, and the country's debt spirals out of control. All of these indicators point to a structural decline in aggregate demand in the economy, and no other factor contributes as much to this economic downfall as the sudden and severe decline in population primarily driven by migration. In a study for the Banco Popular of Puerto Rico,[7] Mario Marazzi-Santiago asserts:

> Annual population estimates for the last decade reveal that the population decline began in 2005, shortly before the current recession began in 2006. Between 2006 and 2010, population and real GDP decreased on average 0.5 and 1.8 percent every year, respectively. A decrease in population leads to fewer income earners, fewer consumers, and fewer taxpayers. More than a quarter of the decline in real GDP can be attributed to the decline in population since the average decline in population (0.5%) represents about 27 percent of the average decline in real GDP (1.8%). The impact on economic growth could have been even larger considering that outward migration has fueled the population decline and that more productive individuals are relatively more likely to migrate. (Progreso Económico 2012)

Given the state of the global economy, Puerto Rico is not alone. In a chapter titled "Lessons from the European Demographic Winter for Puerto Rico," demographer Alejandro Macarrón examines the effects of demographic changes on the economy and society of Puerto Rico. He discusses key lessons that Puerto Rico could learn from studying current demographic changes in Europe. Besides the impact of migration, Macarrón considers the impact of fertility rates dropping below replacement rates and of higher life expectancy. In many European countries fertility levels are below 2.1 children per woman and native populations are shrinking. This phenomenon is dubbed "demographic winter" by many, as the winter in Nordic latitudes of Eurasia and America is a season in which nature seems close to dead. Macarrón refers to this phenomenon as "demographic suicide" (Macarrón Larumbe 2011), because indefinite voluntary sub-replacement fertility would eventually lead to extinction of the population.

Macarrón proposes that the combination of demographic winter and high migration is "very challenging for the economic welfare, the quality of democracy and the richness of interaction in private lives." However, Europe has experienced this demographic winter phenomenon a few decades ahead of Puerto Rico and offers useful lessons to the island from the Old World. In the end, the fate of the island depends on policies to mitigate population loss, especially for keeping on the island—and attracting back to the island—young workers in the prime of their reproductive years.

Since World War II, military service has been one of the constant sources of employment, skills development, and work experience available to Puerto Rican youth both on the island and in the United States. Yet, although many studies have documented the contributions of Puerto Ricans to the military, especially during wars, to date there are very few studies examining military service as an industry that provides career advancement and opportunities as well as spatial mobility. Centro researcher Harry Franqui-Rivera examines those issues in a paper titled "The Well-being of Puerto Rican Veterans and Service Members and Their Place within the Diaspora."

Among the most interesting findings in Franqui-Rivera's paper is that military service and veteran status among Puerto Rican youth are contributing to the growth of communities around military bases and to the dispersion of Puerto Rican migrants. Puerto Rican military service has steadily increased since the first Gulf War and in subsequent wars after September 11, 2001. The surge in troops has led to a subsequent rise in the number of Puerto Rican military veterans. The rate of military participation among Puerto Ricans is higher than it is for the population as a whole, a clear departure from the pattern observed for other Latinos. Puerto Rican veterans enjoy higher median income and lower unemployment and poverty rates than the non-veteran population. In 2009, for example, the median income of island-side Puerto Rican female veterans was \$18,190 while for non-veteran females it was \$10,660; for male veterans it was \$18,926 compared with \$13,101 for non-veterans. For youth serving in the military, serving in the armed forces is a pathway to socioeconomic advancement, and this path is inherently linked to migration to the United States.

Puerto Ricans in this country have the highest rates of cancer, infant mortality, diabetes and asthma. In the chapter titled "Asthma and Diabetes within the Puerto Rican Population," Anna Rosofsky and Judith Aponte examine the two health conditions that have received the most attention in the literature and public discourse over the last decade, and with good reason. Asthma is a chronic disease that has no cure and can be triggered by a host of environmental toxins. Although genetics play a role, such environmental factors as higher exposure to pollutants and allergens have been linked to the spread of asthma. As for diabetes, in 2010 the Centers for Disease Control (CDC) estimated that the rate of diabetes prevalence among Puerto Ricans of 11.2 percent was higher than it was for other ethnic groups. Genetics, cultural factors, and access to health care services, as in the case of asthma, play a role in inducing a high incidence of diabetes among Puerto Ricans. In addition, physical activity and dietary customs also play an important role.

The management of asthma is influenced by access to health insurance, family-based supports, and access to health facilities. Community strategies in prevention and management can help mitigate the incidence and costs to families of both asthma and diabetes. The authors advocate for the implementation of such programs as education, patient navigators, and community health care workers that have proven to be effective in Puerto Rican and other Latino communities. In this context, popular education and healthy neighborhood initiatives focusing on diabetes, asthma, and alcohol consumption may help reduce health disparities.

Most of these health disparities are partly related to environmental, nutritional, and other social conditions. For example, diabetes is related to diet and alcohol consumption, and asthma is related to family poverty and access to health care resources. The CDC has estimated that two-thirds of the disparities in infant-mortality rates between Puerto Rican and non-Hispanic whites are attributable to preterm-related causes of death, while congenital malformations accounted for only 6 percent of the difference.

Civic and political participation play a determinant role in the improvement of social conditions affecting any community. Given the great need for alleviating the adverse circumstances affecting many Puerto Ricans, civic and political engagement should be a high priority. Yet one of the puzzling findings of political science is the low level of participation in electoral processes among stateside Puerto Ricans—in stark contrast with the electoral intensity and voter participation among Puerto Ricans living on the island.

In the chapter titled "Puerto Rican Political and Civic Participation in the United States," Carlos Vargas-Ramos, research associate at Centro, takes a closer look at the stateside Puerto Rican population and its political and civic engagement. Although, voting is the most common form of Puerto Ricans' involvement in the political process, only about half of eligible Puerto Ricans voted in 2008. This turnout rate was commensurate with the Latino population as a whole, higher than the largest Latino subgroups (i.e., Mexicans), but lower than some Latino subgroups, such as Cubans or South Americans. This pattern of political participation is confirmed by other indicators, such as contributing to or working for political campaigns or attending meetings where political issues are discussed.

Despite the overall picture suggested by the data on political engagement, there must be more to the story. Stateside Puerto Ricans have made great strides in the political arena as evidenced by the number of elected representatives serving in Congress and the scores of state legislators, mayors, and municipal officials in office throughout the country. How do we explain that despite showing lower rates of electoral and civic engagement, Puerto Ricans have made significant strides in the political arena and elected a considerable number of state and federal government officials?

Vargas-Ramos asserts that Puerto Ricans benefited from the social and political reforms of the 1960s that created state and local districts, which facilitated the election of previously unrepresented minorities. However, an unintended consequence of Puerto Rican elected officials representing districts with a relatively high percentage of Puerto Rican voters is that lower competition tends to induce lower voter registration and lower turnout rates. Since voter participation levels influence other elected officials, lower participation undermines the political influence of Puerto Rican elected officials.

Researcher Vargas-Ramos concludes, "as Puerto Ricans disperse throughout the country, they are also contributing to the electoral reconfiguration taking place across the country." The results of the 2012 presidential election in Florida show that Puerto Ricans participate in elections when motivated by candidates who take the "right" position on issues. And, when they vote, history and recent experiences suggest, they make a difference. According to Vargas-Ramos, Puerto Ricans were instrumental in the President's victory in Florida. "In all, Puerto Ricans contributed 3.8 percent of the votes Barack Obama received in the state. President Obama won Florida by less than 1 percent."

Despite low participation rates, to the extent that Puerto Ricans become engaged, political and civic participation has served the community well in the past. Social engagement and political mobilization are the institutional and political foundations of the community. Recent events confirm the potential role that civic engagement and political mobilization could play in finding solutions to the many pressing challenges facing Puerto Ricans. There are no more appealing issues to the Puerto Rican community than those that promise to close the social divide and offer hope for a better future. However, the same issues that hinder social advancement for Puerto Ricans also contribute to their below-average involvement in the political process.

Discussion and Conclusions

The New Millennium has opened another chapter in the history of the Puerto Rican community in the United States. More Puerto Ricans now reside on the continent than on the island, and by the end of this decade, the number of those living on the continent may be twice as many as those living in Puerto Rico. Puerto Ricans have become a nomadic people as they search for jobs and economic opportunity to improve the quality of life for their families. It is also likely that in only a few years more Puerto Ricans will reside in Florida than in New York. The factors that contribute to these population changes are not abating: the collapse of the Puerto Rican economy, sizable gaps in education, tighter and more competitive job markets, and more. Yet, our optimism is propelled by the resiliency of the Puerto Rican people.

Undoubtedly, the stateside Puerto Rican community has grown in numbers and complexity since the advent of the new century. As documented in this volume, new social phenomena affecting the stateside Puerto Rican community during the last decade include the following: massive migration from the island; continuous growth in interstate migration and the advent of the South as the new "promised land"; the impact of the Great Recession on the poor and the resiliency of workers in coping with economic adversity; the relative increase in the number of Puerto Ricans who are employed and better educated compared with other ethnic and racial groups; the role of military service as a pathway for upward mobility and as a spur to migration and resettlement; poverty as exacerbated by the wealth gap, and the growing difficulties of youth transitioning to adulthood, especially in New York City. Yet old problems, such as persistent disparities in enrollment in higher education and critical health indicators such as asthma and diabetes, remain to be solved.

The research presented in this volume contributes to identifying and understanding these new social phenomena and solving the enigma of old problems. New evidence presented by Centro researchers challenges long-held beliefs about social conditions among stateside Puerto Ricans and the underlying factors contributing to the entrenchment of disparities and socioeconomic advancement. Just as there is a tendency among mainstream social researchers to lump all Latino groups into one as if they were a monolithic group, there is also a tendency among Latino specialists to lump all Puerto Ricans together as if they, too, were a monolithic group. In actuality, social, demographic, economic, and educational conditions among stateside Puerto Ricans are complex and do not affect all individuals, families, or communities in the same ways. A more detailed analysis of social conditions contributes to identifying patterns not previously evident in the literature and to a deeper understanding of changing social circumstances affecting the stateside Puerto Rican community.

Centro researchers departed from the premise that new social phenomena, such as recent migration and settlement patterns or the adverse impact of the Great Recession, must have affected and had a discernable impact on stateside Puerto Ricans. Contrary to reports from the popular media attributing rapid

Puerto Rican population growth in Florida primarily to recent migration from the island, the research presented in this volume indicates that internal migrants, especially those born in the United States, constitute a sizeable component of this population flow. Florida is driving the advent of the South as a primary destination for Puerto Ricans, but the research presented in the volume also shows that population growth in the South is a more general phenomenon—receiving migrants from the island as well as other states. We predict that this pattern of migration and settlement will continue throughout the decade. Whether these patterns will lead to closing or widening the gap in social disparities remains a topic for future research.

The availability of new data from the ACS and PRCS allowed Centro researchers to challenge and correct some commonly held views reported in the popular media about the existence of a "brain drain" of more educated and skilled workers from the island to the mainland. The currently available evidence controverts such assertions.[8] Although emigrants from Puerto Rico to the United States tend to be younger, they are not overrepresented in high-end managerial or scientific occupations, nor are they any more or less educated than the Puerto Rico population on the island. However, emigrants are more attached to the labor force than the average worker in Puerto Rico. The evidence suggests emigration is about jobs and economic opportunity.

Puerto Ricans in the United States, especially those born in the states, are modern-day nomads. For the first time in the literature, Centro researchers estimate that a sweeping 1.2 million Puerto Ricans, a quarter of the stateside population, moved from one state to another between 2000 and 2011. This is higher than the rate for the general population and contributes notably to the growth of the Puerto Rican population in Florida specifically and in the South more generally. A promising development is that in many of the new settlements in southern states, Puerto Ricans generally have a better educational profile than stateside Puerto Ricans as a whole.

Among the most interesting findings in this volume is that dispersion may be contributing to better socioeconomic outcomes for stateside Puerto Ricans. Military service, for example, is one of the factors contributing to the dispersion of the stateside Puerto Rican community and offers a pathway for socioeconomic advancement to our youth. The evidence presented in this volume shows that veterans have higher median income and lower unemployment and poverty rates than non-veterans. Whether this is an acceptable avenue for social advancement, as opposed to investing in effective educational policies, is a question of political and policy debates and advocacy. Dispersion may be also contributing to lowering social isolation. Between 2000 and 2010, as measured by the dissimilarity index, Puerto Ricans were less segregated from non-Hispanic whites than in prior decades. All in all, our research indicates that dispersion and increased interstate mobility may be strongly related to economic survival. And, to the extent that dispersion contributes to better earnings and settlements in less expensive and segregated housing markets, it may also contribute to the improvement of net worth among Puerto Ricans.

One of the most often researched questions in business and economics since the advent of the Great Recession in December of 2007 is whether the recovery has been strong enough to restore the huge losses in human and financial capital that resulted. Centro researchers have documented that Puerto Ricans experienced a higher increase in unemployment and longterm unemployment than all other ethnic and racial groups represented in the labor force of the United States a full two years after the official end of the recession. As a result, Puerto Rican poverty rates have increased. Yet, mean earnings for full-time, year-round Puerto Rican men stayed about the same while they improved for women, closing the earnings gap between Puerto Rican women and non-Hispanic white women. In short, those workers who remained employed year round were not affected palpably by the recession, and some even improved their relative standing in the labor market two years after the end of the recession.

What explains the relative advancement of Puerto Ricans in labor markets in the aftermath of the Great Recession? An important contribution from Centro researchers is to collect new data for the analysis of critical social indicators otherwise not available. In this volume, we report for the first time findings from the "Puerto Ricans and the Impact of the Recession Study." The findings of the study support an alternative explanation of Puerto Rican workers' behavior in response to adverse economic conditions. The labor-market indicators reported in this volume are consistent with an explanation that emphasizes Puerto Rican resiliency and adaptability when coping with economic adversity. Such an explanation is consistent with other data reported in this volume about interstate mobility and the surge of migration from the island. It also supports other findings suggesting that Puerto Ricans have made some advances over prior decades in narrowing the income gap with non-Hispanic blacks or Latinos of other national origin.

Access to and completion of higher education for stateside Puerto Ricans contributes to how workers fare in job markets and the accumulation of wealth. Over the last decade, stateside Puerto Ricans have improved their rates of high school graduation and completion of a bachelor's degree, although disparities that exist with other groups have remained constant given their overall educational advancement. Strategies for promoting educational advancement among Puerto

Ricans include promoting bilingualism as an asset and focusing on the most disadvantaged group—those out of school and work. Puerto Rican youth appear to have great difficulties transitioning to adulthood, especially in New York City. We propose that part-time employment while finishing high school or attending college might encourage Puerto Rican youth to maintain enrollment in school or college, allow them to support themselves and contribute to family income, and serve as an incentive to continue their education.

We close the volume by taking a fresh look at recurrent problems and new challenges in the literature. One of the most intriguing consequences of the massive exodus of Puerto Ricans from the island is the macro-economic impact of the sharp decline in population. Although the question of migration is gaining recognition from the public and elected officials as a critical component of the economic and social crisis that affects the island, the economic impact of declining population and massive migration is yet to gain general acknowledgment. However, Europe has experienced a similar phenomenon a few decades ahead of Puerto Rico and offers useful lessons. In the end, the European experience suggests that there is relatively little that the government or the business community can do to prevent a "demographic winter" or the massive exodus of workers in their prime productive years.

One of the most pressing paradoxes facing the stateside Puerto Rican community is the fact that socioeconomic disparities, in education and health and many other areas, can be lessened through political participation and civic engagement. Take health as an example. Disparities in breast cancer, diabetes, and asthma—the diseases that show the greatest health disparities for Puerto Ricans—can be successfully addressed through community initiatives. However, strategies to mitigate disparities and the high death rates caused by these diseases require mitigation of environmental, nutritional, and socioeconomic factors, especially in New York City. Yet, often, local elected and appointed officials and the public do not actively engage in finding a solution to these problems affecting the community. Our hope, with this volume, is to contribute to raising awareness among a broad range of stakeholders of the disparities that exist, to supporting social action among those affected by these disparities, and to encouraging civic participation.

NOTES

[1] These estimates of Puerto Rico residents exclude foreign-born populations who are not of Puerto Rican origin.

[2] See the Vargas-Ramos and García-Ellín chapter in this volume. According to decennial census data, the share of Puerto Rican population in the Northeast declined from 69 percent in 1990 to

53 percent in 2010.

[3] Citation for Impact on Puerto Ricans survey and credits.

[4] See Kurt Birson's chapter in this volume. Estimates from the American Community Survey are likely to underestimate the actual outflow of migrants from Puerto Rico to the United States. Marazzi-Santiago (2012) estimates a much higher net migration flow based on the net movement of passengers for the period.

[5] According to the U.S. Census Bureau (SF2, 2010), 2.3 percent of the US population and 2.8 percent of Puerto Ricans moved to a different state the year before. The 1.2 million figure is cumulative and is not comparable to yearly flows.

[6] The dissimilarity index calculates the proportion of a population group (for example, Puerto Ricans) that would have to move from a given geography level in order to achieve parity with another population group (for example, non-Hispanic whites).

[7] Mario Marazzi Santiago (Director Ejecutivo Instituto de Estadísticas de Puerto Rico), Banco Popular of Puerto Rico (Progreso Económico, 2012).

[8] It is possible that when data from larger sample sizes are available to researchers in the future a more detailed disaggregation of occupations and educational attainment will challenge these findings.

REFERENCES

Bloom, D., S.L. Thompson, and R. Ivry. 2010. Building a Learning Agenda around Disconnected Youth. New York: MDRC.

De Jesús, Anthony. 2011. *Abriendo Camino*: An analysis of the three social work pathways initiatives for low-wage Puerto Ricans. *CENTRO: Journal of the Center for Puerto Rican Studies* 23(2): 136–55.

Fernandes, Adrianne L., and Thomas Gabe. 2009. Disconnected Youth: A Look at 16-24 Years Old Who Are Not Working or In School. Rep. no. 7-5700. Congressional Research Service.

Ihrke, David K. and Carol S. Faber (2012) Geographical Mobility: 2005 to 2010. Population Characteristics. P20-567. U.S. Census Bureau. Issued December 2012.

Marazzi-Santiago, Mario. 2012 Demographics and Economics: Puerto Rico 2000–2010. Presentation to the Health and Insurance Conference 2012, San Juan, Puerto Rico. 2 February.

Mercado, Carmen I. 2011. Successful pathways to the teaching profession for Puerto Ricans. *CENTRO: Journal of the Center for Puerto Rican Studies* 23(2): 114–35.

Torres-Vélez, Víctor M. 2011. Puerto Ricans and the green jobs gap in New York City. *CENTRO: Journal of the Center for Puerto Rican Studies* 23(2): 94-113.

Vázquez Calzada, José L. 1988. *La población de Puerto Rico y su trayectoria histórica*. Río Piedras, PR: Escuela Graduada de Salud Pública, Recinto de Ciencias Médicas, Universidad de Puerto Rico.

Visser, M. Anne and Edwin Meléndez. 2011. Low-wage labor, markets and skills selectivity among Puerto Rican migrants. *CENTRO: Journal of the Center for Puerto Rican Studies* 23(2): 38–63.

Puerto Rican Migration and the Brain Drain Dilemma

KURT BIRSON

Introduction

In 2004, the number of Puerto Ricans living in the mainland United States exceeded the population in Puerto Rico for the first time in history.[1] This unprecedented event highlights a new shift in the pattern of Puerto Rican migration, and the now rapidly declining population in Puerto Rico presents serious challenges for the future of the island (see Figure 1).

The 2000 decennial census reported a population of 3.8 million in Puerto Rico, which after growing modestly during the first few years of the decade, began to drop. By the 2010 census, the island registered a population of 3.72 million—an overall decline of more than 2.2 percent.[2] Recent estimates from the annual American Community Survey suggest the population has continued to decrease since then (U.S. Census Bureau 2011).

Accurate estimates of the overall levels of migration between Puerto Rico and the United States are notoriously difficult to obtain. While the American Community Survey and Puerto Rico Community Survey represent relatively new sources of data (ACS and PRCS, respectively), historically other methods have been used to track the flow of migrants between the two regions. Prior to the ACS and PRCS, others have relied on the published figures of net air passenger movement provided by the Puerto Rico Planning Board and the Puerto Rico Port Authority to represent migration.[3] Figures from these local sources generally show much higher levels of net migration from Puerto Rico to the mainland than reported by the ACS, which may also undercount migration flows.[4]

Nevertheless, these U.S. Census Bureau surveys are the most comprehensive national studies to explicitly solicit and track migration data within the United States as well as Puerto Rico from year to year, and the only means of closely examining the social and economic characteristics of migrants.[5] For this study, rather than looking at migration patterns over the period, we concentrate instead on distinguishing the relative characteristics of the migrating cohort. we consider the relative percentages of characteristics across the migrating cohort rather than the total of number of individuals in movement over the period.

FIGURE 1. Population of Puerto Ricans in the United States and Puerto Rico (in millions)

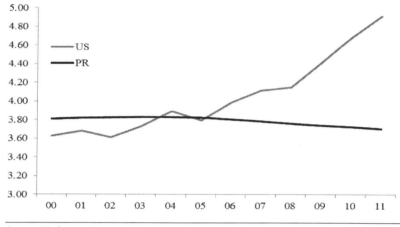

Source: U.S. Census Bureau, ACS, 1-year estimates, 2000-2011, and 2010 Intercensal Estimates.

By creating a profile of Puerto Rican migrants moving between the United States mainland and Puerto Rico we are able to better understand their demographic and human-capital characteristics. Using census data from the ACS and PRCS from 2006 to 2011, we get a clearer picture of the composition of the migrant community and the factors contributing to migration in the first part of the 21st century.

Migration Patterns of Puerto Ricans since WWII

Migration from Puerto Rico to the mainland United States has been a part of the Puerto Rican experience for more than a century, although it accelerated after the 1940s spurred by a variety of economic, social, and political factors. Now, with almost two thirds of Puerto Ricans living abroad, the Puerto Rican community represents the largest diaspora group originating from Latin America and the Caribbean (Duany 2006).

Puerto Ricans are unique among migrant groups, having several advantages over the others. As a territory, or "Commonwealth," of the United States, all Puerto Ricans have U.S. citizenship and can travel freely between the two regions at relatively low cost.[6] Thus, unlike other immigrants to the United States, Puerto Ricans face few barriers to entry aside from the cost of airfare. By the middle of the 20th century, this migration was facilitated by the increasing popularity of air travel and the establishment of Migration Offices for Puerto

Rico's Department of Labor in New York, Chicago, and Philadelphia (Berman-Santana 1998; Acosta-Belén and Santiago 2006; Duany 2007).

Researchers generally recognize four key historical periods affecting the flow of migration between Puerto Rico and the United States following World War II: the "Great Migration" (1940s–1960s), return migration during the 1960s and early 1970s, a period of economic stagnation in the United States and Puerto Rico between the late 1970s and 1980s, and a period of economic expansion during the 1990s (Meléndez 2007; Falcón 1990; History Task Force 1979). During the first half of the 20th century, Puerto Rico experienced incipient levels of emigration to the United States, driven by government policies and the demand for cheap agricultural labor in Hawaii, Louisiana, California, and abroad (Whalen 2005).

The first of these historical periods was that of the era of the Great Migration from the late 1940s to the early 1960s. This was a critical period in the history of Puerto Rican migration, when a massive number of Puerto Ricans left for the United States. According to official sources, a net of nearly 500,000 left from the island in just over a decade — more than 20 percent of the population (Acosta-Belén and Santiago 2006, Vázquez-Calzada 1978). The immediate post-war period was a time of rapid industrialization in Puerto Rico, driven by an influx of private-capital investment from the United States, which displaced agricultural production long dominant on the island. This upheaval of the domestic economic structure, occurring between two major U.S. wars, prompted a movement from rural areas to cities and encouraged migration from the island to the mainland United Sates.[7] During this period, emigrants (those leaving the island) for the United States were "disproportionately young, had higher education levels, and were more skilled than the general population...although agriculture constitute[d] the largest grouping" (Meléndez 2007). These important economic, social, and political changes brought on by industrialization were the result of a U.S.- led development strategy called Operation Bootstrap (in Spanish, *manos a la obra* or "hands to work"). The policy was implemented with the goal of both industrializing the island and reducing the strain of a perceived problem of "overpopulation" believed to be the source of persistent unemployment.[8] However, despite the substantial injection of capital, unemployment still remained stubbornly high and many Puerto Ricans chose to emigrate — a solution the Puerto Rican government would come to rely upon to relieve employment pressures (Berman-Santana 1998;

Martínez-Piva 2005; Bonilla and Campos 1981).[9] Indeed, for many, *manos a la obra* eventually came to mean *manos a las maletas* or "hands to the luggage" (Martínez-Fernández 2008).

The second shift in migration, which occurred during the 1960s and early 1970s, was characterized by continued structural change in the insular economy. Industry shifted from labor-intensive to capital-intensive production, and the service industry and public sector became the largest economic sectors of the domestic economy. Driving this change was the Internal Revenue Service code Section 936—a tax-incentive policy introduced during the previous period that brought hundreds of U.S. corporations to the island, and that, in turn, established petrochemical, pharmaceutical, machinery, and metals industries, among others (Bonilla and Campos 1981; Berman-Santana 1998). New employment opportunities and the prospect of higher wages in Puerto Rico led to decreased out-migration and increased return migration, to the point that some years even recorded positive net immigration (Vázquez-Calzada 1963). Migrants leaving and returning during this phase generally resembled the characteristics of the Puerto Rican population in terms of age, education, and employment (Meléndez 2007).

In the third period, spanning the late 1970s through the 1980s, economic stagnation, both in the United States and Puerto Rico, dampened the flow of migration, and return migration again outpaced emigration for several years (Meléndez 2007; Falcón 1990). From 1970 to 1980, historians place net emigration at just over 65,000 people—a stark difference from prior decades.

The final and fourth shift in the pattern of Puerto Rican migration between Puerto Rico and the United States during the 20th century occurred during the late 1980s to the 1990s. Economic expansion once again led to increased migration, and net outflows of migrants began to rise (Meléndez 2007).

The historical context underscores the importance of such economic factors as unemployment and wage differentials and the long-established reliance on migration as a way of mitigating their effects as the traditional drivers of migration in Puerto Rico.

The first decade of the 21st century now represents a new fifth period for Puerto Rican migration in which emigration from Puerto Rico appears to have increased substantially compared with the numbers of those returning to the island. Estimates vary greatly depending on the source, but range from more than 100,000 to nearly 500,000 net emigration, which would rival or even surpass the figures from the Great Migration era (Duany 2006). Regardless of the source, however, emigration has no doubt been a significant issue in recent years and presents Puerto Rico with some very complex problems.

The massive exodus of Puerto Ricans leaving for the United States, an issue that has garnered much attention among observers, appears to be driven in large part by the deteriorating economic situation on the island beginning in the early part of the decade. This situation was exacerbated by the effects of the Great Recession and fiscal austerity policies, which had a strong impact on employment on the island. Recently, popular sources have also pointed to rising crime in Puerto Rico as another important factor influencing the decision to migrate (Quintero 2011; Greene 2013).

Method and Data

By creating a profile of this movement, we hope to gain further insight into the characteristics of these migrants and shed light on the possible drivers of this most recent phase. We perform cross-tabulations using the U.S. Census Bureau's ACS and PRCS 1-year estimates from 2006–2011 to create a profile of Puerto Ricans migrating between the mainland United States and Puerto Rico during the period.[10] Then, using averages of the data, we make comparisons between the migrating cohort and the non-moving populations in both the sending and receiving regions. Note that the following comparisons include only those individuals who identified themselves as Puerto Ricans migrating between the island and the mainland.[11]

Due to the difficulty of obtaining a more reliable total count of migration figures, this study used relative percentages of estimates from the ACS and PRCS, rather than present-level data. In fact, estimating migration between Puerto Rico and the United States has long been a complicated process. Researchers have relied on a variety of resources to estimate migration numbers, including surveys from various government agencies (from both the United States and Puerto Rican governments), registries from the Port Authority, and air-passenger travel statistics. However, none of these sources were designed specifically to measure migration flows. Still, they remained the only reliable sources for migration data until very recently, including providing figures for the Great Migration of the 1950s (Vázquez Calzada 1978). The ACS was fully implemented by 2005 (U.S. Census Bureau 2009), representing an additional annually updated source for migration estimates.

Migration data from the ACS and PRCS have presented some problems, however. As shown in Figure 2, the magnitude of net migration varies greatly

FIGURE 2. Migration from Puerto Rico as Estimated by Planning Board, Port Authority, and U.S. Census Bureau (in thousands)

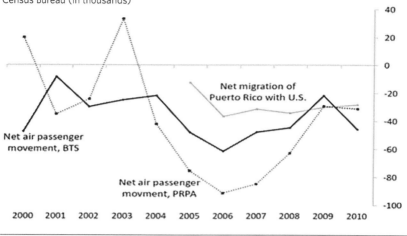

Source: UMarazzi-Santiago, 2012.

between the three principal sources of migration statistics —ACS, PRCS, and net air-passenger movement as measured by the Puerto Rico Port Authority and the Bureau of Transportation Statistics. In general, the ACS and PRCS produce estimates of net migration that are much lower than those derived from net passenger statistics. The fact that these statistics do not fully agree with the overall change in the population of Puerto Ricans living on the Island and in the United States creates an issue that must be addressed.

According to ACS and decennial census data, there were approximately 1.2 million more Puerto Ricans living in the United States in 2010 than in 2000. However, after taking into account natural population growth due to births and deaths, there is a difference of nearly 400,000 people, who are not wholly accounted for by the net emigration figure produced by the ACS of approximately 150,000.[12] Therefore, it appears that there is a portion of population growth among the Puerto Rican community living in the United States that cannot be explained by migration or natural growth. Because this difference exists in decennial censuses (which are full head counts and not estimates), it suggests that net emigration during this most recent decade is much higher than the ACS estimates and more closely resembles that of the Great Migration period of the 1950s. Regardless of the measure, the number of Puerto Ricans leaving the island strongly outweighs the number returning to the island, an effect that is magnified by the falling population of Puerto Rico.

Emigrant Characteristics

Data for emigrants are derived from the ACS 2006–2011.[13] These migrants tended to be younger, neither more nor less educated, more attached to the labor force, and consisted of more blue-collar workers than their counterparts left behind in Puerto Rico. These results challenge the prevailing conventional wisdom that there is a "brain drain" of the island population's highly educated and highly skilled workers, when in fact this migration wave appears underrepresented in these areas. The data suggest that those migrating are probably responding to high unemployment in Puerto Rico.

Table 1 disaggregates the recent migrants by age group and sex and compares them to Puerto Ricans on the island. Migrants under 35 years of age were overrepresented, and those age 35 and up were underrepresented relative to the island population of Puerto Ricans during the same period. This reflects a clear bias towards younger people migrating. More than 77 percent of migrants were younger than 45 years of age, compared with nearly 62 percent in the same age group who remained on the island. Nearly 66 percent of migrants were of working age (between 18 and 65 years old). The highest percentage of migrants (more than 26%) came from the group under 18 years old, suggesting that when people choose to emigrate, they migrate as households.

In Table 2, estimates of educational attainment indicate that emigrants age 25 and older show little particular bias relative to the population they left behind. The only group to show somewhat stronger overrepresentation were those who had a high school education or equivalent. Those with less than a high school education, bachelor's or graduate degrees were underrepresented in the emigrating cohort.

TABLE 1. Age and Sex of Puerto Rican Emigrants (percent)

	Male	Female	Total	Total in PR	Total in U.S.
>18	27.5	25.3	26.4	24.7	33.3
18-24	14.9	15.6	15.2	10.3	11.4
25-34	24.5	22.2	23.4	13.5	15.1
35-44	11.7	12.6	12.1	13.4	12.6
45-54	6.0	7.0	6.5	12.8	11.7
55-64	7.6	8.7	8.2	11.4	7.8
65+	7.8	8.5	8.2	14.0	7.2

Source: U.S. Census Bureau, ACS, 1-year estimates, 2006–2011.

TABLE 2. Educational Attainment of Puerto Rican Emigrants, 25 years or older (percent)

	Male	Female	Total	25-34	35-44	45+	Total in PR	Total in U.S.
Less than HS	31	26	29	18	19	44	32	27
High School	32	30	30	32	39	25	25	30
Some College	16	23	20	26	21	13	21	28
Bachelor's	14	16	15	18	16	13	16	11
Graduate	6	5	5	6	5	5	6	5

Source: U.S. Census Bureau, ACS, 1-year estimates, 2006–2011.

Emigrants with a high school education or less represented more than half of all emigrants during the period of 2006–2011, and more than three-quarters had less than a bachelor's degree. Only 5 percent of emigrants had an advanced degree, compared with 6 percent of those remaining in Puerto Rico. Emigrant men were less educated than women, representing a larger percentage of those with a high school education or less, while a higher percentage of emigrant women had either some college or a bachelor's degree. Males had a slightly higher representation among migrants with a graduate degree, 6 percent compared with 5 percent for females.

According to the data presented in Table 3, emigrants showed a much stronger attachment to the labor force than did the island population. Due to ACS and PRCS survey methodology, it was not possible to determine the labor-force status of migrants prior to leaving the country of origin. Thus, Table 3 and Table 4 refer to an individual's status *after* arriving in the United States.[14]

A greater percentage of emigrants reported being in the labor force, 55.9 percent, which is nearly 10 percentage points higher than the labor-force participation of Puerto Ricans staying on the island. In addition, the difference between the labor-force and civilian-labor-force participation rates suggest that military service is a determining factor in migration (accounting for 3.4 percent of migrants in the labor force), as discussed by Harry Franqui-Rivera in this volume, especially given that this difference in labor-force participation was not evident among the island population that stayed behind. For both emigrants and immigrants, men were more than twice as likely to be in the armed forces as women.

Of the emigrants, labor-force participation was much higher for males than it was for females (64% compared with 49%). This difference may be partly a function of household dynamics, however. According to the Puerto

TABLE 3. Employment Status of Puerto Rican Emigrants, 16 years or older in the U.S. (percent)

	Male	Female	Total	Total in PR	Total in U.S.
Labor-Force Participation	63.6	48.4	55.9	46.8	62.5
Civilian Labor-Force Participation	58.7	46.6	52.6	46.4	61.7
Employment Ratio	34.0	46.3	40.1	38.4	53.7
Unemployment Rate	21.9	28.0	24.6	17.3	12.2
Armed Forces	4.9	1.9	3.4	0.4	0.8
Not in Labor Force	36.4	51.6	44.1	53.2	37.5

Source: U.S. Census Bureau, ACS, 1-year estimates, 2006–2011.

Rico Planning Board's *Encuesta Sobre Información del Viajero* (Survey of Travelers) during the decade of 1990–2000, in more than half the cases, female migrants reported "housewife" as the reason for migration (Meléndez 2007). Nevertheless, the high labor-force participation of the cohort suggests that seeking employment is likely to be a major, if not the primary, purpose for emigration from Puerto Rico during this period.

Despite their attachment to the labor force, Puerto Rican migrants had difficulty obtaining employment in the United States. Emigrants were unemployed at a rate of 24.6 percent after their migration, compared with the 17.3 percent unemployment rate for Puerto Ricans who remained on the island during the same period. This surprising finding may be explained by several factors. First, as evidenced by the data on educational attainment, the majority of Puerto Ricans (59%) coming to the United States who were 25 years of age or older had a high school education or less, and almost 30 percent did not finish high school. Although these figures are comparable to those for all Puerto Ricans living the United States, low educational attainment may be a contributing factor when other labor-force disadvantages, such as English-language skills or work history, are taken into account. As noted by Muschkin (1993), new migrants may lack or have discontinuities in work history in Puerto Rico or the United States and generally experience higher unemployment than the non-migrant labor force. Further limiting employment opportunities for Puerto Rican emigrants moving to the United States is that few have a mastery of English. As of 2011, just 19 percent of Puerto Ricans in Puerto Rico reported speaking English "very well" (U.S. Census Bureau 2011). Finally, upon arriving in the United States, migrants would be faced with a competitive job market still weakened by the effects of the Great Recession.

TABLE 4. Occupation of Puerto Rican Emigrants, 16 years or Older in U.S. (percent)

	Male	Female	Total	25-34	35-44	45+	Total in PR	Total in U.S.
Management, Business, Science, Arts	17	25	21	21	18	27	30	27
Services	18	23	20	22	23	21	20	22
Sales and Office	21	36	28	22	29	24	28	29
Natural Resources, Construction, Maintenance	32	7	20	23	23	18	11	7
Production, Transportation, Material Moving	12	10	11	12	7	9	12	13

Source: U.S. Census Bureau, ACS, 1-year estimates, 2006-2011.

Lastly, for emigrants, Table 4 shows the occupational category of employed Puerto Ricans age 16 or older, who left the island between 2006 and 2011. As with Table 3, Table 4 represents the occupation of the individual *after* having arrived in the United States. Therefore, it is not certain whether an individual emigrating from Puerto Rico would have found employment on the mainland in the same field they were in while residing in Puerto Rico. According to the results shown in Table 4, Puerto Rican emigrants were less likely to be in professional occupations than their island counterparts and instead were more likely to be concentrated in blue-collar, hourly-wage work.

Puerto Ricans who came to the mainland were strongly underrepresented in the "Management, Business, Science, and Arts" categories, consisting of doctors, lawyers, engineers, scientists, and teachers, among others, compared with Puerto Ricans remaining on the island. Migrants were as represented in service, sales, office, and slightly underrepresented in production or transportation occupations, but were strongly overrepresented in the category that includes construction or extraction, agricultural work, or maintenance and repair activities. There are stark differences in occupational representation among emigrants depending on their gender. Although the overall proportion is 20 percent, in the emigrant heavy construction and agricultural sectors, men were overwhelmingly represented among those leaving (32%) relative to women (at 7%). Females were much more concentrated in management, sales and office, or service positions, while men were overwhelmingly employed in construction and maintenance jobs. The weight of these gender differences (and size of the male cohort) led to the relative under- and over-representation in these categories.

Immigrant Characteristics

Those Puerto Ricans returning to the island ("returning migrants" or "immigrants" to Puerto Rico) tended to be more negatively selected than emigrants. Immigrants were slightly older, had slightly lower educational attainment, were less attached to the labor force, and were more linked to blue-collar employment than other Puerto Ricans within the 50 states. Based on estimates from the PRCS, the cohort of returning migrants observed is selected from the years 2006–2011.

In general, returning migrants tended to be slightly older than their Puerto Rican counterparts who remained in the mainland United States, but overall were very similar. Youths under 18 years old were underrepresented, and migrants over the age of 55 were slightly overrepresented. For other age groupings, however, there were no large differences between the migrating and static population. The largest age group among returning migrants was composed of youths under 18 years old, again suggesting that returning migrants also travel as a household. However, when compared with the distribution of the receiving population on the island, these returning migrants were, on average, slightly younger.

Puerto Ricans returning to the island were, in general, slightly less educated than Puerto Ricans in the United States, and they were overrepresented in both ends of the educational spectrum. Return migrants were overrepresented among those with less than a high school education, but were also very slightly overrepresented among those with a graduate degree. Those with a high school education were underrepresented, as were those with some college. The findings from Table 6 show that 32 percent of migrants 25 years of age or older had less than a high school education, compared with 27 percent of Puerto

TABLE 5. Age and Sex of Puerto Rican Emigrants (percent)

	Male	Female	Total	Total in U.S.	Total in PR
>18	31.8	29.7	30.8	33.3	24.7
18-24	11.8	11.4	11.6	11.4	10.3
25-34	14.5	18.4	16.3	15.1	13.5
35-44	15.2	11.3	13.4	12.6	13.4
45-54	11.7	9.8	10.8	11.7	12.8
55-64	8.1	9.8	8.9	7.8	11.4
65+	7.0	9.6	8.2	7.2	14.0

Source: U.S. Census Bureau, ACS, 1-year estimates, 2006-2011.

TABLE 6. Educational Attainment of Puerto Rican Immigrants, 25 years or Older (percent)

	Male	Female	Total	Total in U.S.	Total in PR
Less than HS	33	31	32	27	32
High School	32	22	28	30	25
Some College	22	28	24	28	21
Bachelor's	8	12	10	11	16
Graduate	4	7	6	5	6

Source: U.S. Census Bureau, ACS, 1-year estimates, 2006–2011.

Ricans in the same age group remaining in the United States. The proportion of returning migrants with a high school education or less (60%) was higher than it was for Puerto Ricans in the United States. In terms of higher education, 16 percent of returning migrants had a bachelor's degree or higher, the same as their counterparts remaining in the United States.

Compared with the receiving population in Puerto Rico, returning migrants were also negatively selected in terms of educational attainment as they were slightly more likely to have a high school education or less and were also less likely to have a bachelor's degree than were Puerto Ricans on the island. In the latter case, 10 percent of immigrant Puerto Ricans had earned a bachelor's degree compared with 16 percent of Puerto Ricans on the island who had achieved the same level of education. Returning migrants who had earned a graduate degree were similarly represented in the population of Puerto Rico.

In general, female return migrants had higher levels of educational attainment than did males. Females in this group were much less likely to have a high school education or less, and were more likely to have had some college training or have earned a bachelor's or graduate degree.

Table 7 and Table 8 refer to employment characteristics of return migrants after having arrived in Puerto Rico. Figures from Table 7 suggest that for Puerto Ricans returning to the island, seeking employment was not necessarily a significant reason for their migration. Immigrants to Puerto Rico were not strongly attached to the labor force, with just 47.4 percent in the labor force compared with 62.5 percent of Puerto Ricans living in the United States. Given the slight overrepresentation among returning migrants of those 55 years of age or older, they may be less motivated by employment and instead may be discouraged workers or seeking to retire on the island.

TABLE 7. Employment Status of Puerto Rican Immigrants, 16 years or Older, in Puerto Rico (percent)

	Male	Female	Total	Total in PR	Total in U.S.
Labor-Force Participation	53.5	37.9	45.8	62.5	46.8
Civilian Labor-Force Participation	53.1	37.9	45.6	61.7	46.4
Employment Ratio	26.9	21.6	24.3	53.7	38.4
Unemployment Rate	49.2	43.9	47.0	12.2	17.3
Armed Forces	0.4	0.0	0.2	0.8	0.4
Not in Labor Force	46.5	62.1	54.2	37.5	53.2

Source: U.S. Census Bureau, ACS, 1-year estimates, 2006–2011.

As with the emigrant group, immigrant females were in the labor force at a much lower percentage than males — again, a possible consequence of household dynamics.

Similar to emigrants, immigrants were mostly blue-collar workers. Returning migrants were overrepresented in "Service" and "Natural Resources, Construction and Maintenance" occupations, and underrepresented in "Management, Business, Science, Arts," "Sales and Office," and "Transportation, Material Moving" compared with the stateside Puerto Rican population. This suggests that the flow of migrants from this period was composed of more workers earning hourly wages and fewer professional and office workers.

The percentage of returning migrants who found work in Puerto Rico in the Natural Resources, Construction, and Maintenance category was much higher than it was for the population of stateside Puerto Ricans. In the case

TABLE 8. Occupation of Puerto Rican Emigrants, 16 years or Older in U.S. (percent)

	Male	Female	Total	Total in U.S.	Total in PR
Management, Business, Science, Arts	15	25	20	27	30
Services	24	26	25	22	20
Sales and Office	19	41	28	29	28
Natural Resources, Construction, Maintenance	25	5	17	7	11
Production, Transportation, Material Moving	17	3	10	13	12

Source: U.S. Census Bureau, ACS, 1-year estimates, 2006–2011.

of immigrants, 17 percent found work in this category, compared with just 7 percent in the United States. This is especially significant given that this percentage was more than 50 percent greater than for the island percentage (11%) during the period.

Discussion of Findings

In sum, these findings suggest some important patterns among migrants from Puerto Rico to the United States. First, we see that emigrants in the cohort from 2006–2011 seem to be principally motivated by finding employment, given their age and strong attachment to the labor force, and that this is especially true for men. These job seekers, aided by low transit costs and established stateside social networks, can make the decision to emigrate depending on the relative economic climate in island. Studies have shown a positive correlation between the rate of unemployment and Puerto Rican net migration (Enchautegui and Freeman 2005; Meléndez 2007).

At the same time, contrary to popular perception, the evidence from this study found no evidence of a brain drain at the aggregate educational or occupational categories relative to the Puerto Rican population of the island (Quintero 2011; *Caribbean Business* 2013; Enchautegui 2008). Emigrants, in fact, were less educated, with the majority (59%) of those leaving having a high school education or less. Fifteen percent held a bachelor's degree, and just 5 percent had attained a graduate degree, a slightly smaller representation than among those staying in Puerto Rico. These emigrants were also underrepresented in professional occupations and overrepresented in lower-skill industries, particularly males, who were overrepresented in construction, maintenance, and agriculture activities after arriving in the United States.

Puerto Ricans arriving on the island between 2006 and 2011 were negatively selected; the group was slightly older and less educated, had a low attachment to the labor force, and, among those who did find work, employed in more low-skill jobs.

Migrant characteristics were similar during the previous decades for emigrants. Emigrants during the 1990s were younger, less educated, had a strong attachment to labor force (especially men), and were mostly employed in low-skill occupations before leaving the island. The migrants during this period, however, included a growing number of workers in managerial and office jobs compared with the 1980s. During this time, returning migrants were older, more educated, strongly attached to labor force (also especially true for men), and employed in low-skill jobs despite the growing proportion of managerial and office workers (Meléndez 2007). Therefore, this new wave of migrants is not much different than previous ones.

The flow for emigration during the decade of the 2000s seems strongly linked to employment. Employment has been weak in Puerto Rico and has worsened significantly since 2006, when the island entered into a recession, and beginning in 2009, when Puerto Ricans faced massive public-sector layoffs and budget cuts (Alemán 2012; *Caribbean Business* 2013; *Guardian* 2009). Figure 3 shows the fragile employment situation on the island during the last decade.

According to the US Bureau of Labor Statistics, unemployment remained in double-digit figures throughout the decade, but was greatly affected by the global recession and local budget cuts and layoffs of government workers, who represented 30 percent of all non-farm workers in 2009. (That number has since dropped to 27.7% in 2012.) Puerto Rico has also suffered from extremely low rates of *employment* as a percentage of the population, which has hovered between just 38 percent and 40 percent since 2006, compared with an employment rate of more than 51 percent in the United States in 2011.[15] This means that Puerto Ricans are not only unemployed at a high rate, but also that a large number of people remain out of the labor force entirely.

FIGURE 3. Unemployment in the United States and Puerto Rico (percent)

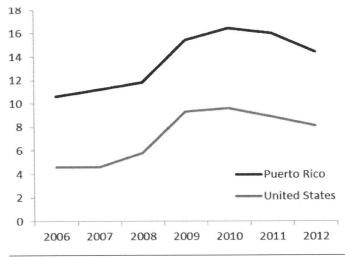

Source: Bureau of Labor Statistics, Local Area Unemployment Statistics.

The net effect of migration outflows during the first decade of the 21st century has meant the loss of a large number of people of working age (between 18 and 65 years old) to the United States. Although, in general, emigrants do not constitute the island's most educated or most skilled workers, these numbers do represent an exodus of a significant portion of the population. This presents severe economic and social consequences for Puerto Rico, constituting a vicious cycle of employment loss, migration, and fiscal pressure. Emigration that is driven by unemployment, in turn, weakens the local economy and drives emigration anew. A report produced by the Puerto Rico Institute of Statistics concluded that more than a quarter of the 1.8 percent reduction in Puerto Rico's real GDP between 2006 and 2010 could be attributed to the loss in population (Instituto de Estadísticas de Puerto Rico 2010).

Emigration patterns in the 21st century induce a range of new challenges for the island—including the potential strain on public finances and the pension system, the loss of federal funds, a continuously shrinking labor force, and an aging population.

Conclusion

The preceding analysis challenges the notion that the island is experiencing a so-called brain drain of its most educated and skilled workers. Rather, the numbers suggest a more representative departure of Puerto Ricans from all corners of society. While in the past, migration has been used as a means of resolving the problem of unemployment on the island, the recent upsurge in the trend significantly lowers aggregate demand and debilitates the Puerto Rican economy. The strain of high unemployment has driven productive members of the population to seek job opportunities in the United States, leaving behind a reduced labor force to bear the effects of a prolonged recession and the costs of an aging population.

This loss in population is problematic for several reasons. First, it means the loss of members of the already small labor force, reducing the island's productive capacity, which, in turn, means reduced employment demand and economic consumption. Second, the loss of the labor force represents a shrinking of the tax base, thus reducing public revenue and resources. Public budgets and spending will have to continually be reduced, and taxes will have to be raised in order for the government to continue to provide public services and pay government employees. Lastly, the loss of population, whether in the labor force or not, will mean reduced capital resources from earnings, pensions, social security, and most importantly, federal funding from Washington. This may lead to economic contraction and further employment difficulties. All of these factors could feed back into the cycle of emigration.

Puerto Rico faces a very uncertain future. Decisions must be made regarding policies to lessen the impact of the current recession, reinforce the structure and health of its public-pension system, and stem the tide of increased emigration and population decline. What is certain, however, is that trends in Puerto Rican migration will play a very significant role in the future of Puerto Rico and merit the continued attention of a wide variety of stakeholders—the most important of whom will be Puerto Ricans themselves.

NOTES

[1] U.S. Census Bureau, ACS and ACS Intercensal Estimates, 2000–2010.

[2] Of these, we estimate that there were approximately 3.5 million Puerto Ricans and 220,000 foreign-born individuals residing on the island.

[3] The decennial census, which included a question about the respondent's residence five years prior, could also be used to establish migration. This, however, does not allow for year-to-year analysis, or the ability to capture (as has become more common) whether individuals move multiple times during that five-year period.

[4] Although the Census Bureau estimates the net migration of some 250,000 Puerto Ricans in the most recent decade, this figure seems too low to explain the drastic change in population. Alternate figures in Duany (2006) derived from net movement of air passengers put the number close to 500,000 for the same period – a number that would rival or surpass that of even the Great Migration period of the 1940s to 1960s.

[5] Due to budget cuts in the Puerto Rican government, programs in several departments, including the census department, have been suspended.

[6] U.S. citizenship was granted to Puerto Ricans in 1917 when congress passed the Jones Act. "Commonwealth" status was designated in 1950, while Puerto Rico was under the governorship of Luis Muñoz Marín (Acosta-Belén and Santiago 2006).

[7] Historians note that more than 65,000 Puerto Ricans served in WWII and 62,000 served in the Korean War. This represented a large percentage of Puerto Ricans of working age and of the population as a whole. In 1950 Puerto Rico had a population of just over 2.2 million.

[8] As health researcher Vázquez-Calzada notes, since the beginning of the 20th century, Puerto Rico had cut mortality rates in half, but still had very high birth rates, causing a rapid increase in population. Many attributed this growth in population to high unemployment.

[9] This strategy of encouraging emigration to reduce employment pressures has been termed the "safety valve" (*válvula de escape*). See Duany (2006) or Berman-Santana (1998) for a more critical view.

[10] Using the ACS and PRCS, we are able to identify migrants by an individual's state/country of residence one year prior to the survey.

[11] During 2000 and 2010 census, there were approximately 200,000 non-Puerto Ricans living on the island.

[12] Author's calculation using ACS data.

[13] For this study, Puerto Rico is the point of reference. Therefore, the term "emigrants" is used to describe migrants leaving Puerto Rico for the United States. "Immigrants" are those Puerto Ricans moving from the United States to Puerto Rico.

[14] Since ACS and PRCS do not contain longitudinal data (tracking a single individual over time) it is not possible to determine whether a particular individual was in the labor force in their residence of origin. Figures represent a representative individual's status once arriving in the receiving region.

[14] The Puerto Rico Port Authority and the Bureau of Transportation statistics both use the same measurements, which are derived from air travel statistics from Puerto Rico's main international airports.

[15] Several studies recognize the sizable role played by underground economic activities, and place its value at over $14 billion for 2006, or about 27 percent of the islands Gross Product.

Estimates are higher if illegal informal activities are considered in the calculation. It is possible that the size of this sector contributes to low employment figures. See Márquez and Ferré (2010), Schneider (2006), Estudios Técnicos (2010).

REFERENCES

Alemán, Eugenio J. 2012. Puerto Rico: Failure of the State. Wells Fargo Securities, LLC: Economics Group

Acosta-Belén, Edna and Carlos Santiago. 2006. *Puerto Ricans in the United States: A Contemporary Portrait*. Boulder: Lynne Rienner Publishers.

Berman-Santana, Déborah. 1998. Puerto Rico's Operation Bootstrap: Colonial Roots of a Persistent Model for "Third World" Development. *Revista Geográfica* 124: 87–116.

Bonilla, Frank and Ricardo Campos. 1981. A wealth of poor: Puerto Ricans in the new economic order. *Daedalus* 110(2): 133–76.

Borjas, George J. 2008. Labor outflows and labor inflows in Puerto Rico. *Journal of Human Capital* 2(1): 32-68.

Caribbean Business. 2013. Census: PR 'Brain Drain' Picking Up. 18 January. Accessed 4 February 2013. http://www.caribbeanbusinesspr.com/news03.php?nt_id=80281&ct_id=1/.

Collazo, Sonia G., Camille L. Ryan and Kurt J. Bauman. 2010. Profile of the Puerto Rican Population in United States and Puerto Rico: 2008. US Census Bureau. Accessed 4 February 2013.

Duany, Jorge. 2006. La nación en la diáspora: las múltiples repercusiones de la emigración puertorriqueña a Estados Unidos. *Revista de Ciencias Sociales* 17: 118–53.

Duany, Jorge, and Félix Matos-Rodríguez. 2006. Puerto Ricans in Orlando and Central Florida. Policy Report 1(1). New York: Centro de Estudios Puertorriqueños, Hunter College, CUNY.

Enchautegui, María E. 2008. La fuga de cerebros en Puerto Rico: su magnitud y causas. Consejo de Educación Superior de Puerto Rico. Universidad de Puerto Rico, Recinto de Río Piedras.

Enchautegui, Maria, and Richard Freeman. 2005. Why Don't More Puerto Rican Men Work? The Rich Uncle (Sam) Hypothesis. No. w11751. National Bureau of Economic Research.

Estudios Técnicos. 2004. Estudio sobre la economía informal de Puerto Rico. Submitted to the Banco Gubernamental de Fomento de Puerto Rico. 3 August 2010.

Falcón, Luis M. 1990. Migration and Development: The Case of Puerto Rico. No. 18. Commission for the Study of International Migration and Cooperative Economic Development.

Greene, Davis. 2013. 'Don't Give Up On Us': Puerto Ricans Wrestle With High Crime. NPR. Accessed 26 March 2013. http://www.npr.org/2013/02/07/171071473/-don-t-give-up-on-us-puerto-ricans-wrestle-with-high-crime/.

History Task Force. 1979. *Labor Migration Under Capitalism: The Puerto Rican Experience*. New York: Monthly Review Press.

Instituto de Estadísticas de Puerto Rico. 2010. Perfil del migrante. Estado Libre Asociado de Puerto Rico.

_____ 2012. Población y crecimiento económico. Progreso Economico. Prepared for Banco Popular de Puerto Rico.

Marino, John 2012. Puerto Rican Migration continues at record pace. 18 January. Accessed February 4, 2013. http://newamericamedia.org/2012/01/puerto-rican-migration-continues-at-record-pace.php/.

Márquez Carlos and James Ferré. 2010. Puerto Rico's underground economy estimated at $20 billion a year. *Caribbean Business* 23 December. Accessed 23 May 2013. http://www.cbonlinepr.com/prnt_ed/news02.php?nw_id=4566&ct_id=0/.

Martínez-Fernández, Luis. 2010. La diáspora en la frontera: retos y oportunidades para el estudio del Orlando puertorriqueño. *CENTRO: Journal of the Center for Puerto Rican Studies* 22(1): 33–55.

Martínez-Piva, Jorge M. 2005. Globalización y desarrollo: desafíos de Puerto Rico frente al siglo XXI. Vol. 84. United Nations–Comisión Económica Para América Latina. United Nations Publications.

Meléndez, Edwin 2007. Changes in the Characteristics of Puerto Rican Migrants to the United States. In *Latinos in a Changing Society*, eds. Martha Montero-Sieburth and Edwin Meléndez. 112–31. Westport, CT: Praeger.

Meléndez, Edwin and M. Anne Visser. 2011. Low-wage labor, markets and skills selectivity among Puerto Rican Migrants. *CENTRO: Journal of the Center for Puerto Rican Studies* 23(2): 39–62.

Moody's Investors Service. 2012. Moody's downgrades Puerto Rico general obligation and related bonds to Baa3 from Baa1 and certain notched bonds to Ba1. 13 December. Accessed 4 February 2013. http://www.moodys.com/research/Moodys-downgrades-Puerto-Rico-general-obligation-and-related-bonds-to--PR_262231/.

Muschkin, Clara G. 1993. Consequences of return migrant status for employment in Puerto Rico. *International Migration Review* 27(1): 79–102.

Pol, Julio C. 2004. Determinantes económicos de la migración entre Puerto Rico y Estados Unidos. Universidad de Puerto Rico, Unidad de Investigaciones Económicas, Ensayos y Monografías, Núm. 119.

Pol, Julio C. and Rafael Silvestrini. 2004. Crimen y economía subterránea en Puerto Rico. Unidad de Investigaciones Económicas, Departamento de Economía, Universidad de Puerto Rico.

Quintero, Braulio. 2011. Fuga de Cerebros. *El Nuevo Día*. Accessed 4 February 2013. http://www.elnuevodia.com/voz-fugadecerebros-968861.html/.

Rodríguez, Clara E. 1989. Puerto Ricans: Immigrants and Migrants: A Historical Perspective. Americans All, A National Multicultural EducationProgram. Washington, DC: Protfolio Project.

Ruggles, Steven, J. Trent Alexander, Katie Genadek, Ronald Goeken, Matthew B. Schroeder and Matthew Sobek. 2010. Integrated Public Use Microdata Series: Version 5.0 [Machine-readable database]. Minneapolis: University of Minnesota.

Schneider, Freidrich. 2006. Shadow Economies of 145 Countries all over the World: What
    do we really know? Working Paper. Presented in Hidden in plain sight: Micro-
    economic measurements of the informal economy: Challenges and opportunities, 4–6
    September. London, UK.

U.S. Census Bureau. 2009. Design and Methodology: American Community Survey.
    Washington, D.C.

Vargas-Ramos, Carlos. 2008. Migration and Settlement Patterns in Puerto Rico: 1985–2005.
    Centro Policy Report 2(1). New York: Centro de Estudios Puertorriqueños, Hunter
    College, CUNY.

Vázquez -Calzada, José. 1963. La emigración puertorriqueña: solución o problema? Sección de
    Bioestadísticas, Escuela de Medicina, Universidad de Puerto Rico.

_____ 1978. La población de Puerto Rico y su trayectoria histórica. Escuela de Salud Pública,
    Universidad de Puerto Rico, Río Piedras.

Whalen, Carmen T. 2005. Colonialism, Citizenship, and the Making of the Puerto Rican
    Diaspora: An Introduction. In *The Puerto Rican Diaspora: Historical Perspectives,*
    eds. Carmen T. Whalen and Víctor Vázquez-Hernández. 1–42. Philadelphia: Temple
    University Press.

A Brief Look at Internal Migration of Puerto Ricans in the United States: 2001–2011

JUAN CARLOS GARCÍA-ELLÍN

Introduction

The main objective of this chapter is to present the state-to-state migration patterns of Puerto Ricans living in the United States after the 2000 census. During the past two decades, available scholarship has analyzed the settlement of Puerto Ricans away from traditional settlement sites, mostly located in the northeastern states, to "new" locations across the country. Most of this scholarship has been focused on the migration between Puerto Rico and different locations across the United States. Yet, the migration experience for Puerto Ricans entails not only migration from the island, but also their movement across state boundaries within the country. The internal migration of the Puerto Rican population within the United States has had a direct and significant impact on these new settlement patterns. This impact is more observable in certain regions of the United States, such as the South, where, besides the migration of people arriving from Puerto Rico a source of increase in the Puerto Rican population has been state-to-state migration. The most common origin of this migration is the Northeast, a region with long-established Puerto Rican communities.

This chapter will demonstrate the significant degree to which internal migrants have contributed to the growth of the Puerto Rican population in areas such as Florida. By examining these internal migration flows, we can better understand the role migrants have played in the increase of the Puerto Rican population in these new places. This knowledge is necessary to form a complete picture of all the sources of Puerto Rican population growth in these new areas. This research will also achieve the goal of identifying not only the new areas of settlement but also the points of origin of the migration flows, and determining if Puerto Ricans share internal migration patterns that are similar to those of the rest of the population.

Finally this chapter will give us a better picture of the characteristics of the Puerto Rican internal migrants and how similar or different this population is from the entire Puerto Rican population living in the United States. Of particular interest is the role that the mainland-born Puerto Rican population plays in maintaining internal migration flows and contributing to the growth of the Puerto Rican population in the new destinations.

Review of Published Research

The subject of Puerto Rican migration to the United States has been thoroughly researched from a wide range of perspectives. It has been documented that Puerto Ricans have migrated to the United States in large numbers since the early twentieth century when Puerto Rican laborers were recruited to perform agricultural work in Hawaii, mostly in the sugar cane fields, and in Arizona, in the cotton fields (Smith 1942, Silva et al. 1984, McCormick and Ayala 2007, Iber and De Leon 2006). It has been also well established that Puerto Ricans have been living in every state since the middle of the twentieth century (Senior 1954).

The large migrations of Puerto Ricans to the United States between the late 1940s and early 1960s, primarily to the Northeast, have been researched extensively and are the subject of a large part of the academic research related to the Puerto Rican population (Centro de Estudios Puertorriqueños 1979, Maldonado-Denis 1980, Ortiz 1986, Rodriguez 1989, Sánchez-Korrol 1994, Ayala 1996). A more current wave of scholarship has analyzed the Puerto Rican migration to Florida and the implications and possible causes of changes in Puerto Rican settlement patterns during the latter part of the twentieth century (Acosta-Belén and Santiago 2006, Duany and Matos-Rodríguez 2006, Concepción-Torres 2008, Vargas-Ramos 2008, Silver 2010, Duany 2011).

Yet, very little attention has being directed to the internal migration of Puerto Ricans within the United States. Only a few scholars have attempted to identify the migration patterns of Puerto Ricans once they have settled in the United States. The bulk of this research has focused on identifying the differences in the internal migration patterns of Puerto Ricans compared with other Latino groups (Boswell 1984, McHugh 1989, Foulkes and Newbold 2000, García-Ellín 2012). The available scholarship that has specifically focused on the internal migration patterns of Puerto Ricans in the United States has mostly analyzed the destinations of Puerto Ricans who have migrated away from New York City (Marzán, Torres and Luecke 2008) or has attempted to examine the different outcomes of Puerto Ricans living in the northeastern United States by their migration status (Marzán 2009). In this context, this chapter provides a more complete view of the internal migration patterns of Puerto Ricans in the United States and their characteristics.

Data and Methodology

The data used in this analysis are drawn from all the one-year samples of the American Community Survey (ACS) conducted by the U.S. Census Bureau for every year between 2001 and 2011 and packaged by the Minnesota Population Center as the Integrated Public Use Microdata Series (IPUMS) (Ruggles et al. 2010). The ACS tracks the mobility of the population by asking those surveyed about their residence the previous year. For this chapter, the place of origin of the migration, as well as the destination, will be the state of previous or current residence, respectively. Thus, only those people who migrated across state lines will be part of the analysis. The use of state-to-state migration data is preferred because such a move implies, with some exceptions, a permanent or at least significant change in the circumstances of the migrant, such as a change in place of employment.

The data analyzed only include those migrants who self-identified as Puerto Rican when answering the question about ethnicity. The results were calculated using the person weights available with the dataset. This methodology was also employed by Foulkes and Newbold (2000) in their analysis of the internal migration of Latino subgroups.

Characteristics of Puerto Rican Internal Migrants

During the entire decade, more than 1.2 million Puerto Ricans migrated across state lines within the United States. This figure is the sum of all the people who at one point during the years 2001 to 2011 informed the ACS that they were living in a different state the previous year. Due to the limits in the data, it is not possible to determine the number of individuals who have engaged in multiple migrations during the period or how many of them were seasonal or temporary migrants. Still, the results present a fairly complete profile of the Puerto Rican domestic migrant.

In regional terms, Puerto Rican migration within the United States is very concentrated. The definitions for the regions are the ones used by the U.S. Census Bureau. The preferred regional destinations of Puerto Rican domestic migrants were the South and the Northeast. Just over 80 percent of Puerto Ricans who migrated across state lines selected these two regions with close

TABLE 1. Destination of Puerto Rican Internal Migrants, 2001-2011 (percent)

Region	Internal Migrants*	All Puerto Ricans in the U.S.**
Northeast	32.6	52.8
South	47.9	29.7
Midwest	7.8	9.4
West	11.7	8.1

Source: *ACS 1-year samples 2001-2011, **2010 US Decennial Census.

to 48 percent settling in the South. A remaining 12 percent migrated to the West and 8 percent settled in the Midwest (Table 1).

The preference among Puerto Rican migrants for relocating in the South is consistent with the migration preferences of the United States population as a whole (Berkner and Faber 2003, Ihrke and Faber 2012). For the past few decades, the South has been the top destination for all domestic migrants and the Puerto Rican population has formed part of this migration. On the other hand, the Northeast has been the least preferred destination of the United States population as a whole, but has been the second-most-preferred destination for Puerto Ricans. While the West has gained popularity as a destination for the United States population as a whole, the Puerto Rican population has not migrated there in greater numbers despite their past history of migrating towards the western states (Silva et al. 1984, Iber and De León 2006, McCormick and Ayala 2007).

The last decade was a period in which Puerto Ricans in the United States changed their settlement patterns in terms of their state of residence. For decades, New York was the preferred destination for Puerto Rican migrants, for those migrating both internally and from Puerto Rico (Maldonado-Denis 1980, Ayala 1996, Duany 2011, García-Ellín 2012). This pattern changed between 2001 and 2011, and the most popular state became Florida, which received 23 percent of internal migrants. This is a very dramatic change, not only because there is a new preferred destination, but also because almost a quarter of all Puerto Ricans migrating across state lines were part of this increasing trend. The other states that were preferred by Puerto Rican migrants were New York at 8.6 percent, Pennsylvania at 8.5 percent, Texas at 5.7 percent, and New Jersey also at 5.7 percent. These five states received a majority (51%) of all Puerto Rican internal migrants between 2001 and 2011 (Table 2).

TABLE 2. Destination of Puerto Rican Internal Migrants, 2001-2011 (percent)

State	Internal Migrants*	All Puerto Ricans in the U.S.**
Florida	22.6	18.3
New York	8.6	23.1
Pennsylvania	8.5	7.9
Texas	5.7	2.8
New Jersey	5.7	9.4

Source: *ACS 1-year samples 2001-2011, **2010 US Decennial Census.

This does not mean that the states that received the higher number of Puerto Ricans through internal migration flows necessarily gained Puerto Ricans overall. Internal, or domestic, migration flows have both inflows and outflows from a particular location. Both the number of in-migrants (inflows) and out-migrants (outflows) from each particular state are considered in calculating net migration, which is the degree to which the population changes through internal migration flows. The analysis is limited to the change in the Puerto Rican population in every state. A positive net migration of Puerto Ricans means that the state has received more Puerto Ricans from other states than the amount it has lost due to migration to other states. A negative net migration means the opposite, that the state has received less Puerto Ricans from other states than the amount it has lost to them. In this study, only migration within the United States, not migration between Puerto Rico and the United States, is considered.

States that received large numbers of Puerto Ricans, such as Florida, Pennsylvania, Texas, North Carolina, and Georgia, also gained Puerto Rican population through relocation from other states. In contrast, other states that received Puerto Rican migrants, such as New York, New Jersey, Massachusetts, California, and Illinois, actually lost Puerto Ricans through relocation to other states (Figure 1). For example, between 2001 and 2011, Florida received over 140,000 more Puerto Ricans from within the United States than it sent to other states. Meanwhile, during the same period, New York had a negative net migration of Puerto Ricans of over 162,000. This means that more Puerto Ricans migrated from New York to other states than the other way around.

The gender composition of Puerto Rican migrants of 51 percent men and 49 percent women is very balanced. However, men are overrepresented among migrants compared with their representation in the total Puerto Rican

FIGURE 1. States with Highest Number of Puerto Ricans Migrating within the U.S., 2001-2011

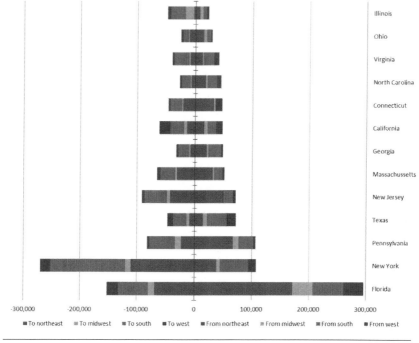

Source: ACS 1-year samples 2001-2011.

population of the United States, which is 49 percent male. As for marital status, only 37 percent of domestic migrants were married, while the remaining 63 percent were single, divorced, or widowed. Although this is a wide gap, it is very similar to the entire Puerto Rican population living in the United States, according to the 2010 decennial census.

There were 846,347 Puerto Ricans who migrated across state boundaries over the age of eighteen. This age group was used to analyze the educational attainment of Puerto Rican domestic migrants. Only 21 percent of those who migrated had not graduated from high school and for 31 percent of migrants, the high school diploma was their highest educational degree; 32 percent had some college experience or an associate's degree; 11 percent had a bachelor's degree; and 5 percent had earned a graduate or professional degree (Table 3). Thus, when compared with the Puerto Rican population as a whole, the

TABLE 3. Educational Attainment of Puerto Rican Internal Migrants at least 18 Years Old, 2001-2011 (percent)

Education	Internal Migrants*	All Puerto Ricans in the U.S.**
Less Than HS	20.8	26.6
High School	30.9	29.9
Some college	32.3	27.6
Bachelor's degree	11.2	10.7
Graduate degree	4.8	5.2

Source: *ACS 1-year samples 2001-2011, **ACS 2006-2010, Table DP02 (persons 25 years old or more).

migrant population is a slightly better-educated group. The number of people who did not finish high school is significantly lower for the migrant group (21% compared with 27%) while the proportion of those who only finished high school is slightly higher (31% compared with 30%). In terms of college experience, the number of people who had some college experience is higher for the migrant population (32% compared with 28%) but the proportion of college graduates is virtually the same (16% compared with 15.9%).

The majority of Puerto Rican domestic migrants were born in the United States. Of all Puerto Ricans who migrated across state borders between 2001 and 2011, 69 percent were born in the United States. A smaller proportion of Puerto Rican migrants, 28 percent, were born in Puerto Rico while the remaining 2 percent were born outside the fifty states and Puerto Rico. These figures are similar to the proportion of the total Puerto Rican population living in the United States, but those born in Puerto Rico are somewhat overrepresented (Table 4).

As for the time spent living in the United States, the largest group, 69 percent, were born in one of the fifty states. Another 13 percent were born outside the fifty states (largely in Puerto Rico) and had lived in the United States for at least

TABLE 4. Puerto Rican Internal Migrants by Place of Birth, 2001-2011 (percent)

Place of Birth	Internal Migrants*	All Puerto Ricans in the U.S.**
United States	69.4	66.4
Puerto Rico	28.4	31.6
Other places	2.2	1.9

Source: *ACS 1-year samples 2001-2011, **ACS 2006-2010, Table B05001.

TABLE 5. Puerto Rican Internal Migrants by Years Living in the U.S., 2001-2011 (percent)

Years in U.S.	Internal Migrants*	All Puerto Ricans in the U.S.**
U.S.-born	69.4	66.4
Less than 10	9.9	7.3
10 to 19	7.3	6.3
More than 20	13.4	19.9

Source: *ACS 1-year samples 2001-2011, **ACS 2006-2010, Table B05005.

twenty years. A smaller proportion, 7 percent, were born outside of the United States and had spent at least ten years in the United States before relocating within the country. Finally, 10 percent of all Puerto Rican domestic migrants were born outside the United States and had lived in the United States for less than ten years, which means that they had migrated to the United States within a decade of this secondary migration (Table 5). The fact that during this last decade, almost seven out of every ten Puerto Rican migrants were born in the United States is very significant, because it reveals that the settlement of Puerto Ricans in new destinations does not exclude migrants arriving directly from Puerto Rico and that Puerto Ricans born in the United States account for a significant portion, and often the majority, of the increase of the Puerto Rican population in these new destinations.

State-to-state Migration Flows
The domestic migration patterns of Puerto Ricans reflect the settlement patterns of this community in the United States. First of all, as Figure 2 shows, the northeastern states of New York, New Jersey, Connecticut, and Pennsylvania and the state of Florida act as both sending and receiving states of domestic migration. Second, there are six migration flows between five northeastern states. New York is the origin of four migration streams (to New Jersey, Pennsylvania, Connecticut, and Massachusetts); New Jersey is the origin of the other two streams (to New York and Pennsylvania). These flows showcase the process of relocation across the region that has been prevalent for the Puerto Rican community since the 1970s (McHugh 1989).

Third, there are five migration flows between four northeastern states (New York, New Jersey, Pennsylvania, and Connecticut) and the state of Florida. Four of these flows are made up of Puerto Ricans migrating from these four states to Florida while the fifth one is made up of Puerto Ricans migrating from Florida

FIGURE 2. Largest State-to-State Migration Flows of Puerto Ricans, 2001-2011

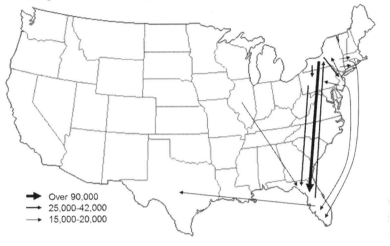

Over 90,000
25,000-42,000
15,000-20,000

Source: ACS 1-year samples 2001-2011.

to New York. These migration flows show a continuation of settlement patterns, evidenced in previous scholarship, of Puerto Ricans relocating to Florida (McHugh 1989, Foulkes and Newbold 2000, García-Ellín 2012). Also, the flows suggest that the Puerto Rican community has created the necessary networks (family members, community organizations, etc.) for Florida to be considered a viable Puerto Rican migration destination during the 1990s and 2000s. During the past two decades, the state of Florida was both a sending and a receiving state of Puerto Rican domestic migrants.

Illinois continues to be an important destination for migration from Puerto Rico, and is now also a sending state to Florida (Table 6). Since the 1990s, it has also become a relevant point of origin for internal migration (Garcia-Ellin 2012). The continuation of Illinois as a sending state accentuates its relevance in the settlement history of Puerto Ricans in the United States. The fact that the flow is from Illinois to Florida is also relevant. This shows that the state of Florida is simultaneously receiving migrants from both the Northeast and the Midwest. This migration flow is a continuation of a pattern of increased migration of Puerto Ricans to southern states first detected during the 1980s (Foulkes and Newbold 2000).

Texas has also emerged as an important destination for Puerto Ricans. For the first time since scholarship on domestic migration has been analyzing the mobility patterns of Puerto Ricans within the United States, Texas has

TABLE 6. Largest State-to-State Migration Flows of Puerto Ricans, 2001-2011

Rank	Flow	Puerto Rican Migrants		
		All	US-born	% US-born
1	NY to FL	92,888	64,988	69.96
2	NY to PA	41,280	30,906	74.87
3	NY to NJ	33,500	25,181	75.17
4	FL to NY	28,565	23,348	81.74
5	PA to FL	26,792	17,171	64.09
6	NJ to FL	19,502	11,823	60.62
7	IL to FL	18,911	12,062	63.78
8	NJ to NY	17,240	12,666	73.47
9	NJ to PA	17,073	11,262	65.96
10	NY to CT	16,732	13,173	78.73
11	NY to MA	16,459	10,917	66.33

Source: ACS 1-year samples 2001-2011.

become one of the more relevant migration flows for Puerto Ricans. The fact that this flow originates in Florida is also relevant, because it adds a dimension to that state's role in the dispersion patterns of Puerto Ricans in the United States. Now, besides its well-established role as a destination for Puerto Rican migrants, Florida is also one of the most important places of origin of Puerto Rican domestic migration.

As previously shown, the Puerto Rican population born in the United States makes up the majority of the migration. Because of the large number of these individuals migrating across state lines, the differences between this subgroup and the subgroup of Puerto Ricans who were born in Puerto Rico are not easily identifiable. Not only were 69 percent of all internal migrants born in the United States, but the largest migration flows also have a high proportion of this subgroup. At least 60 percent of the migrants were born in the United States in all of the twelve state-to-state migration flows with at least 15,000 Puerto Ricans, and six of these migration flows were made up of more than 70 percent from this subgroup (Table 6).

Other differences between these two subgroups are easier to identify in Figure 3 and Figure 4, which demonstrate the differences in their relocation patterns. First, there is more migration to Florida by island-born Puerto

FIGURE 3. Largest State-to-State Migration Flows of U.S.-Born Puerto Ricans, 2001-2011

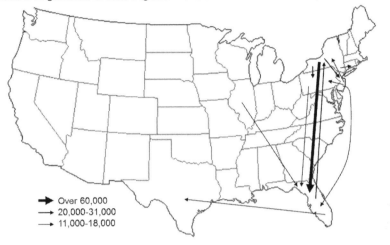

Source: ACS 1-year samples 2001–2011.

FIGURE 4. Largest State-to-State Migration Flows of Island-Born Puerto Ricans, 2001-2011

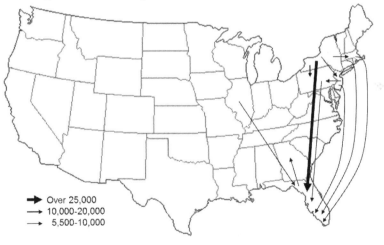

Source: ACS 1-year samples 2001–2011.

Ricans, with six migration flows to Florida compared with four migration flows to Florida of Puerto Ricans born in the United States. This means that even though the state of Florida is the destination of preference for both subgroups of Puerto Ricans, those who were born on the island seem to select Florida more often than other states, particularly when they are migrating from the northeastern region of the United States.

The second difference between the two subgroups is that Puerto Ricans born in the United States are more likely to migrate towards the state of New York than those who are born in Puerto Rico, who appear to be more interested in migrating away from that state. There are four migration flows originating in New York, or out-migration from New York, shown in each of the maps. However, there are two migration flows to New York shown in the map of flows of Puerto Ricans born in the United States, but there are no migration flows for island-born Puerto Ricans that have New York as a destination. This means that the interstate migration in the Northeast is different for each subgroup of Puerto Ricans. While Puerto Ricans born in the United States continue to relocate between New York, New Jersey, Pennsylvania, and Connecticut, those born in Puerto Rico seem to be migrating away from New York and looking for alternate destinations.

The third difference is the role Florida plays as a point of origin for internal migration. As the maps demonstrate, Puerto Ricans born in the United States migrate from Florida to New York and to Texas more than they do to other states. This contrasts with the migration patterns of island-born Puerto Ricans for whom only one of the more important state-to-state flows originates in Florida. Interestingly, the destination of that flow is the state of Georgia. This means that for Puerto Ricans born in the United States, migrating to New York is still socially acceptable and viable in contrast with the migration of the island-born away from that state. Also, during the 2001–2011 period, the migration of Puerto Ricans born in the United States from Florida to Texas is quite significant and is making Texas one of the preferred places of settlement of Puerto Ricans in the United States. Finally, the migration of island-born Puerto Ricans from Florida to Georgia reveals a pattern of dispersion of the Puerto Rican population to other southern states besides Florida and Texas.

Conclusion

To conclude, from 2001 to 2011, the South has gained more Puerto Ricans than any other region in the United States. This change in settlement patterns has been aided by the internal migration of Puerto Ricans into that region of the country. These changes are highlighted by the net gains in the Puerto Rican population of Florida, Georgia, Texas, and North Carolina through internal migration, while, despite continued growth in the Puerto Rican population, New York, New Jersey, and Massachusetts are experiencing negative net internal migration of Puerto Ricans because of relocation to other states. Although arrivals from Puerto Rico account for a large portion of the growth of the Puerto Rican population in the South, during the last decade, this growth has been significantly aided by internal migration.

In general terms, the Puerto Rican population has followed the internal migration patterns of the United States population as a whole by choosing to migrate to the South. On the other hand, even though the West has also experienced an increase in internal migration of Puerto Ricans, this increase is not as large as what has been experienced by the states in the South.

The characteristics of the migrant population are very similar to the Puerto Rican population as a whole. Among the differences between the two is the fact that the migrant population is slightly better educated than the total Puerto Rican population in the United States. Even though the number of college graduates is almost identical in both groups, the proportion of migrants who did not graduate from high school is lower in the migrant population, and at the same time, the proportion of those who had some college experience was higher for this group than it was for the entire Puerto Rican population.

Another significant difference is that the proportion within the migrant population of Puerto Ricans born in the United States is slightly higher than it is within the entire Puerto Rican population living in the United States (Table 4). This overrepresentation in the migrant population together with the data showing a higher proportion of them in all the largest state-to-state migration flows (Table 6) shows that the population of Puerto Ricans born in the United States is driving the new internal migration flows of Puerto Ricans.

Hopefully, this chapter has achieved the goal of providing a more nuanced view of the migration and settlement patterns of Puerto Ricans living in the United States.

REFERENCES

Acosta-Belén, Edna and Carlos E. Santiago. 2006. *Puerto Ricans in the United States: A Contemporary Portrait*. Boulder and London: Lynne Rienner Publishers.

Ayala, César J. 1996. The decline of the plantation economy and the Puerto Rican migration of the 1950s. *Latino Studies Journal*. 7(1): 62–90.

Berkner, Bonny, and Carol S. Farber. 2003. *Geographical Mobility: 1995–2000*. Census 2000 Brief, C2KBR-28. U.S. Census Bureau, Washington, D.C.

Boswell, Thomas D. 1984. The migration and distribution of Cubans and Puerto Ricans living in the United States. *Journal of Geography* 83(2): 65–72.

Centro de Estudios Puertorriqueños-History Task Force, 1979. *Labor Migration under Capitalism: the Puerto Rican Experience*. New York: Monthly Review Press.

Concepción-Torres, Ramón L. 2008. Puerto Rican Migration, Settlement Patterns and Assimilation in the Orlando MSA. Master's thesis, Binghamton University, SUNY.

Duany, Jorge. 2011. *Blurred Borders: Transnational Migration between the Hispanic Caribbean and the United States*. Chapel Hill: University of North Carolina Press.

Duany, Jorge, and Felix Matos-Rodríguez. 2006. Puerto Ricans in Orlando and Central Florida. Policy Report 1, No. 1. Centro de Estudios Puertorriqueños, Hunter College, CUNY.

Foulkes, Matthew and K. Bruce Newbold. 2000. Migration propensities, patterns, and the role of human capital: Comparing Mexican, Cuban, and Puerto Rican interstate migration, 1985-1990. *Professional Geographer* 52(1): 133–45.

García-Ellín, Juan C. 2012. Spatial Aspects of Secondary Migration of Hispanics in the U.S. Ph.D. dissertation. University of California, Los Angeles

Iber, Jorge and Arnoldo De León. 2006. *Hispanics in the American West*. Santa Barbara, CA: ABC-CLIO.

Ihrke, David K., and Carol S. Faber. 2012. *Geographical Mobility: 2005–2010*. Current Population Reports, P20-567. U.S. Census Bureau, Washington, DC.

Maldonado-Denis, Manuel. 1980. *The Emigration Dialectic: Puerto Rico and the USA*. New York: International Publishers.

Marzán, Gilbert. 2009. Still Looking for that elsewhere: Puerto Rican Poverty and migration in the Northeast. *CENTRO: Journal of the Center for Puerto Rican Studies* 21(1):101–17.

Marzán, Gilbert, Andrés Torres and Andrew Luecke. 2008. Puerto Rican Outmigration from New York City: 1995-2000. Policy Report 2, No. 2. Centro de Estudios Puertorriqueños, Hunter College, CUNY.

McCormick, Jennifer and César J. Ayala. 2007. Felícita 'La Prieta' Méndez and the end of Latino segregation in California. *CENTRO: Journal of the Center for Puerto Rican Studies* 19(2): 13–35.

McHugh, Kevin E. 1989. Hispanic Migration and population redistribution in the United States. *Professional Geographer* 41(4): 429–39.

Ortiz, Vilma. 1986. Changes in the characteristics of Puerto Rican migrants from 1955 to 1980. *International Migration Review* 20(3): 612–28.

Rodríguez, Clara E. 1989. *Puerto Ricans: Born in the USA*. Boston: Unwin Hyman.

Ruggles, Steven, J. Trent Alexander, Katie Genadek, Ronald Goeken, Matthew B. Schroeder, and Matthew Sobek. 2010. Integrated Public Use Microdata Series: Version 5.0 [Machine-readable database]. Minneapolis: University of Minnesota.

Sánchez-Korroll, Virginia. 1994. *From Colonia to Community: The History of Puerto Ricans in New York City.* Berkeley: University of California Press.

Senior, Clarence. 1954. Patterns of Puerto Rican dispersion in the continental United States. *Social Problems* 2(2): 93–9.

Silva, Milton N, Blase Camacho Souza, Elvira Craig De Silva and Cristóbal S. Berry-Cabán. 1984. Puerto Ricans of Hawaii: Immigrants and migrants. *Hispanic Journal of Behavioral Sciences* 6(1): 33–52.

Silver, Patricia. 2010. "Culture is more than bingo and salsa": Making Puertorriqueñidad in Central Florida. *CENTRO: Journal of the Center for Puerto Rican Studies* 22(1): 56–83.

Smith, William C. 1942. Minority groups in Hawaii. *Annals of the American Academy of Political and Social Science* 223: 36-44

Vargas-Ramos, Carlos. 2008. Migration and Settlement Patterns in Puerto Rico: 1985-2005. Policy Report 2, No. 1. Centro de Estudios Puertorriqueños, Hunter College, CUNY.

Patterns of Puerto Rican Settlement and Segregation in the United States, 1990–2010

CARLOS VARGAS-RAMOS[1]

The Puerto Rican population in the United States continues to grow in the new millennium. Puerto Ricans also continue to disperse throughout the entire country. Moreover, as they disperse, Puerto Rican settlements throughout the country continue to grow, with the exception of New York City, which continues to lose Puerto Ricans.

This work presents an overview of this population growth in the United States and the extent to which Puerto Ricans have established themselves as neighbors of other ethno-racial groups in the country. It replicates an earlier analysis of decennial census data from 1990 and 2000, updating it with data from the 2010 decennial census. Examination of these data finds that residential segregation from the majority population moderated between the last two decades, decreasing particularly in areas of very high segregation. However, Puerto Rican exposure to non-Hispanic whites decreased throughout the country. In contrast, Puerto Rican residential separation from non-Hispanic blacks and other Latinos continued to decrease from one decade to the next, sometimes in dramatic fashion, while exposure to these groups continued to grow. The trend is positive overall in that fewer Puerto Ricans are living in extremely segregated neighborhoods, even if these data cannot fully characterize the quality of interactions between Puerto Ricans and their non-Puerto Rican neighbors in the neighborhoods they share.

This chapter will first provide an overview of the growth and settlement patterns of Puerto Ricans, focusing on where Puerto Ricans have been concentrated and where they have continued to disperse. The chapter then presents a discussion of Puerto Rican residential segregation from non-Hispanic whites, non-Hispanic blacks, and other Latinos based on analyses of data from selected states and counties.

Settlement

The number of Puerto Ricans in the United States grew by more than 35 percent, a growth rate more than three times that of the population as a whole

TABLE 1. Puerto Rican Population in the United States, 1980–2010

	1980	1990	2000	2010
Total Number of Puerto Ricans	2,013,945	2,727,754	3,406,178	4,623,716
Puerto Ricans (as percentage of total U.S. population)	0.89%	1.10%	1.21%	1.50%
Total U.S. population	226,545,805	248,709,873	281,421,906	308,745,538

	Change		
	1980–1990	1990–2000	2000–2010
Total Number of Puerto Ricans	35.44%	24.87%	35.74%
Total U.S. population	9.78%	13.15%	9.71%

Source: U.S. Census Bureau, Census of the Population and Housing, 1980, 1990, 2000, and 2010.

(see Table 1). Moreover, Puerto Rican population growth during the 2000s was faster than it was during the 1990s, when Puerto Rican population was growing at a rate of 25 percent, and as fast as it was during the 1980s. This sustained growth in the Puerto Rican population in the United States parallels the growth of the Hispanic population in the country, but at a slower rate (Bergad and Klein 2010; Ennis et al. 2011).

This Puerto Rican population growth in the United States stands in stark contrast to the population decline on the island of Puerto Rico. The island of Puerto Rico had a population net loss for the first time in two and a half centuries, declining 2.2 percent, from 3.8 million to 3.6 million, between 2000 and 2010. These demographic trends reaffirm the observation that the majority of the population that self-identifies as Puerto Rican—including 1.5 million people born in Puerto Rico—resides in the fifty states rather than on the island.

Growth of the Puerto Rican population in the United States took place in every state and every region of the country. The majority of the Puerto Rican population was still concentrated in the Northeast, where nearly 53 percent lived in 2010 (see Table 2). However, this settlement concentration continued its decades-long decline. In 1990, more than two-thirds of Puerto Ricans lived in the Northeast. By 2000, three-fifths did so. In contrast, the South continued to increase its concentration of Puerto Ricans. In 2010, approximately 30 percent of

TABLE 2. Regional Distribution of the Puerto Rican Population in the U.S., 1990-2010

	1990	
Region	Puerto Ricans	Percent
Northeast	1,871,981	68.63
South	405,941	14.88
Midwest	257,594	9.44
West	192,238	7.05
Total	2,727,754	
	2000	
Region	Puerto Ricans	Percent
Northeast	2,074,574	60.91
South	759,305	22.29
Midwest	325,363	9.55
West	246,936	7.25
Total	3,406,178	
	2010	
Region	Puerto Ricans	Percent
Northeast	2,443,175	52.84
South	1,373,541	29.71
Midwest	434,735	9.40
West	372,265	8.05
Total	4,623,716	
	Percent Change	
Region	1990-2000	1990-2000	1990-2000
Northeast	29.86	30.27	30.13
South	52.09	50.45	51.03
Midwest	9.99	8.98	9.34
West	8.06	10.29	9.50

Source: U.S. Census Bureau, Census of the Population and Housing, 1990, 2000, and 2010.

Puerto Ricans in the United States lived in the South, twice the proportion that lived there in 1990. In fact, the South trebled its Puerto Rican population in those intervening twenty years, from 400,000 to 1.3 million people. Indeed, Puerto Rican population growth in the United States is driven by the growth in the South of 50 percent every decade since 1990. (For a broader analysis of Puerto Rican population growth in southern states, see Silver's chapters in this volume.)

This population growth and settlement dynamics are seen clearly in the growth in the two states with the largest Puerto Rican populations: New York and Florida. New York was still by far the state with most Puerto Ricans in the United States, with more than one million, or 23 percent of all Puerto Ricans. Florida, however, followed closely behind with nearly 850,000, or 18 percent of all Puerto Ricans. But whereas New York's Puerto Ricans grew by barely 2 percent between 2000 and 2010, Florida's grew by 75 percent; a rate by which Florida is poised to overtake New York as the state with most Puerto Ricans by 2020. States of traditional settlement for Puerto Ricans in the United States, such as New York, had growth rates below the average growth rate nationally of 35 percent. Other examples include Illinois, New Jersey, Connecticut, and Massachusetts, all of which had growth rates below 35 percent. These states with slower growth rates are also the states with the largest Puerto Rican populations.

On the other hand, states of relatively new settlement for Puerto Ricans, such as those in the Sun Belt, exhibited growth rates much faster than the national average. Indeed, the states with the fastest growth in their Puerto Rican populations, at rates that trebled or quadrupled national growth rates, were located mostly in the South or the West. But it should be noted that these were also states that had relatively small shares of the Puerto Rican population in the United States. So, while South Dakota had a Puerto Rican population growth rate of 133 percent, its share of the country's Puerto Rican population was less than one-tenth of one percent, with a total Puerto Rican population of just 1,483 people.

In 2010, the following fifteen states contained approximately 90 percent of the Puerto Rican population in the United States: New York (23%), Florida (18%), New Jersey (9%), Pennsylvania (8%), Massachusetts (6%), Connecticut (5%), California (4%), Illinois (4%), Texas (3%), Ohio (2%), Virginia, Georgia and North Carolina (each less than 2%), Wisconsin (1%) and Hawai'i (1%). The fifteen states with the fastest growth in their Puerto Rican population during the 2000s were: South Dakota (133%), North Carolina (131%), West Virginia (130%), South Carolina (117%), Tennessee (104%), Mississippi (104%), Georgia (103%), Nevada (98%), Arizona (98%), North Dakota (95%), Arkansas (94%), Alabama (93%), Idaho (93%), Maine (92%) and New Hampshire (89%). Despite rapid growth, these fifteen fast-growing states were home to just 6 percent of the Puerto Rican population. Puerto Rican migration patterns continue to mirror those of the population as a whole and other Hispanics generally, settling in fast-growing regions of the country—regions that have experienced large economic growth (Fischer and Tienda 2006; Bergad and Klein 2010).

Puerto Rican Population Concentration

As meaningful as the data on Puerto Rican dispersion throughout the United States are, just as important is the pattern of Puerto Rican concentration in their places of settlement and residence. An initial measure of concentration is their share of the total population, which increased to 1.5 percent in 2010 (see Table 1), more than their population share in 1980 (0.89%), 1990 (1.1%) and 2000 (1.2%).

Using this national share of the total population as a benchmark, it appears that Puerto Ricans are concentrated in nine states: Connecticut (7%), New York (5.5%), New Jersey (5%), Florida (4.5%), Massachusetts (4%), Rhode Island (3%), Hawai'i (3%), Pennsylvania (3%) and Delaware (2.5%). In all of these states, with the exception of New York, Puerto Rican share of population increased from the previous decade. Puerto Ricans were also increasingly overrepresented in these states compared with previous decades. These data indicate that Puerto Ricans (like rest of the population of the United States) are not evenly distributed across the different states, counties, cities, towns, suburbs, and rural areas where they live.

An analysis of county-level data indicates that, as with state-level data, the distribution of Puerto Rican population at the county level was also centered in the Northeast.[2] Of the top ten counties in terms of Puerto Rican population size, six were located in the Northeast: Bronx, Kings, New York (Manhattan), and Queens Counties of New York; Philadelphia County in Pennsylvania; and Hartford County in Connecticut. However, compared with the previous decade, the number of counties in the Northeast has decreased from the time when Hampden, Massachusetts ranked among the top ten counties. Instead, in addition to Cook, Illinois and Orange and Miami-Dade Counties in Florida, Hillsborough County, Florida, has joined the top-ten list. In so far as population growth is concerned, the pattern of growth shifting to the South and to counties of relatively new settlement elsewhere in the Northeast that was observed during the 1990s continued during the 2000s. Thus, among the top ten counties with the fastest growth in Puerto Rican population, six were located in the South (i.e., Lake, Flagler, Polk, Pasco, and St. Lucie Counties in Florida and Hoke County in North Carolina), but four were located in the Northeast, all of them in Pennsylvania (i.e., Union, Luzerne, Lackawanna, and Carbon Counties).

The Puerto Rican population in these counties more than doubled or trebled between 2000 and 2010. In fact, there were twenty-seven counties in which the Puerto Rican population at least doubled, and all of them were in the South, except for those in Pennsylvania and one in Delaware. In addition, there were 81 counties with above-average Puerto Rican population growth. By and large, these counties with above-average growth were not sites of traditional settlement for Puerto Ricans, but were adjacent to such traditional settlement sites (e.g., York County, Pennsylvania; Sussex and Warren Counties in New Jersey, and Putnam County, New York), if not new sites (e.g., Pulaski County, Missouri; Montgomery County, Tennessee; and Hillsborough County, New Hampshire). Counties with below-average Puerto Rican growth were those in or near traditional settlement sites (e.g., Morris County, New Jersey; Providence County, Rhode Island; Lorain County, Ohio; and Hartford County, Connecticut). Counties whose Puerto Rican population decreased were located largely in New York City or its immediate vicinity (e.g., Hudson County, New Jersey). (For a broader discussion of patterns of Puerto Rican migration within the United States, see García-Ellín's chapter in this volume.)

Puerto Rican Segregation

Dispersion of the Puerto Rican population throughout the country, in addition to reducing its concentration in the Northeast, has had a notable impact on how evenly distributed this population is and how much exposure it has to other ethno-racial groups. A common approach to establish statistically how social groups in the United States relate to each other is to analyze how closely or distantly they live from each other at the neighborhood level. Very often this is calculated using aggregate census data, with the census tract standing as proxy for neighborhood in a larger jurisdiction, whether it is a city, county, or metropolitan area. This approach is simply a broad gauge of segregation since it cannot establish the quality of social interaction or whether social interaction takes place at all (Berry 2008). A Puerto Rican, for instance, may live fully surrounded by other Puerto Ricans, but his or her exclusive social interactions with non-Hispanic whites may take place outside the neighborhood, whether in voluntary associations, a community of faith, or other type of group. Alternatively, such a Puerto Rican may be the only one in a neighborhood of non-Hispanic whites, but have no contact with her neighbors. (For a discussion on Puerto Rican levels of civic involvement, see Vargas-Ramos's chapter on the subject in this volume.) In a different scenario, such a Puerto Rican may in fact have contact with neighbors, but the character of such interactions might be positive or negative.

Common statistical indices of segregation cannot ascertain this interaction. Yet, statistical indices of residential segregation allow us to assess the likelihood of such interactions at very broad levels that have a meaningful impact on a person's every day life. For example, educational services are provided at the most local of governmental levels. Knowing that a neighborhood is highly segregated will indicate the likelihood of differential educational outcomes an area may have given the historical association between segregation and the uneven distribution of governmental services (as well as those that are privately distributed by market forces).

The measures used to establish the extent of segregation Puerto Ricans in the United States experience are based on two separate indices: dissimilarity and exposure (cf. Johnston et al. 2007). The dissimilarity index measures the proportion of Puerto Ricans that would have to move in order to achieve parity with another population groups (e.g., non-Hispanic whites).[3] A value of .6 or higher denotes high segregation levels. Values between .4 and .5 are deemed moderate; and those below .3 are seen as low measures of residential separation. The exposure index measures the extent that a Puerto Rican lives in proximity to a person from a different population group (e.g., non-Hispanic black) in the same geographical area.[4] For both indices, the geographical unit of analysis is the census tract within counties, and the data presented is aggregated at the county level. While dissimilarity is the most widely used measure of segregation, using both indices provides a more accurate description of residential distance or closeness (Johnston et al. 2007).

Puerto Rican and non-Hispanic white segregation

Results for the index of dissimilarity for 2010 show that of 71 counties analyzed, segregation of Puerto Ricans from non-Hispanic whites was high in 20 counties, with scores ranging from .6 to .71 (see Table 3).[5] All of these high-segregation counties were located in the Northeast or Midwest, and collectively they contained nearly one-third of the Puerto Rican population in the United States. Dissimilarity was moderate in 14 counties located in a various regions of the country, but mostly in the Northeast and the South. Fifteen percent of Puerto Ricans in the United States lived in these moderate-dissimilarity counties. Dissimilarity was low in eight counties, located largely in the South, where less than 2 percent of Puerto Ricans lived. In addition, 8 percent of Puerto Ricans lived in 14 counties with moderately high levels of dissimilarity, and another 10 percent lived in 14 counties with moderately low dissimilarity.

While a plurality of Puerto Ricans in the United States, 32 percent, still lived highly segregated from non-Hispanic whites, segregation has actually

TABLE 3. Puerto Rican Dissimilarity from Non-Hispanic Whites, 1990–2010

	1990		2000		2010	
Rate	Counties (n=71)	% PR population	Counties (n=71)	% PR population	Counties (n=71)	% PR population
.6 and above	32	57.4	26	45.4	20	31.7
.59 to .51	8	2.9	10	4.1	14	8.5
.50 to .4	10	12	15	12.2	15	15
.39 to .3	14	9	13	12.6	14	10.4
.3 and below	7	>1	7	1.2	8	1.7

Source: Author's calculations based on U.S. Census Bureau, Census of the Population and Housing, 1990, 2000, and 2010.

TABLE 4. Change in Puerto Rican Dissimilarity, 1990–2010

	From Non-Hispanic Whites		From Non-Hispanic Blacks		From Other Latinos	
	1990-2000 as % PR population in 2000	2000-2010 as % PR population in 2010	1990-2000 as % PR population in 2000	2000-2010 as % PR population in 2010	1990-2000 as % PR population in 2000	2000-2010 as % PR population in 2010
Increased	12.7	4.1	5.6	1.1	26.4	20.4
Unchanged	11	12.1	14.9	3.9	1.9	21
Decreased	51.5	51	54.8	62.2	47	25.8

Source: Author's calculations based on U.S. Census Bureau, Census of the Population and Housing, 1990, 2000, and 2010.

improved since 2000 when a greater proportion of Puerto Ricans, 45 percent, lived in 26 counties with high levels of dissimilarity. Indeed, since 1990, Puerto Rican dissimilarity from non-Hispanic whites has plummeted by more than 40 percent. Fifty-seven percent of Puerto Ricans, living in 32 counties, were highly segregated from non-Hispanic whites in 1990.

Change in Puerto Rican dissimilarity from non-Hispanic whites is evident from the data presented in Table 4. Half the Puerto Rican population in the United States resided in counties surveyed where dissimilarity from non-Hispanic whites had decreased between 2000 and 2010 (see Table 4, column 2). The bulk of this reduction in dissimilarity took place in counties with dissimilarity score of .6 or greater, where 30 percent of Puerto Ricans resided. An additional 7 percent resided in counties with dissimilarity ratios between

TABLE 5. Puerto Rican Exposure to Non-Hispanic Whites, 1990–2010

Rate	Counties (n=71)	% PR population 1990	Counties (n=71)	% PR population 2000	Counties (n=71)	% PR population 2010
.9 to 1.0	1	<1	-	-	-	-
.8 to .89	9	1.5	3	<1	1	<1
.7 to .79	14	7.5	9	2	4	1.2
.6 to .69	7	4.6	11	7.4	10	2.7
.5 to .59	14	7.2	13	10.3	12	7.9
.4 to .49	8	8.3	15	11.1	15	12.8
.3 to .39	8	13.8	9	15.3	15	17.9
.2 to .29	8	23.4	6	8.5	10	14.5
.1 to .19	2	15.5	4	10.7	3	3.8
.0 to .09	-	-	1	9.4	1	6.5

Source: Author's calculations based on U.S. Census Bureau, Census of the Population and Housing, 1990, 2000, and 2010.

.59 and .51 in 2010 that experienced a reduction in dissimilarity. Between 1990 and 2000, most Puerto Ricans also lived in counties where dissimilarity form non-Hispanic whites decreased (see Table 4, column 1). Therefore, the trend in declining dissimilarity from non-Hispanic whites extends over two decades. By way of contrast, dissimilarity from non-Hispanic whites increased in counties where 4 percent of Puerto Ricans lived in 2010 and where 13 percent lived in 2000, which is additional evidence of declining dissimilarity. The proportion of the Puerto Rican population that resided in counties where dissimilarity from non-Hispanic whites remained unchanged held steady at 11 percent in 2000 and 12 percent in 2010.

As remarkable as these data on dissimilarity from non-Hispanic whites are, the salient point is one of moderating dissimilarity. As shown in Table 3, while the number of Puerto Ricans living in highly segregated counties decreased, the proportion of those Puerto Ricans living at moderate social distance from non-Hispanic whites has remained steady over twenty years, while the number of those living in low-dissimilarity counties has barely increased. Yet, those living in moderately high-dissimilarity counties have nearly trebled since 1990 and doubled since 2000 to 8.5 percent of the Puerto Rican population.

The index of exposure provides additional evidence for this observation on a moderating dissimilarity. The likelihood that a Puerto Rican would live next door to a non-Hispanic white neighbor in the same county ranged from a low of .08 to a high of .83. Counties where Puerto Ricans were less exposed to non-Hispanic whites tended also to be older sites of traditional settlement, such as Essex County, New Jersey, Philadelphia County, Pennsylvania, or Kings County, New York. In addition, counties with low levels of non-Hispanic whites in their populations, such as Miami-Dade County in Florida or Honolulu County in Hawai'i, also ranked low in Puerto Rican exposure to non-Hispanic whites. On the other hand, counties with high Puerto Rican exposure to non-Hispanic whites were counties with high proportions of non-Hispanic whites in their populations (e.g., Hampshire County, Massachusetts, Pinellas County, Florida, and Ulster County, New York).

An analysis of 71 counties shows that in 2010 a plurality of Puerto Ricans (32%) lived in counties with rates of exposure to non-Hispanic whites between .30 and .50; another 25 percent lived in counties with rates of exposure under .30; and 12 percent lived in counties with exposure rates greater than .50 (see Table 5). In 2000, in contrast, 38 percent of Puerto Ricans lived in counties where exposure to non-Hispanic whites ranged between .30 and .50; 29 percent lived in counties with exposure rates lower than .30; and 20 percent living in counties with rates above .50. Evidently, there was an increase in exposure between 2000 and 2010 as well as between 1990 and 2000 in counties with rates of exposure between .30 and .50, while there were declines in exposure in counties with exposure rates higher than .50 and lower than .30. Table 6 indicates that declines in exposure to non-Hispanic whites at all levels were greater than increases in exposure. Indeed, exposure

TABLE 6. Change in Puerto Rican Exposure, 1990-2010

	To Non-Hispanic Whites		To Non-Hispanic Blacks		To Other Latinos	
	1990-2000 as % PR population in 2000	2000-2010 as % PR population in 2010	1990-2000 as % PR population in 2000	2000-2010 as % PR population in 2010	1990-2000 as % PR population in 2000	2000-2010 as % PR population in 2010
Increased	4.6	11.6	15.5	22.5	73.9	51.3
Unchanged	4.2	10.7	31.7	31.5	1.4	15.8
Decreased	66.5	50.8	28.1	13.2	>1	0

Source: Author's calculations based on U.S. Census Bureau, Census of the Population and Housing, 1990, 2000, and 2010.

declined in the counties where the vast majority of Puerto Ricans lived (see Table 6, columns 1 and 2).

Between 2000 and 2010, half of the Puerto Rican population lived in counties where exposure to non-Hispanic whites decreased; 11 percent lived in counties where exposure increased; and another 11 percent lived in counties where the rate of exposure was unchanged. Between 1990 and 2000, two-thirds of the Puerto Rican population lived in counties of decreasing exposure to non-Hispanic whites; 5 percent lived in counties where exposure increased; and another 4 percent lived in counties where exposure was unchanged. Therefore, the trend has been one of diminishing exposure to non-Hispanic whites across the past two decades, despite some slowing of the trend between 2000 and 2010. Counties of decreasing Puerto Rican exposure to non-Hispanic whites were mostly counties of recent settlement in Florida or Pennsylvania.

These changes in exposure suggest increases in residential segregation because the non-Hispanic white population in these neighborhoods and counties may be decreasing proportionately with the increase of ethno-racial minority groups. Thus, while it is possible that Puerto Ricans may be living in neighborhoods with decreasing separation from non-Hispanic whites, the likelihood of interaction between Puerto Rican and non-Hispanic whites at the county level is nevertheless reduced as the total population of non-Hispanic whites in the county decreases. Some counties may appear to become less segregated by the proportional increase of other populations in the same locations. An analysis of how Puerto Ricans relate to these other social groups is therefore in order.

Puerto Rican and non-Hispanic black segregation

Most analyses of segregation continue to use non-Hispanic whites as the reference point and comparison group, as they have historically been and still are the majority and dominant ethno-racial group in the United States. However, after more than a century of migrating to the United States, the interaction of Puerto Ricans has not been limited to non-Hispanic whites. In fact, in the urban centers of the Northeast, Puerto Ricans have interacted with and lived in close proximity to African Americans (i.e., non-Hispanic blacks). The analyses that follow describe the levels of segregation between Puerto Ricans and non-Hispanic blacks for 1990, 2000, and 2010 in the same 71 counties used in the analysis of segregation from non-Hispanic whites.

TABLE 7. Puerto Rican dissimilarity from Non-Hispanic Blacks, 1990–2010

Rate	1990		2000		2010	
	Counties (n=71)	% PR population	Counties (n=71)	% PR population	Counties (n=71)	% PR population
.6 and above	16	31.5	11	20.7	7	11.1
.59 to .51	19	16.2	11	12.7	9	12.9
.50 to .4	12	13.5	21	19.8	15	13
.39 to .3	15	18.5	16	17.7	22	20.9
.3 and below	9	2.1	12	4.4	18	9.3

Source: Author's calculations based on U.S. Census Bureau, Census of the Population and Housing, 1990, 2000, and 2010.

Dissimilarity between African Americans and Puerto Ricans in 2010 ranged from a very high .78 in Cuyahoga County, Ohio, to a low .09 in Monroe County, Pennsylvania. This segregation measure between Puerto Ricans and African Americans was actually higher in Cuyahoga County, Cook County, Illinois (.77), and Milwaukee County, Wisconsin (.72) than it was in the counties with most dissimilarity between Puerto Ricans and non-Hispanic whites (i.e., Essex County, New Jersey and Berks County, Pennsylvania, each at .7). Yet, Puerto Ricans lived in seven counties with high residential segregation from African Americans, which is half the number of counties with high residential separation between Puerto Ricans and non-Hispanic whites. These seven counties contained 11 percent of the Puerto Rican population in the United States (see Table 7). Puerto Ricans lived in 15 counties (with 13% of the Puerto Rican population in the United States) with moderate dissimilarity from African Americans, and in 18 counties with low dissimilarity. Thus, while some Puerto Ricans did live highly segregated from non-Hispanic blacks, this was not the case for a number of them, in contrast with the experience relative to non-Hispanic whites. Such relatively low levels of dissimilarity from non-Hispanic blacks insinuate a residential *buffering* effect that Latinos seem to serve vis-a-vis non-Hispanic blacks and whites (Fischer and Tienda 2006).

Not only is Puerto Rican dissimilarity from non-Hispanic blacks lower than it is from non-Hispanic whites, the rate of decrease in dissimilarity from the former is greater than it is from the latter. For example, 32 percent of the Puerto Rican population lived in counties with high dissimilarity from non-Hispanic blacks in 1990 compared with 21 percent in 2000 and 11 percent in 2010. An additional

TABLE 8. Puerto Rican Exposure to Non-Hispanic Blacks, 1990–2010

Rate	Counties (n=71)	% PR population 1990	Counties (n=71)	% PR population 2000	Counties (n=71)	% PR population 2010
.9 to 1.0	-	-	-	-	-	-
.8 to .89	-	-	-	-	-	-
.7 to .79	-	-	-	-	-	-
.6 to .69	-	-	-	-	-	-
.5 to .59	-	-	-	-	-	-
.4 to .49	1	1	1	<1	1	<1
.3 to .39	7	17.3	5	4.1	5	7.1
.2 to .29	12	27.2	11	27.2	10	16.6
.1 to .19	24	23.5	30	34.4	33	32.6
.0 to .09	27	12.9	24	9.7	22	10.9

Source: Author's calculations based on U.S. Census Bureau, Census of the Population and Housing, 1990, 2000, and 2010.

16 percent lived in moderately high-dissimilarity counties in 1990, compared with 13 percent in 2000 and 2010. In 1990 and 2010, 13 percent of the Puerto Rican population lived in moderate-dissimilarity counties compared with 20 percent in 2000. Those Puerto Ricans living in counties with lower dissimilarity increased from about 20 to 30 percent between 1990 and 2010. Many more Puerto Ricans lived in counties where dissimilarity from non-Hispanic blacks decreased (62% in 2010 from 55% in 2000) than in counties were dissimilarity increased (1% in 2010 from 6% in 2000) (see Table 4, columns 3 and 4).

While Puerto Rican dissimilarity from non-Hispanic blacks is ostensibly much lower than it is from non-Hispanic whites, Puerto Rican exposure to non-Hispanic blacks is also much lower than it is to non-Hispanic whites. This is the case because the proportion of non-Hispanic blacks in counties in which Puerto Ricans live tends to be much lower than that of non-Hispanic whites. After all, non-Hispanic whites are a numerical majority in this country, even as the proportion of ethno-racial minorities in the population continues to increase. As a result of these demographic realities, exposure to African Americans never exceeded .5 in any of the counties surveyed (see Table 8). In fact, for a plurality of Puerto Ricans (33%), their exposure to non-Hispanic blacks ranged between .10 and .19. For an additional 17 percent, exposure was between .20 and .29.

For nearly one-third of Puerto Ricans, exposure to non-Hispanic blacks did not change over the past two decades. Thirty–two percent lived in counties where exposure did not change between 1990 and 2000 and between 2000 and 2010 (see Table 6, columns 3 and 4). However, a greater proportion of Puerto Ricans lived in counties were exposure to non-Hispanic blacks increased (23%) between 2000 and 2010 than decreased (13%). Moreover, the increase in Puerto Rican exposure to non-Hispanic blacks involved twice as many Puerto Ricans (23%) as did the increase in exposure to non-Hispanic whites (12%) during the same period. During the 1990s, the increase in exposure to non-Hispanic blacks involved three times as many Puerto Ricans (16%) as non-Hispanic whites (5%). (During the 1990s, however, 28% of Puerto Ricans lived in counties that experienced a decrease in exposure to non-Hispanic blacks. Evidently, that trend reversed during the 2000s, when the proportion of Puerto Ricans living in counties of diminished exposure to non-Hispanic blacks decreased to 13%.)

Over time, Puerto Ricans began residing in locations with greater exposure to non-Hispanic blacks, where their numbers began to be more equal. Puerto Ricans appear to be integrating with non-Hispanic blacks to a greater degree than they are with non-Hispanic whites. Nevertheless, the social group with which Puerto Ricans enjoy the closest aggregate space is other Latinos.

Puerto Rican and non-Puerto Rican Hispanic segregation

While discrete Latino groups had historically settled in specific geographic regions of the country, the trend among Latinos (with Cubans as a qualified exception) has been to disperse throughout the country (Bergad and Klein 2010; Fischer and Tienda 2006). Different Latino subgroups may still predominate in particular areas of the country (e.g., Mexican-origin population in the Southwest; Puerto Ricans in the Northeast; Cubans and Cuban-Americans in South Florida). But, with massive Latino internal migration or Latin American immigration into Sun Belt states and other jurisdictions, the opportunity for Latinos of different national origins to live next to each other increases significantly.

As might be expected, Puerto Rican segregation from other Hispanics is relatively low. Most Puerto Ricans (44%) lived in counties with low dissimilarity from other Latinos in 2010 (see Table 9). An additional 15 percent lived in counties of moderately low dissimilarity. No Puerto Rican lived in a county with a dissimilarity ratio greater than .5 in the 71 counties surveyed. Moreover, the results for 2010 are an improvement over those of the previous two decades. For

TABLE 9. Puerto Rican Dissimilarity from Other Latinos, 1990–20

Rate	1990		2000		2010	
	Counties (n=71)	% PR population	Counties (n=71)	% PR population	Counties (n=71)	% PR population
.6 and above	-	-	-	-	-	-
.59 to .51	6	12.8	1	1.3	-	-
.50 to .4	11	11.5	7	13.8	5	9
.39 to .3	16	15.5	15	13.3	17	14.5
.3 and below	38	42	48	47	49	43.7

Source: Author's calculations based on U.S. Census Bureau, Census of the Population and Housing, 1990, 2000, and 2010.

instance, in 1990, 13 percent of Puerto Ricans lived in counties of moderately high dissimilarity, compared with 1 percent in 2000 and none in 2010.

Despite relatively low or moderate levels of dissimilarity from other Latinos, some Puerto Ricans did live in counties that experienced increases in dissimilarity from other Latinos. Between 2000 and 2010, 20 percent of Puerto Ricans lived in counties that had increases in dissimilarity compared with 26 percent between 1990 and 2000 (see Table 4, column 6). Dissimilarity decreased in counties where 26 percent of Puerto Ricans lived in 2010 and where 47 percent lived in 2000. Dissimilarity from other Latinos was unchanged for 21 percent of Puerto Ricans by 2010 and for 2 percent by 2000 (see Table 4, column 5). Evidently, the constancy of Puerto Ricans living relative to other Latinos was much more fluid, especially during the 1990s.

This fluidity is also manifest in the extent to which Puerto Ricans are exposed to other Latinos. Like African Americans, Latinos are a numerical minority in the United States; therefore, while they may share the same immediate space in a given neighborhood, when their exposure is aggregated at a larger jurisdiction, the ratio of interaction is reduced. Consequently, the ratio of Puerto Rican exposure to other Latinos did not exceed .60 in 2010 (or 2000) (see Table 10). (In 1990, Puerto Rican exposure to other Latinos did not exceed .50, and there was barely any exposure above .30.)

Given the growth of the Latino population over the past two decades, increased exposure was not unexpected. In fact, half the Puerto Rican population in the United States lived in counties where exposure to other Latinos increased (as did nearly three-fifths of Puerto Ricans in 2000) (see Table 6, columns 5 and

TABLE 10. Puerto Rican Exposure to Other Latinos, 1990–2010

Rate	Counties (n=71)	% PR population 1990	Counties (n=71)	% PR population 2000	Counties (n=71)	% PR population 2010
.9 to 1.0	-	-	-	-	-	-
.8 to .89	-	-	-	-	-	-
.7 to .79	-	-	-	-	-	-
.6 to .69	-	-	-	-	-	-
.5 to .59	-	-	1	2.4	1	2
.4 to .49	1	1.5	1	1.1	3	1.9
.3 to .39	-	-	4	5.8	6	12.3
.2 to .29	9	13.3	12	28.1	16	20.9
.1 to .19	13	40	15	16.3	19	14.6
.0 to .09	48	27	38	21.7	26	15.5

Source: Author's calculations based on U.S. Census Bureau, Census of the Population and Housing, 1990, 2000, and 2010.

6). Exposure did not decrease in any county surveyed in 2010 (and by less than 1% in 2000). Exposure remained unchanged in counties where 16 percent of Puerto Ricans lived in 2010 (and by 1% in 2000).

Conclusion

The Puerto Rican population in the United States continues to grow. It has grown the fastest in states of recent overall population growth, such as those states in the Sun Belt (Vélez and Burgos 2010), following national trends. The only area of the country that continues to lose Puerto Ricans is New York City. Puerto Ricans also continue to disperse throughout the United States. In a process first observed nearly twenty years ago, Puerto Ricans are moving in growing numbers into every state of the union, by largely abandoning the largest urban centers for Sun Belt metropolitan areas or mid-size cities and exurbs in the Northeast (Rivera-Batiz and Santiago 1996; Acosta-Belén and Santiago 2006).

The first decade of the millennium witnessed an overall improvement in Puerto Rican residential separation from non-Hispanic whites. Fewer Puerto Ricans were living in high-dissimilarity counties in 2010 than in 2000 and 1990. In this sense, Puerto Ricans appeared to benefit from national trends that manifested lower residential segregation between ethno-racial groups. But whereas some of these trends were correctly, if exultantly, touted as the unequivocal end of the most blatant forms of residential separation (Glaeser and Vigdor 2012), national metropolitan trends show that the majority population (i.e., non-Hispanic whites) still lives in neighborhoods that do not exhibit the same extent of ethno-racial diversity that exists in the rest of the country (Logan and Stults 2011). Neighborhoods where minorities live tend to be diverse because they are inhabited by a variety of non-white ethno-racial groups. Neighborhoods where the majority population lives are still overwhelmingly homogeneous (Rugh and Massey 2013).

Insofar as Puerto Ricans are concerned, the positive development in the diminution of extreme residential separation from non-Hispanic whites is tempered by the fact that exposure to non-Hispanic whites over the decades decreased consistently as Puerto Ricans began to occupy new settlement areas. This pattern was evident during the 1990s (Vargas-Ramos 2006) and continued during the 2000s, as the present results show. It seems as if the improvement in residential segregation for Puerto Ricans relative to non-Hispanic whites is temporary and transitional. Migration has contributed to this pattern. Although migration from states and counties of traditional settlement to new locations has contributed to the reduction in Puerto Rican dissimilarity from non-Hispanic whites, the reduction has been from very high dissimilarity to a moderately high dissimilarity. Puerto Ricans are also moving to counties where there are few Puerto Ricans but a large presence of non-Hispanic whites initially that over the decades experience a marked decrease in exposure to non-Hispanic whites. Puerto Ricans may settle in low-dissimilarity or moderate-dissimilarity counties but are likely to encounter increasing segregation as the overall population of counties, states, and the country as a whole continues to change. In fact, the trend is likely to be one of both decreasing and increasing segregation, with the experience of one form or the other determined by local circumstances. As Rugh and Massey have recently noted "...the United States is neither moving toward the end of the segregated century nor resting at a point of stalled integration. Rather, Black and Hispanic segregation and spatial isolation continue to be actively produced in some metropolitan areas while being mitigated in others" (2013: 17).

As counties become more diverse with the natural growth and influx of ethno-racial minorities, exposure to the majority population does not necessarily improve. Rather, minorities come to represent a replacement population to non-Hispanic whites who are either dying off or exiting for more ethnically homogeneous locations. Yet, relative to other Hispanics, it appears as if Puerto Ricans have made greater strides in their residential integration with non-Hispanic whites, even if greater integration is still attainable (Fischer and Tienda 2006; Logan and Stults 2011).

The finding that neighborhoods where distinct ethno-racial minorities live tend to be more diverse than neighborhoods inhabited by non-Hispanic whites because they share residential space with other minorities is evident in the data presented in this chapter. While clear instances of extreme Puerto Rican residential segregation from non-Hispanic blacks exist, the experience is one of largely moderate or low separation. Moreover, the trend is towards relatively greater integration and slowly growing exposure between Puerto Ricans and non-Hispanic blacks. Similarly, and in regards to other Latinos, Puerto Ricans do not seek to stand apart. Rather, Puerto Ricans live in communities with low dissimilarity from other Latinos, in the face of an increasing population growth in this segment of the population. Puerto Ricans are an integral component of the Latino population in the United States.

What then are the prospects for Puerto Rican integration? Thirty years ago Massey and Bitterman (1985) had explained that the standard ecological model of spatial assimilation was applicable to Puerto Ricans despite the paradox of continuing segregation in the wake of socioeconomic advancement. Puerto Ricans with greater socioeconomic resources than other Puerto Ricans appeared to live in neighborhoods that were highly segregated from non-Hispanic whites without much improvement over time. Ecological theory expectations explained that as Puerto Ricans improved their socioeconomic standing, their physical proximity to non-Hispanic whites would improve. This did not happen, because Puerto Ricans, even those of greater socioeconomic standing, were still of lower socioeconomic status than non-Hispanic whites, who shunned them for this reason and not because Puerto Ricans were necessarily ethnically different; and because Puerto Ricans were also more willing to live next to African Americans, partly because of the high proportion of Puerto Ricans of African ancestry, which also kept non-Hispanic whites from those neighborhoods. These explanations were consistent with the ecological model of residential segregation and assimilation. The pattern implicit in the descriptive data presented in this chapter suggests that this pattern of residential integration along socioeconomic and racial factors persists.

Puerto Rican dissimilarity from non-Hispanic whites has improved because fewer Puerto Ricans live in extremely segregated neighborhoods, even if dissimilarity from non-Hispanic whites is still relatively high for many. Puerto Ricans escape these high levels of dissimilarity in a sequential fashion, by moving to progressively less segregated neighborhoods, often in areas that are relatively new to Puerto Rican settlement and not infrequently across county or state lines. In these neighborhoods, exposure to non-Hispanic whites progressively diminishes, while exposure to non-Hispanic blacks and other Latinos increases, which also has the effect of diminishing residential dissimilarity from these other groups. The proportion of minorities continues to increase in the neighborhoods Puerto Ricans inhabit. Minorities are growing more integrated with each other. Although nationally, dissimilarity between African Americans and non-Hispanic whites has improved progressively, it may take more than half a century for their numbers to be equalized if extant conditions persist (Rugh and Massey 2013). The same cannot be said for Hispanics overall and Asians, whose overall relations with non-Hispanic whites appear to be stagnant.

The country, then, is in a process of social flux driven by both upward and downward mobility and migration, with evidence of progress as well as regression. For Puerto Ricans, the process of integration with the majority population appears to continue for many, even if that progress seems tenuous and tentative. Given the large social distance that still remains between Puerto Ricans (and other Latinos and African Americans) and non-Hispanic whites, improvements in segregation are welcome trends. But the fact that social advantages continue to be out of reach for very many Puerto Ricans and other minority groups as a result of the physical and social distance that exists in American society is source of unending concern.

NOTES

[1] With the research assistance of Jennifer Hinojosa. This research has been sponsored by a PSC-CUNY award (PSC-CUNY TRADA- 43 507 2012).

[2] The data presented in this analysis are for 163 counties in 25 states. The selected counties were chosen based on the following criteria: 1) a high number of Puerto Ricans living within their boundaries in 2000 and 2010; 2) an above-average proportion of Puerto Ricans as a percentage of their respective populations in 2000 and 2010; and 3) a relatively rapid growth during the 2000s. The selected counties contained 79% of the Puerto Rican population in the United States in 2010 and 84% in 2000. The fact that these same counties held a smaller share of the Puerto Rican population in 2010 than in 2000 is further evidence of their dispersion across the United States.

[3] Specifically, the index of dissimilarity calculates in the aggregate, at the county level, the proportion of Puerto Ricans who live in a census track relative to their numbers in a given county relative to the proportion of another population group (e.g., non-Hispanic whites, non-Hispanic blacks, other Latinos, Asians, etc.) that lives in the same census track over the numbers of that population group in the same county. Thus, in a neighborhood, Puerto Ricans would be evenly distributed with non-Hispanic whites (or any other comparison group) if their proportions in the neighborhood are the same as their proportions in the county.

[4] Specifically, the index of exposure measures in the aggregate, at the county level, the proportion of Puerto Ricans in a census tract relative to their numbers in the county in relation to the proportion of another group in the census tract relative to county's total population.

[5] As a replication extending a previous study (Vargas-Ramos 2006) with data from 2010, the 71 counties included in this analysis were selected given: 1) a high absolute number of Puerto Ricans within their jurisdiction in 1990 and 2000, 2) an above-average proportion of Puerto Rican as a percentage of their population in 1990 and 2000, 3) a relative high growth during the 1990s. The selected 71 counties included 82% of the Puerto Rican population in 1990, 75% in 2000 and 67% in 2010.

REFERENCES

Acosta-Belén, Edna and Carlos E. Santiago. 2006. *Puerto Ricans in the United States: A Contemporary Portrait.* Boulder, CO: Lynne Reinner Publishers.

Bergad, Laird W. and Herbert S. Klein. 2010. *Hispanics in the United States: A Demographic, Social, and Economic History, 1980-2005.* New York: Cambridge University Press.

Berry, Brent. 2008. Indices of Residential Segregation: A Critical Review and Redirection. In *White Logic, White Methods: Racism and Methodology*, eds. Tufuku Zuberi and Eduardo Bonilla-Silva. 203–16. Lanham, MD: Rowman and Littlefield.

Ennis, Sharon R., Merarys Ríos-Vargas and Nora G. Albert. 2011. *The Hispanic Population.* 2010 Census Brief, C2010BR-04. Suitland, MD DC: U.S. Census Bureau.

Fischer, Mary J. and Marta Tienda. 2006. Redrawing Spatial Color Lines: Hispanic Metropolitan Dispersal, Segregation, and Economic Opportunity. In *Hispanics and the Future of America*, eds. Marta Tienda and Faith Mitchells. 100–37. Washington, DC: National Academies Press.

Glaeser, Edward and Jacob Vigdor. 2012. The end of the segregated century: racial separation in America's neighborhoods, 1890-2010. Civic Report No. 66, Center for State and Local Leadership. New York: Manhattan Institute.

Johnston, Ron, Michael Poulsen and James Forrest. 2007. Ethnic and racial segregation in U.S. metropolitan areas, 1980-2000: The dimensions of segregation revisited. *Urban Affairs Review* 42(4): 479–504.

Logan John R. and Biran J. Stults. 2011. The persistence of segregation in the metropolis: new findings from the 2010 census. Census Brief prepared for Project 2010. Accessed 2 February 2013. http://www.s4.brown.edu/us2010/.

Massey, Douglass S. and Brooks Bitterman. 1985. Explainig the paradox of Puerto Rican segregation. *Social Forces* 64(2): 306–31.

Rivera-Batiz, Francisco L. and Carlos E. Santiago. 1996. *Island Paradox: Puerto Rico in the 1990s.* New York: Russell Sage Foundation.

Rugh, Jacob S. and Douglas S. Massey. 2013. Segregation in post-civil rights America. *Du Bois Review* 1-28. doi: 10.1017/S1742058X13000180.

Vargas-Ramos, Carlos. 2006. Settlement Patterns and Residential Segregation of Puerto Ricans in the United States. Policy Report 1(2): New York: Center for Puerto Rican Studies, Hunter College, CUNY.

Vélez, William and Giovani Burgos. 2010. The impact of housing segregation and structural factors on the socioeconomic performance of Puerto Ricans in the United States. *CENTRO: The Journal of the Center for Puerto Rican Studies* 22(1): 175–95.

Puerto Ricans in Florida
PATRICIA SILVER

> *Florida is a transient state and a state of transience.*
> *The character and composition of Florida changed profoundly after*
> *1950, the result of two powerful forces: migration and immigration.*
>
> Mormino (2005: 14)

Although it seems that most Puerto Ricans have family members living in Florida, there has been surprisingly little written about this important new center of Puerto Rican settlement.[1] This chapter offers a sketch of Puerto Rican settlement in Florida using demographic, historic, and ethnographic data.

In 2010, Hispanics were 22 percent of the total population of Florida. The Puerto Rican population, at about 20 percent of all Hispanics, now rivals the Cuban population, at about 28 percent of all Hispanics (U.S. Census Bureau 2010). By 2020, the number of Puerto Ricans is projected to exceed the number of Cubans in Florida.

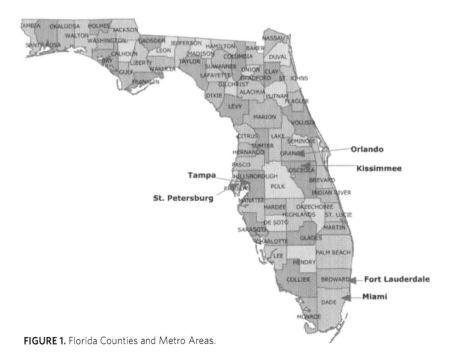

FIGURE 1. Florida Counties and Metro Areas.

Figure 1 identifies Florida counties by name and locates the three metro areas of largest Puerto Rican settlement in the state.[2] Although Puerto Rican communities in the Tampa and Miami areas have longer histories than other areas, Puerto Ricans in the Orlando area, especially in Orange and Osceola counties, predominate over other Hispanic groups. Indeed, Orange County, where Orlando is located, is the leading destination for Puerto Ricans of all the counties in the United States (see Vargas-Ramos 2014).

As a prelude to considering the data for Puerto Ricans in Florida, it is important to note the different regions of this very large state. Floridians refer to North Florida, South Florida, and Central Florida; Central Florida is often divided further into East Central (where Orlando is located) and West Central (where Tampa is located). Jacksonville, not shown in Figure 1, is in North Florida (Duval County). Miami is in South Florida. There is common joking reference that the further north one goes in Florida, the deeper in the South one is.

South Florida is not only the base of Cuban influence and power in Florida, but it is also the area of the state with the largest Hispanic population overall. Bordering Georgia and Alabama, North Florida is often called "Old Florida," suggesting that this part of the state has been less touched by the demographic and cultural changes experienced since the 1960s. Central Florida, where Puerto Ricans are most concentrated, sits geographically and metaphorically between "Old Florida" in the North and the strong Cuban and Hispanic presence in South Florida.

Central Florida has seen a rapid shift in its economic activity in recent decades, as acres of orange groves and the open spaces needed for cattle ranches have been transformed into sites for theme parks, hotels, housing developments, and retail outlet centers. This economic shift has been accompanied by a dramatic demographic shift, and the growth of the Puerto Rican population in Central Florida has been an important part of this transition.

Florida Overview

Figure 2 represents Puerto Rican population by county in Florida. The darker colors indicate the counties with the largest Puerto Rican populations, Broward, Hillsborough, Miami-Dade, Orange, and Osceola.

Table 1 gives the number of Puerto Ricans and their percent of total population for each of the five Florida counties with the largest Puerto Rican populations. Orange County, where Orlando is located, has by far the largest Puerto Rican population, at just under 150,000. Next is Miami-Dade County at about 92,000, followed by Hillsborough County, where Tampa is

FIGURE 2. Puerto Rican Population in Florida Counties, 2010

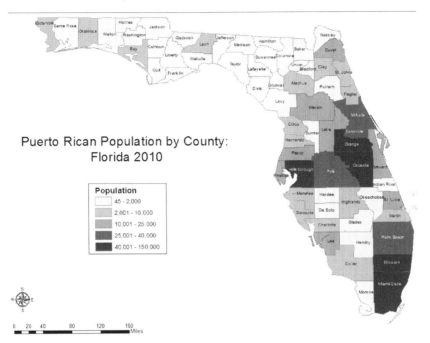

Puerto Rican Population by County:
Florida 2010

Population
45 - 2,000
2,001 - 10,000
10,001 - 25,000
25,001 - 40,000
40,001 - 150,000

0   20   40   80   120   160
                                      Miles

Source: U.S. Census Bureau, 2010 Census SF1, Table PLT11.

located, at just over 91,000. Broward County in South Florida at about 76,000 and Osceola County in Central Florida at about 73,000 are fourth and fifth, respectively, in terms of numbers.

In terms of percentages of total population, Orange and Osceola counties are the largest centers of Puerto Rican settlement in the state. Puerto Ricans in Osceola County, although smaller in number than other counties, make up 27 percent of the total population. In Orange County, they make up 13 percent of the total population. Both counties have a significantly greater concentration of Puerto Ricans than Hillsborough (7%) and the two South Florida counties, Broward and Miami-Dade, where Puerto Ricans make up 4 percent of the population of each. These demographic changes have made an impact on Hispanic influence within the state as the traditional Cuban dominance in South Florida is being challenged by the growth of the Puerto Rican community in Central Florida.

TABLE 1. Florida Counties with Highest Puerto Rican Population, 2010

Rank	State	Percent
Orange County	149,457	13
Miami-Dade County	92,358	4
Hillsborough County	91,476	7
Broward County	75,840	4
Osceola County	72,986	27

Source: U.S. Census Bureau, Census of the Population and Housing, 2010.

TABLE 2. Puerto Rican Population in Florida Metro Areas, 2010

Rank	Puerto Rican	% of Total
Orlando-Kissimmee-Sanford	269,781	13
Miami-FortLauderdale-Pompano Beach	207,727	4
Tampa-St. Petersburg-Clearwater	143,886	5
Lakeland-Winter Haven	34,825	6
Jacksonville	30,532	2

Source: U.S. Census Bureau, Census of the Population and Housing, 2010.

Table 2 gives the numbers and percent of total population for the top five metro areas where Puerto Ricans have settled in Florida. Although Tampa has the longest history of Puerto Rican migration, the 2010 Puerto Rican population in the Tampa metro area of about 140,000 was significantly smaller than in the metro areas of Miami at about 208,000 and Orlando at about 270,000. The difference between the Miami and Orlando communities, however, is evident in the data on percentage of total population. In the Orlando metro area, this percentage (13%) is more than three times that of the Miami metro area (4%).

Located just between Orlando and Tampa is Lakeland, which is home to about 35,000 Puerto Ricans. The area remains largely rural, but as both Tampa and Orlando continue to grow, it sits at the center of what is sometimes called "Orlampa," a part of the state that is predicted to become a mega-region (Griffith 2006). The newest of the top metro areas of Puerto Rican population is Jacksonville, which is home to an emerging Puerto Rican community in North Florida. While still the smallest in both number and percentage of population,

FIGURE 3. Central Florida Counties

this is an area where the Puerto Rican population is expected to grow.

Figure 3 illustrates the counties surrounding Orlando. The counties of Central Florida emerged as key to the isolation and segregation trends that Carlos Vargas-Ramos (2014) has analyzed for Puerto Ricans nationally. Regarding the increasing isolation of Puerto Ricans in Osceola and Orange counties, among others, Vargas-Ramos concludes, "Puerto Ricans gravitate towards other Puerto Ricans as they disperse throughout the United States." Ethnographic data supports this conclusion as Puerto Ricans have moved increasingly to the eastern part of Orlando and Orange County, and to two developments south of Orlando (Meadow Woods and Buenaventura Lakes), which together straddle the Orange/Osceola county line. Political mobilizing for greater Puerto Rican and Hispanic representation has emerged from these areas to the east and south.

Two other counties in Vargas-Ramos' analysis merit attention here. Lake and Polk[3] counties are noted as being among the counties in the United States experiencing the most growth in Puerto Rican population. These two counties, adjacent to the western ends of Orange and Osceola, respectively, are also among the areas experiencing a significant increase in the isolation

TABLE 3. Puerto Rican Education, Income, and Unemployment in Florida and the U.S. (percent)

	High school or higher	Bachelor's or higher	Graduate or professional	Median household income (USD)	Families below poverty	Unemployment
Florida	80	18	5	$41,198	16	11
United States	73	16	5	$38,426	22	13

Source: U.S. Census Bureau, ACS, 5-year estimates, 2010.

of Puerto Ricans. Lake and Polk counties are both relatively rural but show significant signs of "development" in the form of new housing developments and the accompanying shopping and entertainment areas. Ethnographic data suggest that the increase in the Puerto Rican population in Lake County is due in part to some Puerto Ricans choosing to relocate away from the increasing number of Puerto Ricans arriving and settling in Orlando (Orange County) and Kissimmee (Osceola County). Ramón Concepción Torres (2008) found that socioeconomic status among wealthier Puerto Ricans in the Orlando area was a stronger factor than ethnic identification in choice of residence. This prompts a question about the socioeconomic characteristics of those who choose to stay in the Osceola/Orange area compared with those who are moving west to Polk and Lake.

Table 3 gives data on educational attainment, income, and unemployment for Puerto Ricans in Florida compared with Puerto Ricans in the United States as a whole.[4] The median household income for Puerto Ricans in Florida, more than $41,000 per year, is higher than it is for the United States as a whole ($38,426). Puerto Rican unemployment in Florida, at 11 percent, is lower than it is for Puerto Ricans nationally, at 13 percent. The 16 percent of Puerto Rican families in Florida with income below the poverty level during the last 12 months before being surveyed is lower than the national rate of 22 percent. With high school education attainment rates also higher in Florida, 80 percent compared with 73 percent nationally, it begins to look as though Puerto Ricans living in Florida might enjoy a higher socioeconomic status than Puerto Ricans living in other areas of the United States. In terms of the cultural capital of educational attainment at the bachelor's level and beyond, however, Puerto Ricans in Florida look more like Puerto Ricans in the United States as a whole. Puerto Ricans in Florida age 25 and older have only a slightly higher rate of attaining a bachelor's degree or higher (18% compared to 16% nationally), and they are on a par with Puerto Ricans across the United States in terms of graduate or professional degrees, both at 5 percent.

The following two sections will examine these and other data at the metro-area level to show the degrees of variation within the state. The section on Tampa, Miami, and Jacksonville refers to Table 4, Table 5, and Table 6, as does the section covering Orlando. Table 4 shows the percentage of Puerto Ricans in major metro areas relative to the total Puerto Rican population in the state and includes data on birthplace and language use.[5] Table 5 covers educational attainment for Puerto Ricans age 25 and over, median household income,

TABLE 4. Puerto Rican Residence, Birthplace, and Language Use (percent)

	Living in Florida	Born outside 50 states	Born in Florida	English at home	Spanish at home
Jacksonville	3	38	23	34	65
Miami-Fort Lauderdale-Pompano Beach	25	42	26	22	78
Orlando-Kissimmee-Sanford	29	50	18	18	82
Tampa-St. Petersburg-Clearwater	16	40	25	30	70
Total Florida	100	44	23	25	75

Source: U.S. Census Bureau, ACS, 5-year estimates, 2010.

families with incomes below the poverty level during the 12 months prior to being surveyed, and unemployment for Puerto Ricans age 16 and over in the civilian labor force. Table 6 covers occupations in which Puerto Ricans are employed in each of the four metro areas.

Tampa, Miami, and Jacksonville

The history of Puerto Ricans in Florida probably includes a progression from a late-19th-century preference for Tampa, to the Miami area during the 1940s through the 1960s and to Orlando from the 1960s on. Census data indicate that there were 203 Puerto Ricans living in Florida in 1930, and of those 159 were living in the Tampa Bay area.[6] Tampa's appeal during the late 19th and early 20th centuries was due to the cigar-making industry in Ybor City. The Casellas family, for example, were a well-known Afro-Puerto Rican family in Tampa working in cigar making. They were subjected to the onset of segregation in Tampa when Jim Crow laws took hold around the turn of the 20th century (Greenbaum 1986; Vázquez-Hernández 2013). Members of the Casellas family were still in the Tampa area in the 1970s (Vázquez-Hernández 2013).

According to the data presented in Table 4, Puerto Ricans in the Tampa area now constitute 16 percent of all Puerto Ricans in Florida. Of these, 40 percent were born outside the United States;[7] 25 percent were born in Florida; 30 percent speak only English at home; and 70 percent speak Spanish at home. By comparison, among Puerto Ricans statewide there is a higher percentage born outside the 50 states (44%) and a slightly smaller percentage born in Florida (23%). This is reflected in the greater tendency to speak Spanish at home, which is evident in the statewide data (75%).

TABLE 5. Puerto Rican Educational Attainment, Income, and Unemployment (percent)

	High school or higher	Bachelor's or higher	Graduate or professional	Median household income (USD)	Families below poverty	Unemployment
Jacksonville	84	20	6	$46,287	12	9
Miami-Fort Lauderdale-Pompano Beach	79	22	7	$45,990	13	10
Orlando-Kissimmee-Sanford	81	18	5	$40,096	15	12
Tampa-St Petersburg-Clearwater	79	16	4	$39,087	18	11
Total Florida	80	18	5	$41,198	16	11

Source: U.S. Census Bureau, ACS, 5-year estimates, 2010.

Table 5 shows that the percentage of Puerto Ricans age 25 and over in Tampa with a high school degree or higher (79%) is very close to the percentage statewide (80%). The percentage of Puerto Ricans age 25 and over in the Tampa area with a bachelor's degree or higher (16%) is only slightly lower than the statewide rate (18%) and on a par with the percentage nationally (see Table 3). With only 4 percent of Puerto Ricans with a graduate or professional degree, Tampa actually falls below both the U.S. *and* Florida rate of 5 percent.

Table 5 gives the median income for Puerto Rican households in the Tampa metro area as about $39,000, which is the lowest median income of all the major Puerto Rican metro areas in Florida and only slightly higher than U.S. Puerto Rican households as a whole (see Table 3). Among Puerto Ricans in the Tampa area, the percentage of families with incomes below the poverty level during the 12 months prior to being surveyed is the highest of all four metro areas (18%). The 11 percent unemployment rate for Puerto Ricans in the Tampa area is the same as the rate statewide. According to data presented in Table 6, about one third of civilian Puerto Ricans age 16 and over employed in the Tampa metro area work in sales and office occupations. About one quarter work in management, business, science, and arts occupations, and about one fifth work in service occupations. This is very similar to the occupation data for Puerto Ricans statewide.

TABLE 6. Occupations of Employed Puerto Ricans (percent)

	Management, business, science, and arts	Service	Sales and office	Natural resources, construction, and maintenance	Production, transportation, and material moving
Jacksonville	27	19	34	11	9
Miami-Fort Lauderdale-Pompano Beach	31	18	33	9	10
Orlando-Kissimmee-Sanford	24	22	33	9	12
Tampa-St Petersburg-Clearwater	26	20	34	9	11
Total Florida	26	21	33	10	11

Source: U.S. Census Bureau, ACS, 5-year estimates, 2010.

The Puerto Rican community of Miami began to take root in the 1940s, when investors from Puerto Rico's southern coast bought land near the Everglades for sugar production (Duany and Matos-Rodríguez 2006). At around that time, other Florida employers began to hire Puerto Rican farmworkers (Hahamovitch 1997). During the 1950s, Florida-based Caribe Employment Agency placed ads in Puerto Rican newspapers and made radio announcements for agricultural and industrial jobs in the state (Shell-Weiss 2009b). The Puerto Rican Department of Labor reported that during the early 1950s local workers were being recruited directly to Florida, against the directions of the Migration Division and thus with no means of returning to Puerto Rico (Pagán de Colón 1956). Puerto Rican seasonal workers also traveled regularly between Florida and the Northeast, and Florida's garment industry drew Puerto Rican women to the Miami area (Shell-Weiss 2009a). By the mid-1950s, South Florida's Puerto Rican population included wealthy land investors, middle-class professionals, garment factory workers, and migrant farm and hotel workers. Throughout the 1950s and 1960s, many of the Puerto Ricans in the Miami area settled in the Wynwood neighborhood, known locally as "Little San Juan" (Feldman 2011).

Although Miami today is known for its Cuban population, Puerto Ricans in the Miami area make up a fourth all Puerto Ricans in Florida (see Table 4).

Feldman (2011) reports that the Puerto Rican population in the Wynwood area peaked during the 1980s and has since become more dispersed. In 2010, 26 percent of Puerto Ricans in the Miami metro area were born in Florida and 42 percent were born outside the United States.[8] Perhaps reflecting the dominance of Spanish in the Miami area, 78 percent reported speaking Spanish at home and only 22 percent reported speaking only English at home. Puerto Ricans in Miami are on par with Puerto Ricans in Tampa and in Florida as a whole in terms of high school degree (79%), but rank highest among the four Florida metro areas in the number holding a bachelor's degree or higher (22%) and having a graduate or professional degree (7%) (see Table 5).

According to data presented in Table 5, Puerto Rican households in Miami have the second-highest median income (just under $46,000) of the four Florida metro areas and the second-lowest percentage of families with incomes below poverty level in the 12 months prior to being surveyed (13%). The 10 percent unemployment rate for Puerto Ricans in the Miami area is slightly better than the rate for Puerto Ricans in Florida as a whole. In Table 6, the data suggest that, just as in Tampa, sales and office occupations predominate among Miami-area Puerto Ricans (33%), followed by management, business, science, and arts (31%), with service a distant third (18%).

A newly emerging Puerto Rican center in Florida is Jacksonville, located in the northeast corner of the state. Only 3 percent of Florida Puerto Ricans live in the Jacksonville metro area, but the community is growing rapidly. Jacksonville is already home to a Puerto Rican parade.[9] Thirty-eight percent of Puerto Ricans in the Jacksonville metro area were born outside the United States and 23 percent were born in Florida (see Table 4).[10] Jacksonville-area Puerto Ricans have the highest percentage in the state of those who speak only English at home (34%), a fact that may reflect the more English-dominant environment of North Florida. In contrast to Tampa-area Puerto Ricans, who fare the worst in terms of income and unemployment, Puerto Ricans in the Jacksonville area fare the best (see Table 5). Median income for Puerto Rican households in the Jacksonville metro area is just over $46,000, and unemployment is 9 percent, which is the lowest unemployment rate for Puerto Ricans in the four metro areas studied. Similarly, 12 percent of Puerto Rican families in the Jacksonville area had incomes below the poverty level in the 12 months prior to being surveyed, which is the lowest poverty rate for Puerto Ricans in the state and is also lower than the 22 percent rate for all U.S. Puerto Ricans (see Table 3). As in the Tampa and Miami areas, sales and office occupations predominate among Jacksonville

Puerto Ricans (34%), followed by management, business, science, and arts (27%) and service (19%), according to data presented in Table 6.

Orlando Metropolitan Area

The following analysis draws on the data presented in Table 4, Table 5, and Table 6 to sketch a socioeconomic picture of Puerto Ricans in the Orlando-Kissimmee-Sanford area. The Orlando metro area has the largest concentration of Puerto Ricans in the state, at 29 percent of Florida's total Puerto Rican population (see Table 4). Fifty percent of Puerto Ricans in the Orlando metro area were born outside the United States,[11] which is the highest percentage of the four metro areas studied and greater than the total percentage of Puerto Ricans in the state as a whole (44%). The smallest percentage of Puerto Ricans (18%) was born in Florida, which suggests a more dynamic mix of Puerto Ricans from Puerto Rico and from other diaspora communities. The Puerto Rican influence would seem to be strongly felt, however, as more Puerto Ricans in the Orlando metro area report speaking Spanish at home than in any of the other metro areas (82%) and fewer than in any other (18%) report speaking only English at home.

The Orlando metro area is second only to Jacksonville in terms of the percentage of high school graduates (81%), but is on the lower end in terms of bachelor's degrees (18%) (see Table 5), which is still higher than the rate for Puerto Ricans in the U.S. (16%). In terms of graduate or professional degrees, Puerto Ricans in the Orlando metro area are on a par with Puerto Ricans statewide (5%). Puerto Rican households in the Orlando area have the third-lowest median income (about $40,000), which is only slightly higher than the median income of Puerto Rican households in the Tampa metro area. Unemployment for Puerto Ricans in the Orlando area (12%) is the highest of the four metro areas and higher than the unemployment rate for Puerto Ricans statewide (11%). The percentage of Puerto Rican families in the Orlando metro area with incomes below the poverty level in the 12 months prior to being surveyed is 15 percent, which is higher than the poverty rates in both Jacksonville and Miami, and only slightly better than it is for Puerto Ricans in Florida overall.

Employment for civilian Puerto Ricans age 16 and over in the Orlando metro area follows the same pattern seen in the other Florida metro areas (see Table 6). Most Puerto Ricans are employed in sales and office occupations (33%), followed by management, business, science, and arts (24%) and service (22%). Across these four metro areas, however, Orlando has the highest percentage of Puerto Ricans employed in service occupations and the lowest percentage in management, business, science, and arts. This may reflect the prevalence of the theme park tourist industry in the Orlando area.

Although Tampa and Miami have a longer history of Puerto Rican settlement, and the Miami and Jacksonville metro areas seem to have better economic prospects, it is the Orlando area that has held the strongest attraction for Puerto Ricans moving to Florida. With more than a quarter million Puerto Ricans, the Orlando metro area is second only to New York City among U.S. metro areas with large Puerto Rican populations. The following section traces the paths that have brought Puerto Ricans to the Orlando area and gives an ethnographic portrait of the history and actuality of Puerto Ricans in Orlando and Central Florida.

Puerto Ricans in Central Florida: An Ethnographic Portrait

Orlando's Puerto Rican history is longer than generally acknowledged, reaching back at least to the 1940s when Puerto Rican soldiers were stationed at the many Central Florida military bases (Silver 2010).[12] Anecdotal evidence also puts Puerto Rican farmworkers in the celery fields near Sanford in the 1940s and 1950s. Migrant farmworkers and military personnel are both transient populations and the Puerto Rican numbers at the time were not large. Some farmworkers stayed, however, and some former soldiers returned.

In the 1950s, a group of five Puerto Rican women, all married to former U.S. servicemen, were among the Puerto Ricans living in Orlando, and Puerto Rican students attended Central Florida colleges. During the Central Florida land sales that began and developed quickly in the 1960s, Puerto Ricans from Puerto Rico, New York, Chicago, and U.S. military bases around the world invested in Florida. Some were scammed and others obtained legitimate plots of land. Some never came; others did.

When Walt Disney World opened in 1971, Puerto Ricans came as tourists, and many decided to stay (Firpo 2012).[13] At least one of the Puerto Rican women living in Orlando since the 1950s became one of the first Disney workers. Many others followed, recruited from Puerto Rico (Foglesong 2001). Later in the decade, around 1976, NASA began to recruit Puerto Rican engineers from the Mayagüez campus of the University of Puerto Rico, and the Kennedy Space Center in Central Florida began to see a steady stream of Puerto Rican engineers arriving on a yearly basis. As the Puerto Rican population grew, so did the demand for Spanish-language services, prompting further recruitment in Puerto Rico to include contracts for teachers and health care workers.

Although there is not one Puerto Rican barrio per se, the area of East Orlando and beyond into East Orange County is home to a growing number of Puerto Ricans. A neighborhood known as Azalea Park, just east of downtown Orlando, has evidence of Puerto Rican presence since the 1960 census and now serves as something of a gateway to the East Orlando and East Orange area. Another of the oldest Puerto Rican areas is in South Orlando, near the former McCoy Air Force Base, now the Orlando International Airport. Reaching west and south from the airport is also the site of new developments built during the late 1980s and 1990s that straddle the Orange/Osceola county line (Firpo 2012). These developments, Buenaventura Lakes in Osceola County and Meadow Woods in Orange County, are sometimes called "Little Puerto Rico."

Descriptions from many who arrived in Central Florida before the surge in Puerto Rican population during the late 1980s and 1990s suggest that Puerto Rican cultural identification was played out behind closed doors at home. The doorstep came to represent the border crossed from Puerto Rico to mainstream Orlando. At least one family's *parranda navideña* (Christmas carolling) led neighbors to call the police. The Asociación Borinqueña, founded in the late 1970s, provided a space for collectively maintaining cultural traditions in the face of such concerns.

Other Puerto Rican institutions that began to emerge during the late 1970s and 1980s included *La Prensa* newspaper, and a Puerto Rican/Hispanic chamber of commerce. During this time, churches began to have an important presence in the Puerto Rican community of Central Florida, as an increasing number of them began holding Spanish-language services. Orlando is known for mega-churches, and these that have attracted many Puerto Ricans and other Hispanics. Entire church communities have moved to Orlando from both Puerto Rico and New York.

Interviews with Puerto Ricans in Central Florida frequently reference Puerto Rican navigation of the black-white dichotomy of Orlando's social field (Silver 2013). The earliest stories from the mid-century do not generally reference personally experienced discrimination, although they are full of accounts of local ignorance about Puerto Rico and its relation to the United States. As the Puerto Rican population grew, however, so did resistance from non-Hispanics afraid that Orlando would "become another Miami." Accounts from the late 1970s and onward refer to difficulties finding employment, pressure or outright directives not to speak Spanish in the workplace or other public places, and other types of confrontations as Puerto Ricans have been told to go back to where they came from.[14]

By the 1990s, Puerto Ricans were making themselves more visible in public spaces. Orlando's Puerto Rican parade annually brought a loud affirmative Puerto Rican voice to downtown Orlando, and collective voices of protest became louder in response to discrimination. In 1996, for instance, Puerto Ricans organized and led the largest street protest Orlando had ever seen, demanding more—and more balanced—representation of Puerto Rican and Hispanic issues in the press.

Although these events had an impact, Puerto Ricans in the Orlando metro area have not yet gained real access to political power. In Orange County and the City of Orlando, for instance—despite the landscape being dotted with Puerto Rican and other Hispanic businesses both large and small and the prevalence of Spanish being spoken on the radio—there have been only four Hispanics elected to the city and county commissions since the 1980s: Mary I. Johnson as both Orlando City and Orange County Commissioner, Mel Martínez as Orange County Mayor, Mildred Fernández as Orange County Commissioner, and Anthony Ortiz as Orlando City Commissioner. Of these, Martínez is Cuban, Johnson is Cuban and Puerto Rican, and Fernández and Ortiz are Puerto Rican. In Osceola County, a protracted battle for single-member districts to enable more Hispanic representation was finally settled in 2006 by Orlando's U.S. district court, and has resulted in significant political, specifically Puerto Rican, representation in that county (Cruz 2010).

It is also interesting to note that the Puerto Ricans in political positions in Osceola County have been largely Republican. And in Orange County and the City of Orlando, of the elected officials mentioned above, only former Commissioner Johnson is a Democrat. The mix of pro-statehood Puerto Rican politics and the greater wealth of Florida's Republican Party, together with its interest in promoting Hispanic candidates, have had their effect on Puerto Rican political affiliations in Florida. The 2012 elections have perhaps marked a turning point: Puerto Ricans and Hispanics came out to vote in record numbers in 2012; Republican Puerto Ricans lost in their bid for Florida's new congressional district drawn for Hispanic representation; and the Florida state senate now has its first Puerto Rican member, a Democrat. As Florida remains a key player in federal elections, Puerto

Ricans in Central Florida are positioned to be a determining factor in the electoral outcome for the state.

Conclusion

Over recent decades, Florida has become the preferred destination for Puerto Ricans moving from both Puerto Rico and other Puerto Rican diaspora communities in the United States (García-Ellín 2014; Vargas-Ramos 2014). Puerto Rican households in Florida have higher median incomes than Puerto Rican households in the United States as a whole and a smaller percentage of Puerto Rican families in Florida have incomes below the poverty rate over the 12 months prior to being surveyed. While these are markers indicating higher socioeconomic levels for Puerto Ricans living in Florida compared with the rest of the United States, educational attainment among Puerto Ricans in Florida beyond the high school level is not noticeably different.

Research at levels below the state level is needed to assess how the conditions for Puerto Ricans vary in different parts of the state and what kinds of dynamics of community formation are playing out amidst the differing conditions. For instance, although Puerto Ricans in the North and South Florida areas around Jacksonville and Miami have higher incomes and educational attainment as well as lower poverty rates, Central Florida, and especially the Orlando area, is where the large majority of Puerto Ricans relocating to Florida settle. This suggests that something other than economic conditions is drawing Puerto Ricans to the Orlando area. Although the dramatic change in the Central Florida economy following the opening of Disney World in 1971 has undoubtedly been a factor, ethnographic and historical research on Central Florida has identified the important roles played by Puerto Rican participation in the U.S. military, and the targeted marketing of Florida residential developments, in influencing the decision of Puerto Ricans to relocate the the area. Additionally, as the Puerto Rican community in the Orlando area established itself apart from Cuban-dominated Miami, networks of family and friends have swelled the numbers of Puerto Ricans moving to this new center of Puerto Rican migration.

These numbers include both island-born and diaspora-born Puerto Ricans. In the Orlando area, the mix is almost 50/50. As Puerto Rican efforts advance in establishing a political presence in this volatile point on the national electoral map, the dynamic between island-born and diaspora-born Puerto Ricans presents itself as a critical focus of research. One aspect of this is evident in the prevalence of Spanish spoken among Puerto Ricans in the Orlando area. Ethnographic data, for instance, has shown that some English-dominant Puerto Ricans arriving from the Northeast make conscious efforts to improve their Spanish in order to establish themselves in the Puerto Rican community of Orlando.

Although some research has been done on Puerto Rican racialization in the black-white world of Central Florida (cf. Delerme 2013a, 2013b; Silver 2013), there remains much to be done around the state, recognizing the different contexts of South, North, and Central Florida. Further research is also needed into the class dynamics of Puerto Ricans in the different Puerto Rican communities of Florida, not only in terms of their social relations with other ethnic groups in the communities where they settle, but also, and especially, in terms of social relations within the Puerto Rican community itself. Again, this pertains to their ability to form a politically salient presence in Florida, at both local and state levels.

The growth of Puerto Rican communities in Florida has brought change to Florida and to the dynamics of the Puerto Rican diaspora. This brief sketch has served as an introduction to this important new center of the Puerto Rican diaspora. Much remains to be done to document, examine, understand, and facilitate the formation of a Puerto Rican community in Florida.

NOTES

[1] See "Puerto Rican Florida," special issue of *CENTRO: Journal for the Center for Puerto Rican Studies*, Spring 2010. See also Concepción Torres 2008; Delerme 2013a; 2013b; Duany and Matos Rodriguez 2006; Feldman 2011; Firpo 2012; Navarro 2004; Sánchez 2009; Silver 2013. Many of these citations are recent theses and dissertations, which suggests that the coming years may see this body of work grow substantially.

[2] The capital city of Florida is Tallahassee, located in the North Florida panhandle (Leon County). In 2010, the population of the Tallahassee metro area was just under 370,000, of whom 3,444 were Puerto Rican (U.S. Census 2010).

[3] Polk County is where Lakeland is located.

[4] At the time of this writing, parallel data for counties and metro areas were not all available for 2011 and 2012, and so the state-level data here is from the 2006-2010 American Community Survey estimates in order to be consistent with other data in the chapter. Population figures for educational attainment include Puerto Ricans 25 years of age and older. Unemployment figures include Puerto Ricans 16 years of age and older in the civilian labor force.

[5] The Census category for "born outside the United States" references "Puerto Rico, United States island areas, or born abroad to American parent(s)." Thus, the percentage of Puerto Ricans born in Puerto Rico will most likely be lower than the percentages given in Table 4.

[6] Source: Ancestry.com

[7] See Note 5 above.

[8] See Note 5 above.

[9] Other Puerto Rican parades in Florida are in Kissimmee, Melbourne, Orlando, and Tampa.

[10] See Note 5 above.

[11] See Note 5 above.

[12] Much of the evidence for the history presented here has been extracted from the oral history collection, "Puerto Ricans in Central Florida 1940s to 1980s: A History." The project was conducted by the University of Central Florida's Digital Ethnography Lab with support from the Florida Humanities Council, the Orange County Regional History Center, the University of Central Florida's Center for Research and Education in Arts, Technology, and Entertainment (CREATE), and the Center for Puerto Rican Studies at Hunter College, CUNY. A copy of the collection is available in the Centro Library and Archives. Further information on the collection and more detailed accounts of the stories it contains are in Silver 2010.

[13] See also the oral history collection, "Puerto Ricans in Central Florida 1940s to 1980s: A History" at Centro's Library and Archives.

[14] For more on the information in this paragraph, see the oral history collection, "Puerto Ricans in Central Florida 1940s to 1980s: A History" at Centro's Library and Archives

REFERENCES

Concepción Torres, Ramón Luis. 2008. Puerto Rican Migration, Settlement Patterns, and Assimilation in the Orlando MSA. Master's thesis, State University of New York at Binghamton.

Cruz, José. 2010. Barriers to political participation of Puerto Ricans and Hispanics in Osceola County, Florida: 1991-2007. *CENTRO Journal of the Center for Puerto Rican Studies* 22(1): 243–85.

Delerme, Simone. 2013a. The Latinization of Orlando: Race, Class, and the Poltics of Place. PhD dissertation, Rutgers, The State University of New Jersey.

_____. 2013b. The Latinization of Orlando: Language, whiteness, and the poltic of place. *CENTRO: Journal of the Center for Puerto Rican Studies* 25(2): 60–95.

Duany, J., and F. Matos-Rodríguez 2006. Puerto Ricans in Orlando and Central Florida. Policy Report 1(1). New York: Centro de Estudios Puertorriqueños, Hunter College, CUNY.

Feldman, Marcos. 2011. The Role of Neighborhood Organizations in the Production of Gentrifiable Urban Space: The Case of Wynwood, Miami's Puerto Rican Barrio. PhD dissertation, Florida International University.

Firpo, Julio. 2012. Forming a Puerto Rican Identity in Orlando: The Puerto Rican Migration to Central Florida, 1960-2000. Master's thesis, University of Central Florida.

Foglesong, Richard E. 2001. *Married to the Mouse: Walt Disney World and Orlando*. New Haven: Yale University Press.

García-Ellín, Juan Carlos. 2014. A Brief Look at Internal Migration of Puerto Ricans in the United States: 2001–2011. In *Puerto Ricans at the Dawn of the New Millennium*, eds. Edwin Meléndez and Carlos Vargas-Ramos. 24–38. New York: Center for Puerto Rican Studies.

Greenbaum, Susan. 1986. Afro-Cubans in Ybor City: A Centennial History. Tampa: University of South Florida and Sociedad La Unión Martí-Maceo.

Griffith, Kelly. 2006. 'Where East meets West': In the 'new world' of Orlampa, hope grows. *Orlando Sentinel* 17 Dec: J1.

Hahamovitch, Cindy. 1997. *The Fruits of Their Labor: Atlantic Coast Farmworkers and the Making of Migrant Poverty*. Chapel Hill: University of North Carolina Press.

Mormino, Gary R. 2005. *Land of Sunshine State of Dreams: A Social History of Modern Florida*. Gainesville: University Press of Florida.

Navarro, Lydia E. 2004. Lost Identity and Silent Voices: The Academic Struggles of At-Risk Puerto Rican Students in Central Florida. PhD dissertation, University of Central Florida.

Pagán de Colón, P. 1956. Programa de trabajadores migratorios de Puerto Rico a los Estados Unidos. San Juan: Estado Libre Asociado de Puerto Rico, Departamento del Trabajo.

Sánchez, Luis. 2009. *The New Puerto Rico? Identity, Hybridity and Transnationalism within the Puerto Rican Diaspora in Orlando, Florida*. Saarbrücken, Germany: VDM Verlag Dr. Müller.

Shell-Weiss, Melanie. 2009a. *Coming to Miami: A Social History*. Gainesville: University Press of Florida.

_____. 2009b. "I Dreamed I Went to Work": Expanding Southern Unionism in the Mid-Twentieth-Century Lingerie Industry. In *Florida's Working-Class Past: Current Perspectives on Labor, Race, and Gender from Spanish Florida to the New Immigration*, eds. Robert Cassanello and Melanie Shell-Weiss. 227–56. Gainesville: University Press of Florida.

Silver, Patricia. 2010. "Culture is more than bingo and salsa": Making *puertorriqueñidad* in Central Florida. *CENTRO: Journal of the Center for Puerto Rican Studies* 22(1): 57–83.

_____. 2013. Latinization, race, and cultural identification in Puerto Rican Orlando. *Southern Cultures* 19(4): 55–75.

U.S. Census Bureau. American Community Survey, 2006-2010 American Community Survey 5-Year Estimates.

_____. Decennial Census of the Population 2000, 2010.

Vázquez-Hernández, Victor. 2013. The Boricua Triangle: Tampa, Miami and Orlando—A Historical Overview of the Development of a Transnational Puerto Rican Diaspora in Florida. Working paper.

Vargas-Ramos, Carlos. 2014. Patterns of Puerto Rican Settlement and Seggregation in the United States, 1990–2010. In *Puerto Ricans at the Dawn of the New Millennium*, eds. Edwin Meléndez and Carlos Vargas-Ramos. 40–60. New York: Center for Puerto Rican Studies.

New Puerto Rican Diasporas in the Southern United States

PATRICIA SILVER

Perhaps one of the most notable developments in the emerging characteristics of the Puerto Rican diaspora in the United States is the shift to the South as the preferred destination of Puerto Ricans, whether they are moving from the island or from Puerto Rican communities in other parts of the United States. In 2010, the Puerto Rican population of the South was three times the size it was in 1990, growing from about 15 percent to 30 percent of all Puerto Ricans in the 50 states (Vargas-Ramos 2014). The implications of this shift for the sociocultural and political-economic relations of Puerto Rican diaspora communities are significant. In particular, these newer communities bring together island-born and diaspora-born Puerto Ricans in places where both are newcomers.

Figure 1 shows the census-designated regions of the United States. The census identifies 16 states as being in the South, which gives this region the

FIGURE 1. Census Regions and Divisions of the United States

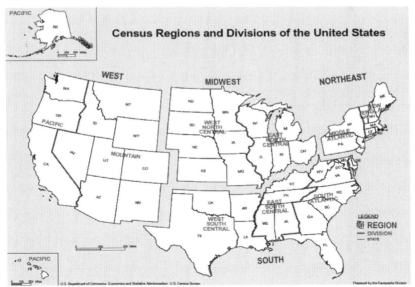

Source: U.S. Census Bureau, 2012.

country's largest population. Historically speaking, however, "the South" has generally referenced the 11 states that formed the Confederacy during the Civil War.[1] Florida and Texas count among those eleven, but these two states are often discounted from historical and sociocultural writing on the South, partly because of their longer Hispanic histories (cf. Bankston 2007; Winders and Smith 2012). It is arguable, for precisely this reason, that research on these two states is especially important in understanding the settlement patterns of Puerto Ricans.

Puerto Rican movement to the South is part of a larger demographic shift over the past several decades. The southern states, largely non-union states, have effectively attracted a range of domestic and international industries by offering corporate subsidies and cheap labor (cf. Cobb 2005). By the 1990s, the South had become the preferred destination for scores of immigrants from around the world. Latin American populations have dominated this movement; in 2005, the six counties with the fastest growing Hispanic populations were all located in the southern states (Cobb 2005).[2]

For Puerto Ricans arriving in the southern states, the context of reception is thus significantly different than it was in New York during the 1950s. Not only are they relocating to areas that are slightly over a generation removed

TABLE 1. Selected Hispanic Populations in the Former Confederate States (percent)

	Cuban to total	Cuban to Hispanic	Mexican to total	Mexican to Hispanic	Puerto Rican to total	Puerto Rican to Hispanic
Alabama	0.1	2	3	70	0.2	7
Arkansas	0.0	0.5	5	77	0.2	3
Florida	7	29	3	15	4	20
Georgia	0.3	3	5	62	0.7	8
Louisiana	0.2	6	2	42	0.2	6
Mississippi	0.1	3	2	68	0.2	7
North Carolina	0.2	2	5	62	0.7	9
South Carolina	0.1	2	3	60	0.6	12
Tennessee	0.1	3	3	66	0.3	7
Texas	0.2	0.5	32	87	0.5	1
Virginia	0.2	3	2	26	0.9	12

Source: U.S. Census Bureau, ACS, 5-year estimates, 2007–2011.

from Jim Crow segregation laws, but, in most cases, the majority Hispanic population in the receiving state is Mexican. Table 1 gives contemporary Cuban, Mexican, and Puerto Rican population percentages relative to total population and to the total Hispanic population for the 11 former Confederate states. For instance, in Georgia, Mexicans make up 5 percent of the total population and 62 percent of all Hispanics compared, with Puerto Ricans who make up less than 1 percent of the total population and 8 percent of all Hispanics. Florida, where the dominant Hispanic group has long been Cuban, is the exception.

Table 2 shows the growth of the Puerto Rican population in each of the 11 former Confederate states between 2000 and 2010.[3] Of these, Florida stands out as having the largest numeric growth, gaining 365,000 Puerto Ricans during the decade to reach nearly 850,000 by 2010. The Puerto Rican population of Texas is a distant second at about 131,000 in 2010. The percentage growth for each of these states points to the increasing popularity of the South for Puerto Rican settlement. The Puerto Rican populations in Georgia, Mississippi, North Carolina, South Carolina, and Tennessee all grew by over 100 percent. North Carolina shows the largest percentage growth at 131 percent and also ranks third in numeric growth at almost 41,000, following Texas whose Puerto Rican population grew by 61,000.

TABLE 2. Puerto Rican Population Growth in the South

	2000	2010	Growth	% Growth
Alabama	6,322	12,225	5,903	93
Arkansas	2,473	4,789	2,316	94
Florida	482,027	847,550	365,523	76
Georgia	35,532	71,987	36,455	103
Louisiana	7,670	11,603	3,933	51
Mississippi	2,881	5,888	3,007	104
North Carolina	31,117	71,800	40,683	131
South Carolina	12,211	26,493	14,282	117
Tennessee	10,303	21,060	10,757	104
Texas	69,504	130,576	61,072	88
Virginia	41,131	73,958	32,827	80

Source: U.S. Census Bureau, 2000 and 2010 Decennial Census.

The following section will consider Puerto Rican social and economic conditions in the seven southern states in Table 2 that had a Puerto Rican population over 10,000 in 2000 and grew by over 10,000 during that decade. These seven states are: Florida, Georgia, North Carolina, South Carolina, Tennessee, Texas, and Virginia. Although there is a small but growing body of literature on Hispanics in the South, there are few studies that focus on or even mention Puerto Ricans. The purpose here is to prompt questions and encourage further research on these new areas of Puerto Rican settlement.

Puerto Ricans in the South

One characteristic of these new diaspora settlements is the diversity of birthplace and migration experiences among Puerto Ricans (García-Ellín 2012). This, in turn, indicates divergent experiences in Puerto Rican cultural and social identification. Many of those who come directly from a life in Puerto Rico experience discrimination as a minority for the first time in their lives; many island-born Puerto Ricans have negative stereotypes about Puerto Ricans born and raised outside Puerto Rico (cf. Dávila 1997; Findlay 2009; Ramos-Zayas 2003; Rivera 2007; Sánchez 2009). Those who have lived and struggled for equality in Puerto Rican diaspora communities in the United States, who proudly embrace identification as *Nuyorican* or *ChicagoRican* and so on, may have their own negative views of those arriving directly from Puerto Rico (cf. Findlay 2012; Ramos Zayas 2003). When faced with claims from islanders that they are "not really Puerto Rican," Puerto Ricans from the diaspora express hurt and anger (cf. Silver 2010). In new Puerto Rican diaspora settlements, negotiations on both sides of this dynamic are an important aspect of efforts to form community and establish a Puerto Rican economic and political presence.

There is limited ethnographic and historical data available from southern Puerto Rican diaspora communities that would allow deeper understanding of Puerto Rican community building in the context of these divergent experiences (Capeles-Delgado 2006; Concepción Torres 2008; Delerme 2013; Eichenberger 2004; Feldman 2011; Firpo 2012; Sánchez 2009; Silver 2010, 2013). However, U.S. Census data allow a comparison of Puerto Rican communities in different states in terms of birthplace and language spoken at home, which may give some indication of cultural orientation vis-à-vis the surrounding community. Table 3 gives data on birthplace and language use for Puerto Ricans in the seven southern states selected from Table 2 compared with Puerto Ricans in the United States as a whole.

TABLE 3. Birthplace and Language Use (percent)

	Born outside 50 states	English at home	Spanish at home
Florida	44	23	69
Georgia	31	38	50
North Carolina	28	41	46
South Carolina	27	47	42
Texas	37	32	59
Virginia	30	42	46
U.S. Puerto Ricans	34	31	60

Source: U.S. Census Bureau, ACS, 5-year estimates, 2007-2011.

The data category used for birthplace outside the outside the United States includes "Puerto Rico, United States island areas, or born abroad to American parent(s)." Thus, the percentage of Puerto Ricans in each of these states born in Puerto Rico will most likely be lower than the percentage given in Table 3. That said, Florida has the highest percentage (44%) of Puerto Ricans not born in the 50 states, which is higher than the rate for the United States as a whole (34%). Florida also has the highest percentage of Puerto Ricans who speak Spanish at home (69%), which again is higher than the rate for the United States as a whole (60%). Texas follows Florida with 37 percent not born in the 50 states and 59 percent who speak Spanish at home. Across the other states presented in Table 3, the percentage born outside the 50 states is less than the rate for Puerto Ricans in the United States as a whole (34%) and the percentage speaking only English at home is higher than it is for Puerto Ricans in the country as a whole (31%). Fewer than one third of Puerto Ricans in Georgia were born outside the 50 states, but half of them speak Spanish at home. Puerto Ricans in South Carolina have the smallest percentage who were born outside the 50 states (27%), and they also have the smallest percentage who speak Spanish at home (42%).

Other census data describe the range of educational attainment and economic activity of Puerto Ricans in these seven southern states, which then allows some comparison with these class markers for Puerto Ricans in the United States as a whole as well as non-Hispanic whites in each state. Table 4 gives data for educational attainment among Puerto Ricans 25 years of age and older in the seven southern states in comparison with non-

TABLE 4. Educational Attainment (percent)

		High school or higher		Bachelor's or higher		Graduate or professional degree	
		Puerto Rican	Non-Hispanic White	Puerto Rican	Non-Hispanic White	Puerto Rican	Non-Hispanic White
Florida	2007	79	89	18	28	5	10
	2011	80	91	18	29	5	10
Georgia	2007	87	86	27	30	8	11
	2011	86	88	24	31	7	11
North Carolina	2007	82	86	19	28	6	9
	2011	86	89	23	30	7	10
South Carolina	2007	N/A	85	N/A	27	N/A	9
	2011	82	88	19	29	4	10
Tennessee	2007	N/A	82	N/A	23	N/A	8
	2011	88	85	26	24	10	9
Texas	2007	85	90	27	33	9	11
	2011	89	92	28	34	10	11
Virginia	2007	89	88	29	36	12	15
	2011	89	90	32	38	13	16
United States	2007	72	89	15	30	5	11
	2011	74	91	16	32	5	12

Source: U.S. Census Bureau, ACS, 5-year estimates, 2007–2011.

Hispanic whites in these states and Puerto Ricans in the United States as a whole. The data presented are from the American Community Survey (ACS) 3-year estimates from 2007 and 2011. These data allow a comparative view that encompasses pre- and post-recession. In the case of South Carolina and Tennessee, the data are only available in the 2011 estimates because there was not a large enough sample size in the 2007 estimates, which points to growth of the Puerto Rican population in those states.

Puerto Ricans in these seven southern states have generally been able to achieve higher educational attainment than Puerto Ricans in the United States as a whole. For instance, the percentage of Puerto Ricans 25 years of age and older with a high school degree or higher in these states ranges from 6 to 15 percentage points higher than the percentages for Puerto Ricans in the United States as a whole. The exception is the percentage of Puerto Ricans with graduate or professional degrees in Florida and South Carolina. In Florida, Puerto Ricans are on a par with Puerto Ricans in the United States as a whole, but in South Carolina, the percentage of Puerto Ricans with graduate and professional degrees is 1 percentage point below what it is for Puerto Ricans in the United States as a whole (4% compared with 5%). The percentage of Puerto Ricans holding a bachelor's degree or higher is greater in these southern states than it is in the United States as a whole, although exceeded by only a few percentage points in Florida and South Carolina. Puerto Ricans in Virginia have the highest educational attainment across all the states represented in the table. Graduate and professional degrees among Puerto Ricans in Virginia, Texas, and Tennessee range from 5 to 8 percentage points ahead of Puerto Ricans in the United States as a whole.

TABLE 5. Income, Poverty, and Unemployment (percent)

		Median household income (USD)		Family poverty rate		Unemployed	
		Puerto Rican	Non-Hispanic White	Puerto Rican	Non-Hispanic White	Puerto Rican	Non-Hispanic White
Florida	2007	$40,961	$50,887	14	5	8	5
	2011	$39,427	$50,377	18	7	15	11
Georgia	2007	$47,255	$56,274	12	6	8	5
	2011	$47,085	$56,291	17	8	16	9
North Carolina	2007	$43,356	$49,701	13	7	9	5
	2011	$46,165	$51,020	18	8	14	10
South Carolina	2007	N/A	$50,148	N/A	7	N/A	5
	2011	$46,210	$50,939	20	8	10	10
Tennessee	2007	N/A	$44,807	N/A	10	N/A	6
	2011	$37,004	$45,918	20	10	12	10
Texas	2007	$46,914	$57,321	12	6	8	5
	2011	$47,280	$61,918	14	6	9	7
Virginia	2007	$58,073	$63,374	9	5	5	4
	2011	$66,445	$67,841	11	5	9	6
United States	2007	$37,152	$54,189	22	6	11	5
	2011	$37,668	$56,229	24	7	16	9

Source: U.S. Census Bureau, ACS, 3-year estimates, 2007 and 2011.

When compared with non-Hispanic whites in each state, however, Puerto Rican educational attainment is almost consistently lower. According to the 2007 estimates, Puerto Ricans in Virginia had a slightly higher rate than non-Hispanic whites for high school and higher. A more noticeable exception is Tennessee, where Puerto Ricans have higher rates of educational attainment than non-Hispanic whites across the three educational levels listed in the table: (1) high school degree or higher, (2) bachelor's degree or higher, and (3) graduate or professional degree. In Georgia and Virginia, although Puerto Ricans and non-Hispanic whites have similar rates of high school education, Puerto Ricans fall behind in higher education.

Table 5 gives data on income, poverty, and unemployment for Puerto Ricans 16 years of age and older in the seven southern states considered here. The table includes comparative data for non-Hispanic whites in each state as well as for Puerto Ricans in the United States as a whole.

Median household income for Puerto Ricans in each of the seven states, both pre- and post-recession, is higher for non-Hispanic-white households than it is for Puerto Rican households, although the gap is smaller than it is between non-Hispanic-white and Puerto Rican households in the United States as a whole. With the exception of Texas and Virginia post-recession, the difference in median household income between non-Hispanic-white and Puerto Rican households in the seven states represented in the table ranges from about $5000 to $11,000. In Virginia, the 2011 data show a difference in household income of under $2000. In Texas, however, the difference in median household income between non-Hispanic-white and Puerto Rican households grew from about $10,000 pre-recession to about $15,000 post-recession. The 2011 data for Texas thus approach the higher discrepancy between non-Hispanic-white and Puerto Rican households in the United States as a whole.

As expected given the recession, the poverty rates for Puerto Rican and non-Hispanic-white families increased across the five states with data available from both the 2007 and the 2011 estimates. As with median household income, there is a discrepancy between Puerto Rican and non-Hispanic-white poverty rates, but the difference is smaller when the two groups are compared with the United States as a whole. The post-recession 12-percentage-point difference in South Carolina between Puerto Rican and non-Hispanic-white families is the largest across the seven states represented in the table. For the United States as a whole, the difference is about 16 percentage points in both estimates.

Across the five states with pre- and post-recession data available, as for the United States as a whole, Puerto Rican unemployment in 2011 was higher than it was in 2007, showing the impact of the recession. Although the same was true for non-Hispanic-white unemployment in these states, Puerto Rican unemployment rose by a greater percentage in each state except North Carolina and Texas. In North Carolina, Puerto Rican and non-Hispanic-white unemployment both increased by 5 percentage points. In Texas, Puerto Rican unemployment increased by only 1 percentage point, and non-Hispanic-white unemployment increased by 2 percentage points during the same period. The 2011 estimates indicate that in South Carolina, Puerto Rican and non-Hispanic-white unemployment were both at 10 percent. Puerto Rican unemployment in these southern states, however, was lower than it was for Puerto Ricans in the United States as a whole both pre- and post-recession.

Table 6 gives percentages for civilian-employed Puerto Ricans 16 years of age and older in the three occupational categories employing the majority of Puerto Ricans for each of these seven states and for the United States as a whole.[4] The table also includes comparative data for non-Hispanic whites in each state as well as for Puerto Ricans in the United States as a whole. With the exception of Florida in both estimates and South Carolina in the 2011 estimates, employment for Puerto Ricans in management, business, science, and arts occupations dominates across the states considered, with the second-largest occupational category being sales and office occupations. In Florida, as it is for Puerto Ricans across the United States, the opposite is true. In the 2011 estimates for South Carolina, the two occupational categories are the same at 28 percent.

The 2011 estimates for South Carolina also show that state with the largest percentage of Puerto Ricans 16 years of age and older employed in service occupations (26%). This is greater than for Puerto Ricans in the United States as a whole (23%). Across the states in the table and in the United States as a whole, the percentage of Puerto Ricans employed in service occupations is consistently higher than the percentage of non-Hispanic whites.

Table 6 also includes percentage of employment in the armed forces because of the large number of military bases located in the southern states. The data for employment in the armed forces shows that a larger percentage of Puerto Ricans in the South are employed in the armed forces than in the United States as a whole, both pre- and post-recession (under 1%). In the 2011 estimates, North Carolina and Virginia had the highest percentage of Puerto Ricans employed in the armed forces (6%).

TABLE 6. Occupations Employing Puerto Ricans and Non-Hispanic Whites (percent)

		Management, business, science and arts		Service		Sales and office		Armed Forces	
		Puerto Rican	Non-Hispanic White	Puerto Rican	Non-Hispanic White	Puerto Rican	Non-Hispanic White	Puerto Rican	Non-Hispanic White
Florida	2007	25	37	20	15	32	30	0.4	0.4
	2011	26	38	22	17	32	29	0.4	0.4
Georgia	2007	34	39	14	12	31	28	5	0.8
	2011	34	41	16	13	29	26	3	0.8
North Carolina	2007	30	37	20	13	29	26	6	1
	2011	33	40	20	15	31	25	6	1
South Carolina	2007	N/A	36	N/A	13	N/A	27	N/A	0.9
	2011	28	37	26	15	28	27	5	1
Tennessee	2007	N/A	32	N/A	14	N/A	27	N/A	0.3
	2011	31	36	22	15	27	26	1	0.3
Texas	2007	33	42	16	12	28	28	3	0.6
	2011	37	44	19	12	26	27	4	0.7
Virginia	2007	36	44	17	12	26	25	5	2
	2011	39	47	18	13	26	23	6	2
United States	2007	26	38	22	14	29	27	0.8	0.4
	2011	27	40	23	15	29	26	0.9	0.5

Source: U.S. Census Bureau, ACS, 3-year estimates, 2007 and 2011.

Puerto Ricans also have consistently higher rates of employment in the armed forces than non-Hispanic whites across these seven states and in the United States as a whole. Like Puerto Ricans, a greater percentage of non-Hispanic whites are employed in the armed forces in North Carolina (1%) and Virginia (2%) than in the other states. The Puerto Rican rates of employment in the armed forces in these two states, however, remain 5 and 6 percentage points above those of non-Hispanic whites.

As with the civilian employment data, Florida is the exception to the data on Puerto Rican employment in the armed forces. In Florida, both pre- and post-recession, Puerto Rican and non-Hispanic-white employment in the armed forces were the same (0.4%). In comparison to Puerto Ricans in the United States as a whole, Puerto Ricans in Florida are actually less likely to be in the armed forces.

The combined data on income, poverty, educational attainment, and employment for Puerto Ricans in these seven southern states support the view that Puerto Ricans in this region have higher socioeconomic status than Puerto Ricans in the United States as a whole. Compared with non-Hispanic whites in most cases, however, Puerto Ricans in these states are not doing as well.

More research is needed to give life to these numbers and render a more nuanced understanding of these new Puerto Rican diasporas in the South. For instance, each of these state overviews needs further data at county and place levels to learn about where Puerto Ricans are settling in the state, how long they are staying, and who their neighbors are. Puerto Rican social relations and economic and political incorporation in each locale will vary according to distinct contexts of reception and local histories. Ethnographic research in individual communities is thus needed to learn more about the kinds of challenges and successes Puerto Ricans in the South are experiencing and how these intersect with Puerto Rican histories in other places.

Conclusion

Puerto Ricans are coming to the South in increasing numbers and there is to date limited research to assess the issues and challenges they face. These emerging Puerto Rican diasporas in the South differ in significant ways from those that developed as a result of mid-20th century migrations. New Puerto Rican diasporas have the common condition of incorporating both island- and diaspora-born, and that fact alone will challenge previous research frameworks. In addition, compared with the largely working-class migration of the mid-20th century, the Puerto Rican communities emerging in the 21st century include both island- and diaspora-born with higher educational attainment and higher-paying employment opportunities.

As Puerto Ricans from diverse backgrounds seek to establish themselves politically, economically, and socially in these new spaces, new Puerto Rican identifications will undoubtedly emerge. The present moment offers the research opportunity to observe these processes as they are happening. The study of any one place will not provide a blanket explanation for the increased settlement of Puerto Ricans in the South, but research in each area will raise questions to guide research in other areas in an effort to develop the necessary data for comparing how Puerto Rican issues and challenges are expressed in the new diaspora communities of the South. Puerto Rican community formation in these new diaspora spaces is challenged by both the widely diverse backgrounds and experiences that Puerto Ricans bring to their new communities and the demands that stem from the environment in which they now find themselves. The following summary offers suggestions for research directions and urges that locally specific studies be conducted with Puerto Rican diaspora communities in the South to develop the resources required for comparative analyses:

1. Among other characteristics of interest for Puerto Ricans in these new diaspora communities is the difference in the context of reception from what Puerto Ricans experienced in New York. Because Puerto Ricans are often newly arriving in areas that may have already been home to other Hispanic groups for a significant time, the receiving society may well incorporate Puerto Ricans into their own pre-existing definition of "Hispanic." How Puerto Ricans navigate, challenge, or accommodate this, and to what effect, are important questions.

2. The southern legacy of segregation and Jim Crow still plays out in many places. In Orlando, for instance, Puerto Ricans were told they had to decide to be white or black to be part of a public-school bi-racial parent committee, originally founded in the Civil Rights era of the 1960s (Silver 2013). The question of how Puerto Ricans are racialized by others and how they racialize themselves and others is significant on various levels, not the least of which is the kinds of alliances Puerto Ricans make in an effort to establish political and economic presence.

3. The "right to work" statutes in the southern states have also had a significant impact on work conditions affecting Puerto Ricans. Unions have often served as the foundation of social networks in both Puerto Rico and northern diaspora communities. What have Puerto Rican experiences been in these "right-to-work" states? How has this impacted migration and livelihood decisions?

4. Military service and veterans' organizations may also provide a social network for Puerto Ricans in states where unions are not as strong. In his chapter in this volume, Carlos Vargas-Ramos (2014) attributes the growth of the Puerto Rican populations of Texas and Georgia to military bases being located in those states. Research in Central Florida has also pointed to the military's role in the history of that community

(Silver 2010). Given the large number of military bases in the South, to what degree, and with what impact, does participation in the armed forces connect Puerto Ricans in the southern states to the communities in which they have settled?

5. It will also be important to investigate the impact of Protestantism in the South, especially Southern Baptist and Evangelical/Pentecostal denominations, on Puerto Rican religious affiliation and political participation. To what degree have Puerto Ricans remained in their original faiths brought from their home communities or been influenced by the dominant presence of Protestantism in the Bible Belt?

6. Florida's importance in federal-level elections has put the spotlight on Puerto Ricans in that state. While areas of the South may differ from each other in terms of political dynamics, there is still a line of inquiry to be pursued about the degree to which the meanings of Republican and Democrat are changing, as increasing numbers of Puerto Ricans and other Hispanics adopt and adapt these political parties to their own needs and uses.

In brief, research on the state of Puerto Ricans in the South as the 21st century unfolds will undoubtedly bring new questions and new frameworks for analysis. It will also be important, however, to compare data across time and space to look for similarities as well as differences in the Puerto Rican experience. The history of Puerto Rican activism in New York and Chicago and the development of Puerto Rican Studies in the latter part of the 20th century are integral to the development of new Puerto Rican diasporas in the 21st century.

NOTES

[1] The Confederate states were Alabama, Arkansas, Florida, Georgia, Louisiana, Mississippi, North Carolina, South Carolina, Tennessee, Texas, and Virginia. Of these, Alabama, Florida, Georgia, Louisiana, Mississippi, South Carolina, and Texas were the seven that formed the Confederacy in 1861. The other four joined soon after that. In this writing, "the South" will refer to these eleven states.

[2] For other scholarship on the Latinization of the South, see Mantero 2008; Mohl 2008; Smith and Furuseth 2006, Odem and Lacy 2009, Winders and Smith 2008, 2010). See also the 2012 special issue of *Latino Studies* vol. 10(1-2).

[3] I am grateful to Kurt Birson and Surey Miranda for their work in generating tables for this chapter.

[4] The two categories not shown here are "natural resources, construction, and maintenance" and "production, transportation, and material moving" in the 2011 estimates. Occupations included in these categories shifted slightly from 2007 to 2011, making comparison unreliable. The three occupations listed are consistently the largest employers of Puerto Ricans across the seven southern states and in the United States as a whole.

REFERENCES

Bankston, Carl L., III. 2007. New People in the New South: An Overview of Southern Immigration. *Southern Cultures* 13(4): 24–44.

Capeles-Delgado, Julio C. 2006. Ethnic Identity Construction: Puerto Ricans in El Paso, Texas. Ph.D. dissertation, New Mexico State University.

Cobb, James C. 2005. Beyond the "Y'all Wall": The American South Goes Global. In *Globalization and the American South*, eds. James C. Cobb and William Stueck. 1–18. Athens: The University of Georgia Press.

Concepción Torres, Ramon L. 2008. Puerto Rican Migration, Settlement Patterns, and Assimilation in the Orlando MSA. Master's thesis, State University of New York at Binghamton.

Dávila, Arlene M. 1997. *Sponsored Identities: Cultural Politics in Puerto Rico*. Philadelphia: Temple Univiversity Press.

Delerme, Simone. 2013. The Latinization of Orlando: Race, Class, and the Politics of Place. Ph.D. dissertation, Rutgers, The State University of new Jersey.

Eichenberger, Susan E. 2004. Where Two or More Are Gathered: The Inclusion of Puerto Ricans in Multiethnic Latino Parishes in Southeastern United States. Ph.D. dissertation, University of Florida.

Feldman, Marcos. 2011. The Role of Neighborhood Organizations in the Production of Gentrifiable Urban Space: The Case of Wynwood, Miami's Puerto Rican Barrio. Ph.D. dissertation, Florida International University.

Findlay, Eileen J. 2009. Portable roots: Latin New Yorker community building and the meanings of women's return migration in San Juan, Puerto Rico, 1960–2000. *Caribbean Studies* 37(2): 3–43.

Firpo, Julio. 2012. Forming a Puerto Rican Identity in Orlando: The Puerto Rican Migration to Central Florida, 1960–2000. Master's thesis, University of Central Florida.

García-Ellín, Juan C. 2012. Spatial Aspects of Secondary Migration of Hispanics in the US. Ph.D. dissertation, University of California, Los Angeles.

Mantero, José M. 2008. *Latinos and the U.S. South*. Westport, CT: Praeger.

Mohl, Raymond A. 2008. Globalization, Latinization, and the Nuevo New South. In *Other Souths: Diversity and Difference in the U.S. South, Reconstruction to Present*, ed. Pippa Holloway. 408–22. Athens: University of Georgia Press.

Odem, Mary E. and Elaine C. Lacy. 2009. *Latino immigrants and the transformation of the U.S. South*. Athens: University of Georgia Press.

Ramos-Zayas, Ana Y. 2003. *National Performances: The Politics of Class, Race, and Space in Puerto Rican Chicago*. Chicago: University of Chicago Press.

Rivera, Raquel Z. 2007. Will the "Real" Puerto Rican Culture Please Stand Up? Thoughts on Cultural Nationalism. In *None of the Above: Puerto Ricans in the Global Era*, ed. Frances Negrón-Muntaner. 217–32. New York: Palgrave MacMillan.

Silver, Patricia. 2010. "Culture is more than bingo and salsa": Making *puertorriqueñidad* in Central Florida. *CENTRO: Journal of the Center for Puerto Rican Studies* 22(1): 57–83.

_____. 2013. Latinization, race, and cultural identification in Puerto Rican Orlando. *Southern Cultures* 19(4): 55–75.

Smith, Heather A. and Owen J. Furuseth. 2006. *Latinos in the New South: Transformations of Place*. Aldershot, England and Burlington, VT: Ashgate.

Sánchez, Luis. 2009. *The New Puerto Rico? Identity, Hybridity and Transnationalism within the Puerto Rican Diaspora in Orlando, Florida*. Saarbrücken, Germany: VDM Verlag Dr. Müller.

U.S. Census Bureau. Census Regions and Divisions of the United States. Accessed 28 December 2012. https://www.census.gov/geo/www/us_regdiv.pdf/.

_____. Decennial Census of the Population 2000, 2010.

_____. American Community Survey, 2007 3-year estimates, 2011 3-year estimates, and 2011 5-year estimates.

Vargas-Ramos, Carlos. 2014. Patterns of Puerto Rican Settlement and Seggregation in the United States, 1990–2010. In *Puerto Ricans at the Dawn of the New Millennium*, eds. Edwin Meléndez and Carlos Vargas-Ramos. 40–60. New York: Center for Puerto Rican Studies.

Winders, Jamie and Barbara E. Smith. 2008. Nashville's New "Sonido": Latino Migration and the Changing Politics of Race. In *New Faces in New Places: The Changing Geography of American Immigration*, ed. Douglas S. Massey. 249–73. New York: Russell Sage.

_____. 2010. New pasts: Historicizing immigration, race, and place in the South. *Southern Spaces*. http://southernspaces.org/2010/new-pasts-historicizing-immigration-race-and-place-south#content_top/.

_____. 2012. Excepting/accepting the South: New geographies of Latino migration, new directions in Latino studies. *Latino Studies* 10: 220–45.

Puerto Rican Economic Resiliency after the Great Recession

KURT BIRSON and EDWIN MELÉNDEZ

Several years after one of the longest and deepest recessions since the 1930s, we have the opportunity to look back at its long-term impact on Puerto Ricans in the United States. The Great Recession of 2007–2009 had a devastating effect on millions of people in the United States, but its consequences were not felt equally. National data tend to obscure differences across demographic groups and thus merit a deeper look into economic indicators in order to reveal individual trends that may exist.

Those most negatively affected by the Great Recession were male workers, youths 16 to 25 years of age, the less educated, and racial minorities (Van Horn 2013; Sierminska and Takhtamanova 2011). Hispanics as a group were hit particularly hard with sharp increases in unemployment and poverty, declining income and some of the largest losses in asset wealth of all the ethnic and racial groups. One significant gap in the literature is the assessment of the impact of the Great Recession on Puerto Ricans. Our study analyzes long-term effects of the Great Recession on the stateside Puerto Rican community. By and large, Puerto Ricans lost a lot of ground. Unexpectedly, however, our study shows that by most measures Puerto Ricans fared relatively better than other Latinos and reduced the earnings gap relative to non-Hispanic whites.

Our findings show that, despite the many challenges faced during the recession, Puerto Ricans in the labor force have proven to be relatively adaptable and resourceful in the face of changing economic conditions. Puerto Rican workers were among the most active groups in terms of taking steps to improve their labor-market standing and finding work, while also being the most adaptable in terms of surviving the effects of prolonged unemployment and financial hardship. Moreover, other studies in this volume show Puerto Ricans to be a very mobile community, moving from state to state and returning to Puerto Rico in search of better opportunities. Internal migrants tended to be a selection of the most educated Puerto Ricans, while Puerto Ricans arriving in the United States were more generally representative of educational attainment in Puerto Rico. Migrants from the island comprised more blue-collar workers and were more attached to the labor force, however (Birson; García-Ellín, in this volume).

We use one-year estimates of Census Bureau data from the U.S. Census Bureau's American Community Survey (ACS) for the analysis and focus on four racial and ethnic groups within the United States: Puerto Ricans, non-Hispanic whites, non-Hispanic blacks, and non-Puerto Rican Latinos. We separated Puerto Ricans from Latinos as a whole for the purpose of making comparisons between Puerto Ricans and the other groups. Thus, any figures presented here referring to Latinos exclude data on Puerto Ricans. Additionally, we include a selection of data collected in a 2012 survey for the Center for Puerto Rican Studies entitled "Puerto Ricans and the Impact of the Recession (or PRIR)."[1] The survey divides respondents into the same four racial and ethnic categories above and includes only those who are between the ages of 18 and 65 and in the labor force.[2]

According to the National Bureau of Economic Research, the most recent recession officially began in December 2007 and lasted until June 2009. Our analysis using ACS estimates covers the period from 2007 to 2011, the most recent year when U.S. Census Bureau data were available on the subject, which allows us to capture the changes of certain economic indicators both before the onset of the recession and two years following its official end. Using these sources of data, we focus our analysis on whether the Puerto Rican community has recovered from the adverse impact of the recession and which factors mitigated the relative standing of Puerto Ricans in the job market. In general, despite high levels of unemployment and losses in earnings, Puerto Ricans were able to maintain their financial standing relative to other Latinos and non-Hispanic blacks and reduced the earnings gap relative to non-Hispanic whites.

Employment

The primary concern coming out of the Great Recession has been not just the great losses in employment across all sectors, but also that employment has not recovered to pre-recession levels, and in many cases, continues to stagnate in what many consider a jobless recovery (Knoteck and Terry 2009; Valletta and Kuang 2013). The employment rate peaked in January of 2008 before falling precipitously in the years that followed. During the recession, the overall seasonally adjusted unemployment rate nearly doubled, from 5 percent to 9.5 percent, as monthly job losses averaged up to 712,000 unemployed from October 2008 to March 2009 (Goodman and Mance 2011; U.S. Department of

Labor 2011). Due to the crisis in the housing market, losses during the recession were heaviest in traditionally cyclical industries, such as manufacturing and construction, but also quickly grew in other, more resilient industries, such as retail trade, hospitality and leisure industries. In absolute terms, losses occurring in the private services sector were second only to those in manufacturing. Unemployment levels did not peak until February of 2010, before job growth began to pick up its pace (Goodman and Mance 2011). As our analysis shows, unemployment remained a serious problem for many by 2011.

The situation has been especially bleak for Puerto Ricans and other racial and ethnic minorities. Puerto Ricans experienced the highest increase in unemployment during the period considered for this study, seeing a 6 percent jump from 10 percent in 2007 to 16 percent in 2011 (see Table 1). Just over 51 percent of Puerto Ricans in the labor force were employed in 2011, a decrease from about 55 percent in 2007. Unemployment rose 5.7 percent for non-Hispanic blacks, 4.9 percent for Latinos, and 3.5 percent for non-Hispanic whites.

Table 2 shows the ways in which people have had to cope with losses during the Great Recession. According to data from the PRIR study, Puerto Ricans, especially those who were employed at the time of the survey, were the most likely among respondents to have resorted to things like borrowing money or moving in with friends and family, taking jobs below their education or skills or that they did not like. The results also show that those who were unemployed had to rely on these measures much more heavily than their employed counterparts. For instance, almost twice as

TABLE 1. Employment and Labor-Force Participation (percent)

	Total		Puerto Rican		Non-Hispanic White		Non-Hispanic Black		Other Latino	
	2007	2011	2007	2011	2007	2011	2007	2011	2007	2011
Labor-Force Participation	64.8	64	61.8	61.9	64.8	63.9	62.8	62.0	68.6	68.0
Civilian Labor Force	64.4	63.6	61.0	61.3	64.4	63.5	62.3	61.6	68.2	67.7
Employment Ratio	60.5	57	54.9	51.4	61.0	57.8	54.8	50.6	63.5	59.7
Unemployment Rate	8.6	13.6	10.0	16.0	5.3	8.8	12.0	17.7	6.9	11.8
Armed Forces	0.4	0.4	0.8	0.7	0.4	0.4	0.5	0.4	0.4	0.3
Not in Labor Force	35.2	36	38.2	38.1	35.2	36.1	37.2	38.0	31.4	32.0

Source: U.S. Census Bureau, ACS, 1-year estimates.

TABLE 2. Economic Survival Strategies During the Recession (percent)

Employed	Puerto Rican	Non-Hispanic White	Non-Hispanic Black	Other Latino	Total
Borrowed money from family or friends	22	20	18	20	20
Moved in with family or friends to save money	6	3	9	3	4
Taken a job you did not like	15	6	12	13	8
Taken a job below your education or experience level	11	5	10	8	6
Moved to a different house or apartment or living arrangement	11	5	11	9	6
Unemployed	Puerto Rican	Non-Hispanic White	Non-Hispanic Black	Other Latino	Total
Borrowed money from family or friends	42	37	45	33	38
Moved in with family or friends to save money	22	13	12	4	11
Taken a job you did not like	17	25	21	12	22
Taken a job below your education or experience level	14	21	17	5	17
Moved to a different house or apartment or living arrangement	16	15	7	10	12

Source: Puerto Ricans and the Impact of the Recession Study
Note: Response to the question, "Have you done any of the following because of the economic recession?" *Sample:* respondents in the labor force.

many unemployed Puerto Ricans (42%) reported borrowing money than did those who were employed (22%), and nearly four times as many (22%) unemployed Puerto Ricans moved in with friends and family. However, Puerto Ricans exhibited differences in labor-market behavior depending on their labor status. Employed Puerto Ricans were more likely than other groups to either take jobs they didn't like or jobs that were below their education level and were therefore more adaptable than unemployed Puerto Ricans in this dimension. Although less likely than non-Hispanic whites or non-Hispanic blacks to have resorted to these strategies, unemployed Puerto Ricans were still more likely than other Latinos to have done so.

The recession has also sparked another troubling pattern in terms of the increase in long-term unemployment (unemployment lasting more than twenty-seven

TABLE 3. Long-term Unemployment During the Recession (percent)

	Total		Puerto Rican		Non-Hispanic White		Non-Hispanic Black		Other Latino	
	2007	2011	2007	2011	2007	2011	2007	2011	2007	2011
age 16-25	34.0	49.6	38.2	53.7	32.1	47.8	39.3	54.8	34.2	49.8
age 25-55	26.6	43.0	29.4	46.9	21.8	37.9	30.5	48.7	26.0	42.6
age 55 or older	31.5	46.7	31.2	43.9	31.2	46.4	32.8	48.1	30.4	47.6
Total	30.7	46.4	32.9	48.2	28.4	44.0	34.2	50.5	30.2	46.7

Source: U.S. Census Bureau, ACS, 1- year estimates.
Sample: unemployed workers.

weeks), which grew to a record level of more than 40 percent of the unemployed during the recession (Alegretto 2010). As with overall unemployment, long-term unemployment has continued to rise even after its recessionary peak affecting close to 46 percent of all unemployed workers in 2011.

Table 3 shows long-term unemployment estimated for four ethnic and racial groups in the labor force divided into three age groups: 16–25 years old, 25–55 years old, and over age 55.[3,4] Long-term unemployment remained substantially higher in 2011 than in 2007 among all ethnic, racial, and age groups. Among 25–55 year-old workers, nearly 47 percent of Puerto Ricans –17.5 percent higher than in 2007 — had been out of work for more than six months, second only to non-Hispanic blacks with over 48 percent in that category. Latinos followed with over 42 percent, and non-Hispanic whites had the lowest percentage of the groups with just over 37 percent unemployed long-term. Youths between the ages of 16 and 25 experienced the highest rates of long-term unemployment both before and after the recession. Over that period, the increase was spread equally among all four ethnic and racial groups, averaging nearly 16 percent.

Puerto Ricans older than 55 years of age fared slightly better than their younger counterparts and relative to other ethnic and racial groups — rising 12.7 percentage points to 43.9 percent — the lowest percentage increase for workers 55 or older. However, Puerto Ricans also have the highest proportion of the population out of the labor force among the groups studied, which contributes to the lower rate of long-term unemployed among the elderly.

One of the more pernicious effects of long-term unemployment is the difficulty in finding subsequent re-employment, which has had its worst

TABLE 4. Employment Instability: Frequency of Unemployment since Recession (percent)

	Puerto Rican	Non-Hispanic White	Non-Hispanic Black	Other Latino	Total
Never	50	77	55	66	72
Once	20	10	23	16	13
2 or 3	17	9	12	11	10
4 or more	11	4	8	6	5

Source: Puerto Ricans and the Impact of the Recession Study.
Note: Response to the question, "In the last 5 years, how many times were you unemployed and looking for work or between jobs for at least 3 months?" *Sample*: workers in the labor force.

TABLE 5. Time at Current Job (percent)

	Puerto Rican	Non-Hispanic White	Non-Hispanic Black	Other Latino	Total
1 year	23	16	20	16	16
2-5 years	43	32	40	43	35
5 or more years	33	52	39	39	48

Source: Puerto Ricans and the Impact of the Recession Study (employed respondents only).

impact on older workers (Farber 2011; Valletta and Kuang 2012; Van Horn 2013). As unemployed workers get closer to retirement age, it can be difficult to find employment when competing against younger workers and new graduates in the labor market. As a result, many older workers have left the labor force following the Great Recession.

Participants from the PRIR were asked about their employment experience over the previous five years (between 2007 and 2012). During this time, non-Hispanic whites had relatively the most stable employment experience through the recession, with the largest percentage of respondents (77 percent) reporting having never been unemployed more than three months during this period. Puerto Ricans, in contrast, had the lowest percentage of respondents reporting to have never been unemployed at any time since the recession. Rather, Puerto Ricans have faced the most challenges finding stable work. Puerto Rican respondents reported the highest percentage of workers having been unemployed more than twice in the five years in question.

In table 5 we see that for those currently employed, Puerto Ricans had the shortest job tenure. Puerto Ricans had the highest percentage of workers

TABLE 6. Strategies for Finding Employment (percent)

	Puerto Rican	Non-Hispanic White	Non-Hispanic Black	Other Latino	Total
Moved to find job	26	20	23	15	20
Took new job from temporary job	13	8	17	18	11
Took reduction in pay or benefits	4	7	8	12	8
Took training or class for new skills to get job	25	9	17	10	11
Job in new field or career	24	18	31	21	20

Source: Puerto Ricans and the Impact of the Recession Study (Employed respondents only).
Note: Response to prompt: "The following are a list of ways people have found new jobs. Please select any of the following that you did in order to find employment."

employed for just one year (23 percent), and the lowest percentage of workers in the same position for five or more years (33 percent). This was compared to 16 percent of non-Hispanic whites at their job for one year, and 52 percent in their current job for five or more years.

Long-term unemployment has been a growing problem for workers over the last several decades, having reached historically high levels during and after the Great Recession (Valletta and Kuang 2012; Van Horn 2013). Researchers have pointed to several factors contributing to this phenomenon, including the effect of increased global competition, the shift of economic activities towards service industries, and the ascent of "just-in-time" hiring practices involving the use of temporary workers. Following the Great Recession, long-term unemployment worsened due to the combination of massive job losses and weak aggregate demand that delayed new hiring (Goodman and Mance 2011; Knoteck and Terry 2012; Valletta and Kuang 2012).

Despite the challenges in finding employment, survey results suggest that Puerto Ricans were among the most resourceful and adaptable members of the labor force following the Great Recession, actively taking steps to either find work wherever available or acquiring new skills to become more competitive. Table 6 shows that, among employed respondents, Puerto Ricans were most likely of the four racial and ethnic groups to have moved to find a new job or to have taken training or a class to learn new skills and were more likely than the employed respondents to have gotten a job in a new career to have gotten a job after having worked in a temporary job.

TABLE 7. Strategies for Improving Competitiveness (percent)

Employed	Puerto Rican	Non-Hispanic White	Non-Hispanic Black	Other Latino	Total
Taken an education class useful for job hunting	17	8	7	8	8
Taken a class or training course for skills to get a new job	25	21	27	13	20
Went to a One-stop Career Center or government agency for help	13	5	7	10	6
Looked for a job using Internet job boards or employer websites	36	28	32	24	28
Attended a job fair	15	12	24	15	14
None of the above	40	52	43	53	51

Unemployed respondents	Puerto Rican	Non-Hispanic White	Non-Hispanic Black	Other Latino	Total
Taken an education class useful for job hunting	19	19	21	26	21
Taken a class or training course for skills to get a new job	27	31	23	21	27
Went to a One-stop Career Center or government agency for help	25	35	37	18	32
Looked for a job using Internet job boards or employer websites	64	68	56	43	60
Attended a job fair	28	27	43	28	31
None of the above	12	19	23	22	20

Source: Puerto Ricans and the Impact of the Recession Study (Employed respondents only).
Note: Response to the question, "Which of the following have you done to help make yourself more competitive in the job market?"

Table 7 shows some of the steps that workers took in order to become more competitive in the labor market. These results were also split among unemployed and employed respondents. We can see that, again, employed Puerto Ricans were more assertive in their efforts to find employment. These Puerto Ricans were the most likely to have taken a class or training course to improve their skills, made use of government resources to find work, and searched for employment opportunities online. It is interesting to note, however, the stark difference between the unemployed and employed respondents.

Unemployed Puerto Ricans did not have the same success as other racial and ethnic groups in these categories, or as their currently employed counterparts. Of the unemployed, Puerto Ricans more closely resembled unemployed non-Hispanic whites in terms of taking educational or training classes or using the Internet. The one strategy that unemployed Puerto Ricans used to a greater degree than unemployed non-Hispanic whites was One-stop Career Centers and government agencies. This outcome may be affected by the implementation of local workforce development services, and representative of ethnic and racial differences in access to government programs.

Income and Earnings

Losses in employment among Puerto Ricans and other minorities led to losses in income and wealth relative to non-Hispanic whites. In general, two years after the Great Recession ended, earnings remained below their 2007 levels. In 2011, average real annual earnings for full-time, year-round working individuals (adjusted for inflation) decreased from their levels in 2007 for most of the ethnic and racial groups.[5] Non-Hispanic blacks experienced a small gain in average earnings ($121) between 2007 and 2011, driven by the ability of non-Hispanic black women to increase their earnings. Puerto Ricans saw a decrease of $138 and non-Puerto Rican Latinos lost $52 on average during the period. Non-Hispanic whites lost the most ground of all groups, at ($1,675). There were some important differences between men and women, however. For all groups except Latinos, men lost more money than women. Puerto Rican women experienced an increase in earnings of $1,556 between 2007 and 2011, and non-Hispanic black women had an increase of $568. Non-Hispanic white women suffered a loss in earnings of $323 and non-Puerto Rican Latinas gained $291.

Despite the losses in earnings, the recession did not affect the relative financial standing of racial and ethnic groups. Non-Hispanic whites had by far the highest earnings among full-time workers employed for at least fifty weeks in the past year. Their earnings averaged $55,960, which was more than $13,000 higher than the next highest group, Puerto Ricans, at $42,404. Non-Hispanic blacks ($39,537) and non-Puerto Rican Latinos ($34,361) had the lowest earnings, among the ethnic groups. Because non-Hispanic whites lost the greatest amount in average earnings, all minority groups narrowed their earnings gap relative to non-Hispanic whites. By 2011, Puerto Ricans earned 76 cents for every dollar of non-Hispanic whites' earnings, and non-Hispanic blacks and Latinos earned 71 cents and 61 cents, respectively, relative to the

TABLE 8. Individual Earnings for Full-time, Year-round Workers

	Total		Puerto Rican	
	2007	2011	2007	2011
Mean earnings for full-time, year-round workers:	$52,381	$51,080	$42,542	$42,404
Difference		($1,300)		($138)
Ratio to whites				0.76
Male	$59,347	$57,851	$47,029	$45,585
Female	$42,280	$42,137	$36,839	$38,395

	Non-Hispanic White		Non-Hispanic Black		Other Latino	
	2007	2011	2007	2011	2007	2011
Mean earnings for full-time, year-round workers:	$57,635	$55,960	$39,416	$39,537	$34,413	$34,361
Difference		($1,675)		$121		($52)
Ratio to whites		1.00		0.71		0.61
Male	$66,164	$64,254	$42,818	$42,710	$36,366	$36,481
Female	$44,973	$44,650	$36,145	$36,713	$30,633	$30,924

Source: U.S. Census Bureau, ACS, 1-year estimates.
Note: Figures have been adjusted for inflation (2007=100).

majority group. Earnings disparities were even larger among males, with non-Hispanic whites earning $64,254 on average — nearly $18,000 higher than Puerto Rican men at $45,585. In all cases, income for males exceeded that of females, but female Puerto Ricans and non-Hispanic black women saw sizable increases in earnings over the period. It is also worth noting the more than $8,000 difference in earnings between Puerto Ricans and non-Puerto Rican Latinos in this case, a fact that points to the different social characteristics of the two groups.

We further disaggregated income and earnings disparities by low-wage and non-low-wage workers in the United States. Following (Visser and Meléndez 2011), we defined low-wage workers as any worker whose total income was below two-thirds of the median in the metropolitan area in which they lived. Using the metropolitan area provides a more accurate measure of income relative to the cost of living than the simple national average. The results are shown in Table 9. Since fewer low-wage workers are employed full-time and at least fifty weeks a year, we removed this restriction and simply measured income for those employed workers who had positive income.

Table 9 shows a dramatic difference between low-wage and non-low-wage workers. Interestingly, average earnings of low-wage workers were lowest for non-Hispanic whites both prior to and after the recession, if by 2011, all four groups had similar average earnings in this category. These low-wage earnings notwithstanding, non-Hispanic whites have the lowest proportion of low-wage workers by a large margin. Only 28 percent of non-Hispanic-white workers were in the low-wage category in 2011 compared with 41 percent of Puerto Ricans and non-Hispanic blacks and 53 percent of Latino workers. Thus, more Puerto Rican, non-Hispanic- black, and Latino workers have significantly lower incomes than non-Hispanic whites. Still, all groups saw the proportion of low-wage workers decline in the years

TABLE 9. Individual Earnings by Wage Type (with income and worked in last 12 months)

	Total		Puerto Rican	
	2007	2011	2007	2011
Individuals	143,630,939	141,360,039	1,628,753	1,834,110
Not low wage	63.77	66.09	56.5	58.9
Low wage	36.2	33.9	43.5	41.1
Average Income				
Not low wage	$63,669	$59,538	$53,808	$50,756
Low wage	$13,333	$11,609	$14,239	$12,203

	Non-Hispanic White		Non-Hispanic Black		Other Latino	
	2007	2011	2007	2011	2007	2011
Individuals	99,234,183	94,460,483	15,159,684	14,959,416	18,220,364	19,650,775
Not low wage	69.4	71.7	54.7	58.8	43.1	47.1
Low wage	30.6	28.3	45.3	41.2	56.9	52.9
Average Income						
Not low wage	$66,442	$62,392	$50,457	$48,179	$50,095	$45,848
Low wage	$12,606	$11,084	$14,145	$12,043	$14,582	$12,448

Source: U.S. Census Bureau, ACS, 1-year estimates.
Note: Figures have been adjusted for inflation (2007=100).

TABLE 10. Mean Individual Earnings by Educational Attainment (full-time, year-round, 25 years or older)

	Total		Puerto Rican	
	2007	2011	2007	2011
Less than high school diploma	$30,101	$28,139	$30,191	$29,788
High school graduate (or GED)	$38,770	$36,682	$35,894	$35,020
Some college or associate's degree	$47,363	$44,257	$43,272	$41,456
Bachelor's	$71,278	$67,129	$61,826	$58,797
Higher than bachelor's	$99,894	$93,303	$81,706	$81,684

	Non-Hispanic White		Non-Hispanic Black		Other Latino	
	2007	2011	2007	2011	2007	2011
Less than high school diploma	$36,257	$33,803	$27,413	$26,860	$25,827	$24,634
High school graduate (or GED)	$41,508	$39,276	$32,165	$31,575	$32,162	$30,455
Some college or associate's degree	$49,717	$46,808	$39,106	$37,435	$41,673	$38,294
Bachelor's	$75,395	$70,646	$54,901	$52,517	$53,569	$53,541
Higher than bachelor's	$104,031	$96,531	$73,163	$70,226	$78,736	$79,339

Source: U.S. Census Bureau, ACS, 1-year estimates.

following the recession, which may be due, in part, to some workers exiting the labor force.

To get a fuller picture of earnings and income, we also compared earnings of workers relative to their education levels. Table 10 shows mean individual earnings of full-time, year-round workers age 25 and older. Relative earnings disparities remained similar among the ethnic and racial groups, and the level of earnings correlated strongly and positively with the level of education (those with less than a high school education earned the least and those with a graduate-level education earned the most). We can also see that earnings in all categories fell since the beginning of the recession in late 2007.

Table 11 more fully illustrates the differences within educational attainment that drive earnings disparities among the ethnic and racial groups. Minority groups had similar proportions of the population with a high school education, some college, or a bachelor's degree. The key difference lies in the proportions of workers at either end of the educational spectrum — those with less than a high school education and those with a bachelor's degree or graduate-level education. Non-Hispanic white workers held bachelor's or graduate degrees

TABLE 11. Educational Attainment, 25 Years of Age or Older (percent)

	Total		Puerto Rican	
	2007	2011	2007	2011
Less than high school diploma	15.5	14.1	27.6	24.9
High school graduate (or GED)	30.8	28.4	30.6	29.5
Some college or associate's degree	27.2	29	25.9	29.3
Bachelor's	16.9	17.9	10.8	10.9
Higher than bachelor's	9.7	10.6	5.0	5.4

	Non-Hispanic White		Non-Hispanic Black		Other Latino	
	2007	2011	2007	2011	2007	2011
Less than high school diploma	10.6	8.9	19.8	17.3	40.9	38.2
High school graduate (or GED)	30.7	29.1	34.4	31.5	27.7	26.7
Some college or associate's degree	28.2	30.1	28.5	32.6	19.1	22.1
Bachelor's	19.0	19.9	11.4	12.1	8.5	9.0
Higher than bachelor's	11.5	12.0	5.9	6.6	3.8	4.0

Source: U.S. Census Bureau, ACS, 1-year estimates.

at nearly double the rate of the other ethnic groups — and thus had a higher proportion of high earners — both before and after the recession. The number of minority workers with less than a high school education is more than double the number for non-Hispanic whites. For Puerto Ricans, this was 25 percent in 2011. Non-Hispanic blacks had a lower proportion at 17 percent. Other Latinos differed greatly from Puerto Ricans, having the highest rate at over 38 percent. In sum, lower educational attainment translates into lower earnings potential for these groups and makes them especially vulnerable during bouts of prolonged unemployment.

For comparison, Table 12 shows educational attainment for those working full time and year round. Here we can see that educational disparities persist between the same groups, and that non-Hispanic whites have the highest percentage of workers with a bachelor's degree or above, though not by the same degree. Importantly, we observe that for all the groups, shares of full-time, year-round workers were generally skewed toward those with higher levels of education than for the general population shown in Table 11. Further, these percentages increased over the period. This demonstrates that not

TABLE 12. Educational Attainment for Full-time, Year-round Workers with Income (percent)

	Total		Puerto Rican	
	2007	2011	2007	2011
Less than high school diploma	9.1	7.8	13.7	11.5
High school graduate (or GED)	28.1	24.7	33.3	28.7
Some college or associate's degree	29.8	31.1	31.9	35.5
Bachelor's	21.2	22.7	14.7	16.2
Higher than bachelor's	11.8	13.7	6.4	8.1

	Non-Hispanic White		Non-Hispanic Black		Other Latino	
	2007	2011	2007	2011	2007	2011
Less than high school diploma	4.8	3.7	8.4	6.9	34.3	29.8
High school graduate (or GED)	27.7	24.4	33.6	28.4	29.6	27.6
Some college or associate's degree	31.1	31.9	34.2	37.2	21.7	25.5
Bachelor's	23.4	24.9	16.2	17.7	10.2	11.7
Higher than bachelor's	13.1	15.0	7.6	9.9	4.2	5.4

Source: U.S. Census Bureau, ACS, 1-year estimates.

only were those working full time more likely to be better educated, but also that the labor market became more competitive following the recession in terms of requiring a more highly educated workforce. This situation makes it increasingly difficult for those less educated to find work, and underscores the importance of education for competing in the United States economy.

In addition, we note that Latinos had by far the highest concentration of workers with less than a high school education in Table 12, suggesting that a relatively large proportion of its workers are engaged in lower-wage work — an observation corroborated by the findings presented in Table 9.

Poverty

Finally, studies from the period find that the recession took a toll in the form of higher poverty levels across the board. Jacobsen and Mather (2011) note that the number of people in poverty increased more between 2009 and 2010 than in the year following any other recession since 1962. As in the case of unemployment and earnings, poverty was highest among minorities. Non-Hispanic blacks and Puerto Ricans led with the highest levels of individual

TABLE 13. Individual Poverty (percent)

	Total		Puerto Rican	
	2007	2011	2007	2011
All People	13	15.9	24.3	27.4
Under 18 years	18	22.5	32.3	35.5
18 to 64 years	11.6	14.8	20.1	23.6
65 years and over	9.5	9.3	22.6	22.1
People in families	10.6	13.4	22.1	25.0
Unrelated individuals 15 years and over	23.6	27	35.3	39.3

	Non-Hispanic White		Non-Hispanic Black		Other Latino	
	4.8	3.7	8.4	6.9	34.3	29.8
All People	10.2	13.0	24.7	28.1	22.5	26.6
Under 18 years	13.3	17.8	34.5	39.4	29.9	34.7
18 to 64 years	9.6	12.5	20.5	24.5	18.7	22.8
65 years and over	8.0	7.8	20.6	18.9	20.6	20.8
People in families	7.7	10.3	22.8	26.1	20.7	24.7
Unrelated individuals 15 years and over	21.2	24.2	32.6	36.5	33.1	37.5

Source: U.S. Census Bureau, ACS, 1-year estimates.

poverty, at 28.1 percent and 27.4 percent, respectively. This is more than double the rate of poverty for all non-Hispanic whites in 2011 (13 percent).

However, perhaps most alarming has been the rise in childhood poverty levels: studies estimate that there were approximately 6.5 million children in the United States living in poverty. This trend has been driven by persistent and long periods of unemployment that have lowered household incomes (Isaacs 2011). The rate of child poverty for Puerto Ricans in 2011 was 35.5 percent compared with 39.4 percent for non-Hispanic blacks and 34.7 percent for other Latinos. The poverty rates for these three ethnic groups were nearly double the rate of 17.8 percent for non-Hispanic whites under 18. For Hispanics, poverty rates were more tied to educational attainment. According to Lopez and Velasco (2011), between 2007 and 2010, poverty rates among Latino children grew the most among those in families with parents who have a high school diploma or less and the least among those where the parent had a college degree.

TABLE 14. Childcare Needs (percent)

Employed respondents	Puerto Rican	Non-Hispanic White	Non-Hispanic Black	Other Latino	Total
Not look for or apply for work	8	2	2	13	4
Turn down job offered	3	2	5	3	3
Late for work	13	3	3	10	4
Absent from work	15	6	3	11	7
Change hours of work	4	9	6	6	8
Unemployed respondents	Puerto Rican	Non-Hispanic White	Non-Hispanic Black	Other Latino	Total
Not look for or apply for work	19	16	17	12	16
Turn down job offered	17	11	11	6	10
Late for work	13	5	3	7	5
Absent from work	15	4	9	8	6
Change hours of work	8	15	3	6	10

Source: Puerto Ricans and the Impact of the Recession Study.
Note: Female respondents only. Response to question, "In the past 12 months has a concern about your childcare needs caused you to do the following?"

Survey results from the PRIR showed that childcare needs had an important effect on the professional lives of women—especially among Puerto Ricans and Latinos. Participants were asked how childcare needs affected their employment experience. Men overwhelmingly reported "no concerns," and were thus not shown here. Puerto Rican respondents were most likely to report not looking for work, being late or absent, or turning down a job due to childcare needs. However, what stands out is the fact that the consequences of childcare needs were much more prevalent among unemployed Puerto Rican women than employed women.

Conclusion

Although the Great Recession is officially several years in the past, its effects are still being felt by many. The so-called jobless recovery has led to prolonged hardship for millions struggling with unemployment and poverty and has only shown modest signs of improving.

The evidence presented in this chapter underscores the demographic differences that exist within the United States economy. Unemployment, especially lasting more than six months, remains stubbornly high among Puerto

Ricans and other minorities. As a direct result, household incomes fell and poverty rose sharply, particularly for children. Puerto Ricans, as well as other minorities, continue to struggle with higher incidence of low-wage jobs and lower earnings potential based on their deficient levels of educational attainment.

Further, the results of this study point to the importance of distinguishing Puerto Ricans from Latinos as a whole, in their unique characteristics in terms of employment, education, English proficiency, earnings, and poverty. When compared with the overall impact of the recession in term of earnings and employment, Puerto Ricans fared better than other Latinos and non-Hispanic blacks both in terms of substantially higher earnings and the impact of the recession as measured by loss in earnings. Findings from the PRIR demonstrate that perhaps the greatest asset of Puerto Ricans during the recession has been their adaptability and resilience.

Nonetheless, Puerto Ricans have relatively high rates of poverty, especially among children. This fact highlights the diversity in the experiences of Puerto Ricans in the workforce — some fare relatively well, while others continue to struggle. We observe sharp differences in terms of the impact of the recession among who are employed and those who are unemployed, underemployed, employed in low-wage jobs, or out of the labor force. Those who were employed and had higher levels of education appear to have weathered the recession well and made progress, while unemployed and low-wage workers were more negatively affected. The improvement according to certain indicators underscores the resilient behavior of those workers whose ability to be were more strategic increased their competitiveness.

The severe losses in employment and subsequent increases in poverty levels highlight the importance of policy responses at the federal and local levels, as well as the need for robust safety-net programs intended to lessen the impact suffered by workers during recessions and workforce training programs. Specifically for Puerto Ricans, policy responses should be focused on addressing the needs of the most vulnerable members of the community, such as those with low levels of education, low-wage workers, and low-income families. In light of the evidence presented in this study, these may include childcare needs to support female-headed households and increased education and workforce training programs for disadvantaged workers. Cuts to the federal budget, including unemployment benefits, will likely prolong the recovery for the millions of Americans still struggling. "Belt-tightening" at a time when many have still not recovered from the Great Recession is likely to have devastating consequences.

NOTES

[1] The authors acknowledge the financial support of the "Puerto Ricans and the Impact of the Recession" study from the Ford Foundation and the Center for Puerto Rican Studies for conducting the study. The survey was designed by Edwin Meléndez (principal investigator) and M. Anne Visser (project manager), and the data were collected by GfK Custom Research, LLC.
[2] Data for this survey were weighted to be nationally representative.
[3] Calculations for long-term unemployment were based on the number of workers who were employed less than 25 weeks as a percentage of workers who were not employed for at least 50 weeks in the year, according to ACS figures. It is worth noting that ACS estimates tended to be higher compared to estimates from Current Population Statistics of the Bureau of Labor Statistics in 2007. ACS estimates were used since it was possible to disaggregate Puerto Ricans from Latinos.
[4] ACS methodology was changed after 2008 in order to more closely resemble CPS figures. For more information on the difference between ACS and CPS employment, see "Comparison of ACS and CPS data on Employment Status" by Braedyn Kromer and David Howard. www.census.gov/people/laborforce/publications/ACS_CPS_Comparison_Report.pdf
[5] Full-time, year-round workers are those who worked at least 35 hours a week for at least 50 weeks of the year.

REFERENCES

Alegretto, Sylvia and Devon Lynch. 2010. The composition of the unemployed and the long-term unemployed in tough labor markets. *Monthly Labor Review* October: 3–18.

Aaronson, Daniel, Ellen Rissman and Daniel G. Sullivan 2004a. Assessing the jobless recovery. *Economic Perspectives-Federal Reserve Bank of Chicago* 28: 2–20.

_____. 2004b. Can sectoral reallocation explain the jobless recovery? *Economic Perspectives-Federal Reserve Bank of Chicago* 28: 36–49.

Adda, Jerome, Christian Dustmann, Costas Meghir and Jean-Marc Robin. 2013. Career Progression, Economic Downturns, and Skills. NBER Working Paper No. w18832. National Bureau of Economic Research.

DeNavas-Walt, Carmen, Bernadette D. Proctor and Jessica C. Smith. 2011. Income, Poverty, and Health Insurance Coverage in the United States: 2010. U.S. Census Bureau, Current Population Reports, P60-239.

Engemann, Kristie M. and Howard J. Wall. 2009. The Effects of Recessions Across Demographic Groups. Federal Reserve Bank of St. Louis Working Paper Series.

Fang, Lei and Pedro Silos. 2012. Wages and Unemployment Across Business Cycles: A High-Frequency Investigation. Working Paper No. 2012-16. Federal Reserve Bank of Atlanta.

Farber, Henry. 2011. Job Loss in the Great Recession: Historical Perspective from the Displaced Workers Survey 1984-2010. NBER Working Paper No. 17040. National Bureau of Economic Research.

Goodman, Christopher J., and Steven M. Mance. 2011. Employment loss and the 2007-09 recession: an overview. *Monthly Labor Review* April: 3–12.

Hipple, Steven. 2009. The labor market in 2009: recession drags on. *Monthly Labor Review* March: 3–22.

Hoynes, Hilary W., Douglas L. Miller and Jessamyn Schaller. 2012. Who Suffers During Recessions? NBER Working Paper No. w17951. National Bureau of Economic Research.

Isaacs, Julia. 2011. The Recession's Ongoing Impact on America's Children: Indicators of Children's Economic Well-Being in 2011. Brookings Institution.

Jacobsen, Linda A., and Mark Mather. 2011. A Post-Recession Update on US Social and Economic Trends. Population Bulletin Update. Population Reference Bureau.

Knoteck, Edward S., and Stephen Terry. 2009. How will unemployment fare following the recession? *Federal Reserve Bank of Kansas City Economic Review* Third Quater: 5–33.

Lopez, Mark H., and Gabriel Velasco. 2011. Childhood Poverty Among Hispanics Sets Record, Leads Nation. Washington, DC: Pew Research Center.

Oberg, Charles N. 2011. The great recession's impact on children. *Maternal and Child Health Journal* 15(5): 553–4.

Rothstein, Donna. 2012. Young Adult Employment During the Recession. Issues in Labor Statistics, May 2012. Washington, DC: Bureau of Labor Statistics.

Sum, Andrew, Ishwar Khatiwada, Allison Beard and Sheila Palma. 2010. Labor Underutilization Impacts of the Great Recession of 2007–2009: Variations in Labor Underutilization Problems Across Age, Gender, Race-Ethnic, Educational Attainment and Occupational Groups in the US, 2009 Fourth Quarter. Boston: Northeastern University, Center for Labor Market Studies.

Sierminska, Eva and Yelena Takhtamanova. 2011. Job flows, demographics, and the Great Recession. *Research in Labor Economics* 32: 115–54.

Taylor, Paul, Rakesh Kochhar, Richard Fry, Gabriel Velasco and Seth Motel. 2011. Wealth Gaps Rise to Record Highs between Whites, Blacks and Hispanics. Washington, DC: Pew Research Center.

U.S. Department of Labor. 2010. The Long Term Unemployment Experience of the Jobless. Issues in Labor Statistics, June 2010.

_____. 2011. The Hispanic Labor Force in the Recovery. Bureau of Labor Statistics Special Report. http://www.dol.gov/_sec/media/reports/HispanicLaborForce2011/HispanicLaborForce.pdf/.

_____. 2012. Latino Labor Force at a Glance. Bureau of Labor Statistics.

Valletta, Rob, and Katherine Kuang. 2013. Why is unemployment duration so long? *FRBSF Economic Letters* 30 January.

Van Horn, Carl E. 2013. *Working Scared (or Not at All)*. Lanham, MD: Rowman & Littlefield.

Visser, M. Anne and Edwin Meléndez. 2011. Puerto Ricans in the US low-wage labor market: Introduction to the issues, trends, and policies. *CENTRO: Journal of the Center for Puerto Rican Studies* 23(2) 4-19.

Wolff, Edward N. 2012. The Asset Price Meltdown and the Wealth of the Middle Class. NBER Working Paper No. w18559. National Bureau of Economic Research.

Rebuilding the Puerto Rican Education Pipeline for a Multilingual and Multicultural Future

LUIS O. REYES

In New York City, the historical gateway of Puerto Rican migration to the United States, and in New York State, Puerto Ricans continue to experience chronic, academic underachievement as measured by their relatively low enrollment levels at various points in the "education pipeline" (De Jesús and Vasquez 2005) and by the low education attainment levels of the adult Puerto Rican population over 25 years of age. Puerto Ricans in New York City make up 26 percent of Hispanic youth (ages 16 through 24) and 8 percent of the city's youth overall, according to a merged sample from the United States Census Bureau American Community Survey (ACS) from 2006, 2007 and 2008 (Treschan 2010). Data from this report, derived from the Census Bureau, indicate that Puerto Rican youth are the most disadvantaged of all comparable groups in terms of access to services, educational attainment, and rates of poverty, with 33.4 percent of Puerto Rican households having incomes under the Federal Poverty Level (Treschan 2010). A more recent study by researchers at the Center for Puerto Rican Studies confirmed persistent disparities for youth in New York City (Reyes and Meléndez 2012).

Paradoxically, educational attainment among Puerto Ricans in the United States as a whole has been slowly improving over the past decade. In 2000, 63 percent of Puerto Ricans 25 years of age and older had a high school degree or higher compared with 75 percent in 2011 (U.S. Census Bureau 2011). Similarly, only 12.5 percent of Puerto Ricans had a bachelor's degree or higher in 2000 compared with 16 percent in 2011 (U.S. Census Bureau 2011). Even though educational attainment has been steadily increasing, the disparities in educational attainment among Puerto Ricans, non-Hispanic whites, and other Hispanic subpopulations has remained constant (Reyes and Rosofsky 2013). For instance, the disparity between Puerto Ricans and non-Hispanic whites earning a bachelor's degree has hovered around a 9-percentage-point difference over the past decade (U.S. Census Bureau 2011).

In this chapter, I present the latest educational data on Puerto Ricans in New York City, New York State, and the United States (U.S. Census Bureau 2011). The data demonstrate that Puerto Ricans are taking longer to graduate from high school and are enrolling in college and graduate school at lower percentages than their non-Hispanic white and other Hispanic counterparts, especially in New York City. Also, disparities in educational achievement for Puerto Ricans in New York City compared with the population of the United States as a whole are almost twice as large across all levels of educational attainment (Reyes and Rosofsky 2013). Additionally, the gap in educational attainment beyond high school that exists between Puerto Ricans and non-Hispanic whites is greater among males than it is among females. A similar gender gap in educational attainment exists for Hispanics as a whole (Reyes and Meléndez 2012).

Beyond presenting detailed findings on disparities in school enrollment and educational attainment, I discuss various factors that contribute to these educational disparities. I review the history of the Puerto Rican community's traditional civil rights approach that championed Transitional Bilingual Education (TBE) and ESL programs as the means by which Puerto Rican and other Latino English Language Learners (ELLs) could transition as rapidly as possible to the monolingual educational mainstream. I propose that Puerto Rican educators and policymakers rethink the traditional civil rights approach and explore the utility of an additive educational framework that embraces the development of Puerto Rican students' academic, linguistic, and cultural knowledge and competence and builds upon the existing strengths within Puerto Rican and Latino communities (Bartlett and Garcia 2011). This additive educational framework builds on Puerto Rican students' home languages, culture, and ethnicity, addresses social inequality, prepares teachers for diversity with an emphasis on culturally responsive teaching and learning practices, and helps students acquire social and cultural capital (Nieto, Rivera and Quiñones 2010).

Finally, I highlight a set of policy and programmatic solutions that build upon the existing strengths of Puerto Rican and Latino communities, including academic, linguistic, and cultural competence. These solutions include culturally and linguistically appropriate child care and early education that uses Puerto Rican children's home languages, engages Puerto Rican parents and community members in culturally competent ways, has school-based staff who acquire Spanish-language skills and value bilingualism and biliteracy, features a well-rounded, rigorous curriculum in middle school and high school coupled with academic, social, and emotional supports for all students, and strengthens the pathways into higher education and STEM-based careers in the workforce.

A Brief Profile of Puerto Ricans in New York City Public Schools

As of 2010, Puerto Ricans remained the largest national subgroup of Latinos in New York State at 31.6 percent (U.S. Census Bureau 2011) and 30.8 percent of the total Latino population of New York City that same year. However, Puerto Ricans made up just 26 percent of Latino youth (ages 16 through 24) in New York City compared with Dominican youth who made up 29 percent (Treschan October 2010). Puerto Ricans in New York City, along with Dominicans and the more recently arrived Mexicans, continue to face numerous social and economic barriers along with poor academic achievement, high dropout rates, and low college enrollment and graduation rates.

Among New York City Latinos, Puerto Ricans have the highest rates of poverty with 33.4 percent of Puerto Rican households living below the federal poverty level (Treschan 2010: 11). According to Treschan, Puerto Ricans, especially males, are "the most disadvantaged youth group in New York City, with rates of school enrollment, educational attainment and employment status lower than any other comparable group" (2010: 4). Almost 42 percent of Puerto Rican male 16 to 24 year-olds in New York City were without a high school diploma compared with more than 32 percent of Puerto Rican females (Treschan 2010: 9). Approximately 17 percent of these Puerto Rican males were not in school, employed, or looking for work, compared with 9 percent of Dominicans and 8 percent of Mexicans (Treschan 2010: 9).

In New York City, Latinos make up 39 percent of public school students and 67 percent of all enrolled ELL students. Many Puerto Rican enrolled youth attend segregated and low-performing public schools with the least experienced teachers and fewer and fewer Puerto Rican teachers. A large number of 16 to 24 year-olds are "disconnected" (i.e., living in poverty, lacking family supports, and neither attending school nor employed) (Treschan 2010).

In addition to these realities, fewer and fewer Puerto Rican students are eligible for and enrolled in bilingual or English-as-a-Second-Language (ESL) instructional programs. According to the 2010 American Community Survey 1-year estimates for the city population five years of age and older (U.S. Census Bureau 2011), nearly 28 percent of Puerto Ricans speak English only at home compared with 9 percent of Mexicans and 15 percent of all Latinos. More than

72 percent of Puerto Ricans speak a language other than English, but only 21 percent speak English less than "very well." The comparable statistics for Mexicans five years of age and older are 9 percent, 92 percent, and 60 percent, respectively. Among the overall Latino city population, 15 percent speak English only at home, 85 percent speak a language other than English, and 41 percent speak English less than "very well." While the majority of Puerto Ricans report speaking Spanish, only one out of five report having limited English proficiency.

In a recent policy brief on Latino youth in New York City, the Community Service Society (CSS) summarized these statistics as follows: "Latino youth are largely English-speaking" and "Since relatively few Mexican young people enroll in school, school-based English Language Learning (ELL) programming should not be the predominant policy concern for Latino youth" (Treschan 2010: 4). This policy position, thus, abandons even the limited TBE mandate of the 1974 Aspira Consent Decree (*Aspira of New York v. Board of Education of the City of New York* 1974), not to mention abandoning the Puerto Rican community's historical support for bilingualism and biculturalism as reflective of its individual and collective identity. In fact, the CSS assertion about the irrelevance of ELL programming given the limited number of enrolled Mexican young people (20% of males and 39% of females) ignores the fact that Mexicans make up only 13 percent of Latino youth (Treschan, p. 7). Further, the U.S. Census Bureau's ACS data on Puerto Ricans' language proficiency is based on self-reported proficiency in English and is not based on any objective assessment of English proficiency and as such is not a reliable measure of language proficiency. The Spanish LAB-R and English LAB-R language proficiency assessments, which are administered to Spanish-surnamed pupils entering the New York City public school system based on their parents' responses to the Home Language Survey, would be more reliable measures. However, such data are not available for all Puerto Ricans living in New York City.

This policy position is occurring at a time when public schools in New York, as in the nation at large, are being challenged to respond to the rapid growth of other Latino immigrant populations and bilingual education has come under political attack.

Disparities in School Enrollment, Population Three Years and Older Enrolled in School

Reyes and Rosofsky (2013) examined the most recent school enrollment and attainment data from the U.S. Census Bureau for the year 2011 for the United States, New York City, and New York State. As expected, Puerto Ricans, non-Hispanic whites, and Hispanics have relatively equal rates of enrollment in these three areas from nursery school through elementary school and from age 3 to 16. Enrollment disparities don't begin to appear until age 16 (see Figures 1a, 1b and 1c).

At ages 16 to 18, a higher percentage of Puerto Ricans are enrolled in high school, and fewer Puerto Ricans are enrolled in college or graduate school than both non-Hispanic whites and all Hispanics in all three geographic locations. Another noticeable difference is that non-Hispanic whites in New York City are doing much better in higher education enrollment from ages 16 to 18 than their peers in the rest of the state and the country. On the other hand, the percentage of Puerto Ricans enrolled in college and graduate school in this age bracket is approximately the same in the three areas examined. In New York City, Hispanics as a whole are also doing slightly better than they are nationwide in terms of higher education enrollment.

The disparity in enrollment becomes even more pronounced at ages 19 to 24. In New York City, almost twice as many Puerto Ricans remain in high school (20%) than do Puerto Ricans in the United States (11%) (Reyes and Rosofsky 2013). Furthermore, there is an 18-percentage-point difference in this same age bracket between Puerto Ricans in high school in New York City (20%) and non-Hispanic whites (2%), while the reverse is true for college or graduate school. Puerto Ricans in New York City in the 19-to-24 age bracket are also falling behind in higher education enrollment compared with Puerto Ricans in the country as a whole. The higher education enrollment of all Hispanics and Puerto Ricans is relatively equal in the United States, but that of Puerto Ricans is lower in both New York City and New York State relative to all Hispanics.

Overall, there is a 10-percentage-point disparity in the college or graduate school enrollment of Puerto Ricans and Latinos compared with non-Hispanic whites in the United States and New York State (Reyes and Rosofsky 2013). However, the disparity in college or graduate school enrollment grows to 16 percentage points in New York City, (20.5% for Puerto Ricans and 36.4% for non-Hispanic whites). Latinos in New York City (24.2%) and New York State

FIGURE 1A. School Enrollment of Puerto Ricans, 2011

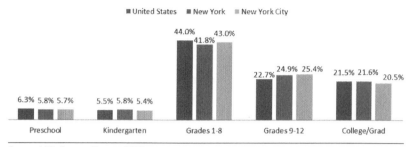

Source: U.S. Census Bureau 2011.

FIGURE 1B. School Enrollment, Non-Hispanic White Alone, 2011

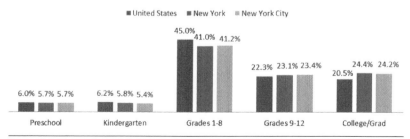

Source: U.S. Census Bureau 2011.

FIGURE 1C. School Enrollment of Hispanics, 2011

Source: U.S. Census Bureau 2011.

(24.4%) have a higher college or graduate school enrollment than Latinos in the rest of the United States (20.5%). However, the higher education enrollment of Puerto Ricans in New York City (20.5%) and New York State (21.6%) is approximately equal to that of Puerto Ricans nationally (21.5%). In short, these enrollment data demonstrate that Puerto Ricans are taking longer to graduate from high school and are enrolling in college and graduate school at lower rates than their non-Hispanic white and other Hispanic counterparts, especially in New York City.

Disparities in Educational Attainment (25 and Older)

In the United States, 16 percent of Puerto Ricans 25 and older received a bachelor's degree or higher compared with 32 percent of non-Hispanic whites, a 16-percentage-point differential (U.S. Census Bureau 2011). The respective statistics for New York State were 14 percent for Puerto Ricans and 37 percent for non-Hispanic whites, a 23-percentage-point differential. As of 2010, according to ACS 1-year estimates (U.S. Census Bureau 2011), Puerto Ricans in New York City have the greatest disparity in college attainment when compared with non-Hispanic whites. While 25.2 percent of whites completed a bachelor's degree and 20.23 percent a graduate or professional degree (45.4% combined), only 8.1 percent of Puerto Ricans completed a bachelor's degree and 4.1 percent a graduate or professional degree (12.5% combined), a 34-percentage-point difference.

What should also be noted is that non-Hispanic whites and all Hispanics in New York City have higher rates of attaining bachelor's and graduate degrees than non-Hispanic whites and all Hispanics in New York State and the United States. As previously noted, the opposite is true for Puerto Ricans.

Gender Disparities

In addition to educational attainment disparities among white, all Hispanic, and Puerto Rican populations in the United States, disparities in educational attainment at the college and graduate level are more pronounced for Puerto Rican men than they they are for Puerto Rican women age 25 and older (Reyes and Rosofsky 2013; Reyes and Meléndez 2012). Referring to Figure 4 and Figure 5, the percentage of non-Hispanic white men in the United States in 2011 who completed or were enrolled in college or graduate school (60.6%) was almost double that of Puerto Rican men (32.3%). The disparity was not as great for women. For example, 65 percent of non-Hispanic white

FIGURE 2. Educational Attainment 25 Years and Over in the United States, 2011

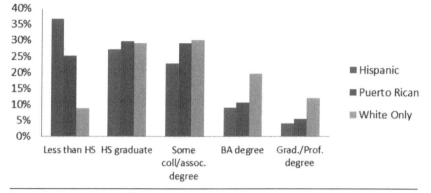

Source: U.S. Census Bureau 2011.

TABLE 1. Bachelor's Degree and Graduate School Attainment (Percent)

	Non-Hispanic White		Puerto Rican		Hispanic	
	Bachelor's	Graduate	Bachelor's	Graduate	Bachelor's	Graduate
U.S.	19.9	12	10.7	5.4	9.1	4.1
New York State	20.1	16.5	8.7	5.2	10.4	5.4
New York City	25.2	20.2	8.1	4.4	10.2	4.9

Source: U.S. Census Bureau 2011.

women had completed or were enrolled in college or graduate school, while only 43 percent of Puerto Rican women had similar rates of educational attainment (Reyes and Rosofsky 2013).

What are the conclusions to be taken from these census findings? First, school enrollment disparities for Puerto Ricans (when compared with non-Hispanic whites) are more pronounced for New York City than for New York State or the nation as a whole. Second, educational attainment disparities for Puerto Ricans (when compared with non-Hispanic whites) are more pronounced for New York City than for New York State or the nation as a whole, even more so when disaggregating by gender. Third and last, there are sizable gaps in college and graduate school attainment in New York City and New York State for Puerto Ricans compared with non-Hispanic whites, especially men.

Assessing the Education Pipeline

Puerto Rican and other Latino students, both native-born and foreign-born, in large part, face similar school conditions and academic outcomes, as reflected in what has been characterized as a "leaky education pipeline" (De Jesús and Vasquez Fall 2005). Many Puerto Rican students in public schools in the United States live in low-income neighborhoods and have been concentrated in middle and high schools where students have less than a 50 percent chance of graduating on time (Balfanz and Letgers 2004). These schools also spend less per pupil, are more segregated (Fessenden 2012; Orfied, Kucsera, and Siegel-Hawley 2012), more overcrowded, and have high rates of teacher turnover and low rates of graduation when compared with their affluent white majority counterparts (New York City Coalition for Educational Justice 2007; Reyes 2012). While in general, these students have extensive needs, many teachers in these low-performing schools are inexperienced,

FIGURE 4. Male College and Graduate Level Educational Attainment, United States

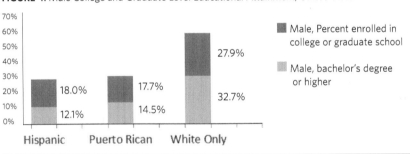

Source: U.S. Census Bureau 2011.

FIGURE 5. Female College and Graduate Level Educational Attainment

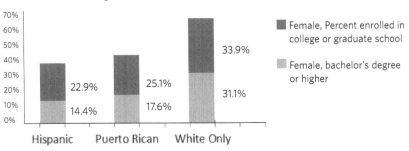

Source: U.S. Census Bureau 2011.

do not have advanced degrees, and are in need of instructional support and professional development (Meade and Gaytan 2009).

Those who do graduate find themselves unprepared for college-level academic courses. Now, many of these so-called "dropout factories" (Balfanz and Letgers 2004) in Puerto Rican and Latino neighborhoods are being subjected to closing, restructuring, or phasing out (Reyes 2012). The discontinuities and disparities in the school experiences and outcomes of these Puerto Rican and Latino students are also reflected in the disconnection that large numbers of them face as young adults transitioning from school to work (Reyes and Meléndez 2012). One of the main consequences of a broken educational pipeline and the significant educational disparities that result is that Puerto Ricans are concentrated in low-wage jobs and experience higher rates of unemployment and poverty than other Latino subgroups.

There are several in-school and out-of-school factors that may be contributing to the disparities in educational enrollment and attainment among the Puerto Rican population, especially those prevailing in New York City, including lack of human and financial capital, few family resources, less access to early education, and residential segregation (Kasinitz et al. 2009). These conditions expose youth to structural disadvantages resulting in the higher likelihood of dropping out of high school. In New York City, many families are not likely to go outside of the public school system, which typically receives less funding in poorer areas than it does in neighborhoods with lower rates of poverty. Additionally, many families have little knowledge about academically selective high schools that require students to take an entrance test. (Kasinitz et al. 2009).

Educating Puerto Ricans for a Multilingual/Multicultural Future

Researchers, community leaders and educators have traditionally looked at the education of Puerto Rican students in New York City and the United States within the framework of equal educational opportunities, especially for those students with limited English proficiency (LEP) (Santiago-Santiago 1978; Reyes 2006). Today, fewer and fewer Puerto Rican students are eligible for and enrolled in bilingual or ESL instructional programs. Of particular relevance for policymakers studying the "Puerto Rican educational pipeline" is the overarching demographic reality that 91.4 percent of Puerto Rican youth who were born in the United States (and 85% of Latino youth) report speaking English well or very well (Treschan 2010).

As a result, some policymakers suggest that ELL programming should not be the predominant policy concern for Latino youth. The relevance of bilingual or ESL program models of instruction for the academic achievement of Puerto Rican students in New York City is not known, given the absence of disaggregated Puerto Rican student data (Reyes 2012) not to mention the continuing decrease in the number of available bilingual programs for ELL students, in general (New York City Department of Education 2013). A large majority of ELL students (nearly 76% of ELLs or more than 120,000 of the nearly 160,000 ELL students) were enrolled in ESL programs during the 2011–2012 school year. Only 17.7 percent were enrolled in TBE programs (84% of whom, or fewer than 24,000, were Spanish-speaking students) and 4.0 percent were enrolled in Dual Language (DL) programs (New York City Department of Education 2013).

During the last decade, the New York City Department of Education has been dismantling bilingual programs and increasing the number of ESL programs even as the numbers of immigrant and language-minority students have increased in city schools (Reyes 2012). Between 1999 and 2012, in fact, the percentage of eligible ELL students in New York City participating in TBE programs fell from about 50 percent to about 18 percent. In effect, the 1974 Aspira Consent Decree that established the right of Puerto Rican and Latino LEP/ELL students to attend TBE programs, is no longer feasible as an educational remedy for the vast majority of Puerto Rican students, especially the 91.4 percent who were born in the United States and report speaking English well or very well. Similar demographic and linguistic patterns are likely to prevail in New York State and in the United States as a whole.

Fewer and fewer Puerto Rican students are eligible for and enrolled in TBE or ESL instructional programs. At the same time, public schools in the United States are being challenged to respond to the rapid growth of other Latino immigrant populations in an era that has seen bilingual education come under attack from the political right. I propose that Puerto Rican educators and policymakers rethink the traditional civil rights approach embedded in New York City's Aspira Consent Decree that provided TBE and ESL programs as the means by which ELLs could transition as rapidly as possible to the monolingual educational mainstream.

I explore the utility of an additive educational framework that builds on Puerto Rican students' home languages, culture, and ethnicity, addresses social inequality, prepares teachers for diversity with an emphasis on culturally responsive teaching and learning practices, and helps students acquire social and cultural capital (Nieto, Rivera and Quiñones 2010).

I present testimonial evidence in the following pages that this alternative education framework is actually reflective of the original vision of Puerto Rican educators and researchers like Dr. Antonia Pantoja, the pioneering founder of Aspira, Inc., and Dr. Frank Bonilla, the founding director of the Center for Puerto Rican Studies.

Limitations of the Civil Rights Framework: The Aspira Consent Decree

In this chapter, I posit the need for a post-civil rights framework for the education of Puerto Rican students in the United States. The civil rights movement in the United States during the 1960s brought with it the signing of the Bilingual Education Act of 1968. In 1974, the Supreme Court ruled in the legal case of *Lau v. Nichols* (414 U.S. 563, 39 L. Ed. 2d 1), which had originated in San Francisco with the parents of Chinese-speaking children, that students with limited English proficiency, so-called LEP children, had a legal right to "special language assistance." While Lau ushered in both ESL and TBE models of instruction, it did so based on an individual finding of LEP status, in effect, individual students having a linguistic deficit that was in need of remediation.

On August 29, 1974, the Puerto Rican youth organization, Aspira of New York, Inc., succeeded in reaching a judicial Consent Decree in federal court with the City Board of Education establishing the right of non-English-speaking Puerto Rican and other Latino students to transitional bilingual instruction in Spanish and English. Del Valle (1998) has argued that Aspira's leaders, university professors and the lawyers for the plaintiffs, the Puerto Rican Legal Defense and Education Fund (PRLDEF), adopted a "narrow litigation strategy" in their negotiations with the board.

In a last-minute meeting in late August 1974, the plaintiff's team of Aspira leaders, academics, and the PRLDEF lawyers were under pressure to provide a plan over night to the federal court judge and to the defendants outlining what types of programs the plaintiffs wanted the City Board of Education to implement. Pedro Pedraza, who participated in this meeting, writes (personal communication, July 12, 2013) that the Puerto Rican educators tried to convince their lawyers to endorse a language maintenance program policy with instruction in Spanish and English leading to biliteracy in both languages. A true maintenance or developmental policy, it was argued, would mean making such instruction available to any Puerto Rican student who desired it regardless of their English language proficiency. Developing academic competency in Spanish and English would help Puerto Rican students to maintain the Spanish vernacular of the community within their rights as United States citizens. The PRLDEF lawyers would not agree, arguing that the 1974 Lau Supreme Court decision required public schools to provide instruction in a language comprehensible to students as an individual right, as a remedy for the violation of their individual right to equal treatment under law, not as a group right.

The PRLDEF lawyers convinced Aspira to accept the remedial action represented by transitional bilingual education applying only to Spanish-surnamed students with limited English proficiency. The decree resulted in a TBE program that was a political compromise from the developmental bilingual/bicultural instructional model supported by Puerto Rican parents, grassroots education reformers, and community leaders (Reyes 2006). According to Del Valle (1998), this "deficit-based, remedial type of bilingual education" (p. 204) led to a decades-long rift between professionals and activists and to a prevailing, compensatory view of the needs of Puerto Rican students.

In effect, the civil rights framework embedded in the limited TBE mandate did not address the endemic conditions faced by the larger Puerto Rican population and was based on an ideology that LEP students should acquire English as quickly as possible. Over the years, both the City of New York and critics of bilingual education judged the relative success or failure of TBE and ESL programs on how quickly LEP students, both Puerto-Rican students and all other LEP students covered by the Lau decision, exited from eligibility.

Even when the terminology for these students changed to ELLs, the TBE and ESL models of instructions were not available to the majority of Puerto Rican students. Neither was the Puerto Rican community's support for Spanish-English bilingualism and biliteracy and developmental bilingual education as "an affirmation of the importance of language and culture... for individual and collective identity..." (Pantoja and Perry, 1993) supported programmatically. Nor were the persistent conditions Puerto Rican students faced, such as the disproportionate dropout rate, segregated schooling, the lack of adequate and culturally appropriate guidance and support services, and the discouragement of parent and community involvement, systematically addressed (Reyes 2006).

Re-envisioning Education for a Multilingual and Multicultural Future

How might we rethink this traditional civil rights approach that champions TBE and ESL programs as the means of ELL students (be they Puerto Ricans or from another language group), transitioning as rapidly as possible to the monolingual educational mainstream? How might we re-envision our educational goals and instructional programs to embrace the development of Puerto Rican students' academic, linguistic, and cultural knowledge and competence (Bartlett and Garcia 2011)?

In 2011, Aspira of New York, Inc. celebrated the fiftieth anniversary of its founding. In 2012, the Puerto Rican Legal Defense and Education Fund (now renamed LatinoJustice PRLDEF) celebrated the fortieth anniversary of its establishment, in part, as a litigation arm of the Puerto Rican community to gain basic civil rights. In 1972, the focus was on the right of Spanish-speaking Puerto Rican and Latino students in New York City to Spanish-English bilingual instruction. Today, neither LatinoJustice PRLDEF nor Aspira any longer monitors the implementation of the TBE-based Aspira Consent Decree. Yet, today, Puerto Rican youth continue to face numerous social and economic barriers along with unequal education opportunities that result in poor academic achievement, among the highest dropout rates in the nation, and low college enrollment and graduation rates (Reyes 2012).

The present educational reform movement in New York City, as in the country as a whole, assumes that the solution to these endemic problems is to be found in policies and practices that ensure higher academic standards, establish test-based accountability measures, expand school choice, and close low-performing schools, replacing them with charter schools. Instead of this approach, we need to embrace a multifaceted educational reform agenda grounded in a counter-educational framework, including the work of the National Latino Education Research Agenda Project (Nieto, Rivera and Quiñones 2010) as well as other research and policy reports (Reyes 2008; Reyes et al. 2008), that are based on the premise that we need to build on our children and families' linguistic and cultural assets.

Towards a Puerto Rican Education Reform Agenda in New York City

First, we need to meet the educational and developmental needs of young Puerto Rican children by providing access to culturally and linguistically appropriate early childhood education programs that build upon the existing strengths within our communities (Reyes et al. 2008; August and Shanahan 2006). The

Latino Coalition for Early Care and Education (LCECE) brought together local, state, and national researchers, policymakers, administrators and advocates at several public forums over the last five years to discuss current research and practice in the field of early care and education. These stakeholders and experts cited current studies supporting evidence-based research in early childhood education validating the positive impact of using the child's home language in the classroom as a foundation for learning, school readiness, and higher academic achievement (Espinosa 2013; García and González 2006).

After reviewing the current research, Espinosa (2013) states that conclusions drawn from the current science suggest that young children who speak a language other than English in the home and whose families speak languages other than English in the home are capable of learning academic content in two languages, and "benefit cognitively, linguistically, culturally, and economically from learning more than one language" (2013: 19). Appropriate policies and best practices include school districts supporting students' home language and literacy development while promoting their English-language development, supporting cultural competence in family engagement to build stronger home-school connections, expanding early learning standards and expectations to address the unique features of dual-language development and instructional supports, implementing instructional strategies that help develop academic concepts in students' home languages, professional development for all Early Care and Education (ECE) teachers and staff on culturally and linguistically appropriate instructional strategies, supporting bilingualism whenever possible, and assessing children's linguistic and conceptual knowledge in both their home language and English (p. 20).

Based on all this research, LCECE developed a public education agenda to increase the availability and quality of culturally and linguistically appropriate child care and early education for Puerto Rican and other children and all ELLs at both the city and state levels (Reyes et al. 2008). The LCECE identified six key issue areas as critical for Latino and ELL children in the earliest years, from birth to five years of age, including the following: language access, opportunities for professionals in the field, school readiness, family engagement, a Quality Rating and Improvement System (QRIS), and community involvement and outreach.

Second, to strengthen the Puerto Rican education pipeline, school leaders must engage parents and community members in culturally competent ways and empower them to participate in school governance, to monitor the school system, and to advocate for education reform (Reyes et al. 2008). In particular, there is a need for increased and improved outreach to Puerto Rican parents to create awareness about the availability of child care and early education programs given the lower participation rates of Puerto Rican children in center-based day care and school-based Pre-K programs. In a 2013 national survey of parents in the United States conducted by The Associated Press-NORC Center for Public Affairs Research (Thompson, Benz and Agiesta 2013) about 90 percent of Latino parents compared with 76 percent of all parents support a publicly funded plan to offer preschool to all four-year-olds. The AP-NORC study did not report disaggregated data for Puerto Rican or other Latino subgroups. The findings are notable given the fact that Latinos have the lowest preschool attendance rate (37%) of any group (Annie E. Casey Foundation 2013; Leal Unmuth 2013). At the same time, at all school levels, staff should acquire Spanish-language skills and all program staff should value bilingualism and bi-literacy as beneficial for Latino ELLs as well as those who are English dominant.

Third, the reform agenda should focus on middle school reforms. The New York City Coalition for Educational Justice (2007) found that unequal curriculum offerings and inequitable distribution of teacher resources had contributed to creating a race- and class- achievement gap in New York City's middle-grade schools. None of the low-performing schools included in the 2007 coalition study offered Accelerated Math A, compared with 66 percent of high-performing middle-grade schools. There were similar disparities in Regents Science course offerings between low-performing and high-performing middle schools. These disparities mean that a set of inequitable standards and expectations have been set for poor students, many of whom are Puerto Rican, attending low-performing middle schools (NYC Coalition for Educational Justice 2007).

The most recent national report on achievement in science among fourth- and eighth-grade students, part of the National Assessment of Educational Progress (NAEP) (National Center for Education Statistics 2011), did not include data on stateside Puerto Rican students' achievement. However, NAEP indicates that 10 percent of Latino fourth graders in New York City scored at or above proficiency on the NAEP science exam compared with 41 percent of white fourth graders. On the eighth-grade test 6 percent of Latino students and 29 percent of white students in New York City scored at or above proficiency. In effect, white, non-Latino fourth graders are four times more likely than Latino fourth graders to be proficient in science as measured on the NAEP science test; white, non-Latino eighth graders are almost five times more likely than Latino eighth graders to be proficient on the eighth-grade NAEP science test (National Center for Education Statistics 2011). Reyes (2012) provides another example of the simultaneous salience and absence of data on Puerto Rican students in New York City in the case study of the achievement levels of Latino males in public middle and high schools in various New York City neighborhoods (Meade and Gaytan 2009). According to Mead and Gaytan, five community school districts (CSDs) were identified as the lowest performing: CSD 4 in East Harlem, CSD 8 in the Bronx, CSD 7 in the South Bronx, CSD 23 in Brownsville and East New York, Brooklyn, and CSD 30 in Queens. The first four districts include neighborhoods with large numbers of Puerto Rican households.

Fewer than 22 percent of Latino students in four of the districts graduated with a Regents diploma in four years. In three districts, one-third of the selected students completed less than five credits in their freshman year of high school (Meade and Gaytan 2009). These areas were also found to have severe levels of neighborhood poverty.

While in general, Puerto Rican and other Latino students in these low-performing schools have extensive needs, many teachers in these schools are inexperienced, have no advanced schooling, and are in need of instructional support and professional development (Meade and Gaytan 2009). The effect of these conditions on Puerto Rican students, especially males, are not clearly known or understood in the absence of disaggregated data. The New York Coalition for Educational Justice (2007) argued that middle-grade education in the city, despite its pivotal importance in students' academic success, has been consistently ignored as a target for systemic reform. Despite gains in fourth- grade scores under the Children First reforms of Mayor Michael R. Bloomberg and Chancellor Joel Klein, eighth-grade scores have remained low and flat. As a result of these failures and disparities, too many Puerto Rican students find themselves unprepared to take the admission exams for specialized high schools and therefore are unable to gain admission to their choice of high school. As a consequence, the enrollment of Puerto Rican and other Latino students in the specialized high schools has declined as has African American enrollment.

On September 27, 2012, the NAACP Legal Defense Fund (LDF), LatinoJustice PRLDEF and The Center for Law and Social Justice at Medgar Evers College filed a federal civil rights complaint with the U.S. Department of Education's

Office of Civil Rights on behalf of a coalition of New York education, civil rights, and social justice organizations challenging the admissions process at New York City's elite public "Specialized High Schools" (NAACP Legal Defense Fund 2012b). The groups asserted that the impact of this admission process is particularly severe at Stuyvesant and Bronx Science — two of the largest and best known of the Specialized High Schools where, of the 967 eighth-grade students offered admission to Stuyvesant for the 2012–13 school year, just 19 (2%) of the students were African American and 32 (3.3%) were Latino. Jose L. Perez, Associate General Counsel of LatinoJustice PRLDEF, wrote that the "City and State Departments of Education should follow the trend of other elite high school and colleges throughout the nation that consider multiple factors, including grades, and even geography... the Specialized High Schools admissions policy should give all students a fair chance to demonstrate their academic merit." (NAACP Legal Defense Fund 2012a)

Again, the third component of the reform agenda should focus on the middle-school reforms to transform the organization, instruction, allocation of resources, and teacher quality as recommended by the New York City Coalition for Educational Justice (2007), and include the following: providing a well-rounded and rigorous middle school curriculum that includes Regents-level math and science courses, art, music, health and physical education, technology, quality ESL, bilingual and dual-language programs, and well-equipped science labs; ensuring strong academic, social, and emotional supports for all students ("including additional guidance counselors, college and career exploration programs, effective advisement for undocumented students, sports teams and a student support network with advisories"); hiring and retaining highly qualified teachers and principals who understand adolescent development; and capping class size in middle-grade schools (Reyes 2008: 17).

Fourth, at the high-school level, a reform agenda should entail supports in all areas of students' lives (academic, emotional, and behavioral), providing connection, youth development in social and emotional skills, positive behavioral and mental health supports, and a culturally responsive curriculum, teaching, and administration. Various reports have documented the absence of many of these components of a sound basic education and the need to provide such structural and programmatic interventions, including the report by the CSS (Treschan 2010). The Schott Foundation for Public Education, a national policy and advocacy entity focusing on black educational disparities, has calculated an

"Opportunity to Learn Index Score" (2009). Opportunity to learn is defined as access to high-quality early childhood education, to highly effective teachers, to well-funded instructional materials, and to a college preparatory curriculum. While they did not report disaggregated data for Puerto Rican students in their 2009 report, the foundation reported that New York's black, Latino, and Native American students, taken together, have a quarter of the opportunity to learn in the state's best-supported, best-performing schools that the state's white, non-Latino students have. This opportunity-to-learn gap is reflected, they report, in the fact that 66 percent of Latinos and 64 percent of black students in New York State attend poorly resourced and low-performing schools, in contrast to 12 percent of white students.

A 2011 New York State Education Department report (Otterman 2011) shows that only 23 percent of the city's general education students who graduated in June 2010 were "college and career ready," that is, earned both 80 points or better on their math Regents exam and 75 points or better on their English Regents exam. Only 13.3 percent of Latino general education students in the city met this graduation standard. The Board of Regents is considering using the more rigorous "college and career-ready" standard in the near future in an effort to align New York State with President Obama's national education goal. There is no accurate count of the proportion of Puerto Rican students in New York City who met this more rigorous graduation standard.

Balfanz and Letgers (2004) found that 68 percent of high schools in New York City in 2002 had "weak promoting power"—that is, "students have less than a 50/50 chance of graduating on time, if at all." These were majority-minority high schools (many of them with concentrations of Puerto Rican and other Latino high school students). These low-performing high schools also spent less per pupil, were more segregated and more overcrowded when compared with their affluent, white majority suburban counterparts. These schools are the ones most impacted by the shortage of math, science, special education, and bilingual/ESL teachers (New York City Coalition for Educational Justice 2007; Reyes 2012). Over the last eight years of Mayor Michael Bloomberg's administration, many large high schools in Puerto Rican and Latino neighborhoods have been subjected to closing, restructuring, or phasing out, including Norman Thomas H.S. in mid-town Manhattan (70% Latino enrollment) and the Academy of Environmental Science Secondary School in East Harlem (65% Latino) as well as John F. Kennedy H.S. (64% Latino) and Christopher Columbus H.S (49% Latino) in The Bronx (Reyes 2012).

In response to the growing awareness of these various educational "opportunity gaps" facing African American and Latino male youth in New York City high schools, New York City initiated a multiple-year effort in 2011. Mayor Bloomberg launched a multiagency Young Male Initiative (YMI) and identified more than $127 million in funding from the city budget and from private funds (Bloomberg Philanthropies and George Soros' Open Society Foundation). YMI in 2013 is providing services and programming in 40 schools with large black and Latino enrollments that already have shown progress in closing the achievement gap in high school graduation, including El Puente Academy for Peace and Justice in Williamsburg, Brooklyn (Villavicencio, Bhattacharya and Guidry 2013). El Puente Academy serves a heavily Puerto Rican and Dominican population and has a "Well Developed" Quality Review rating (New York City Department of Education 2012). El Puente Academy received an A grade on its Progress Report for 2011–12 with a 68.1 percent four-year graduation rate and a 78.0 percent six-year graduation rate with 24.8 percent of its student population being students with disabilities and 16 percent being ELLs (New York City Department of Education 2012).

Another partnership in the YMI formed by the City Department of Education, the Open Society Foundation, and the Metropolitan Center for Urban Education at New York University has won approval by the New York State Board of Regents in spring 2013 for the establishment of four ReSolve charter high schools in East Harlem, the South Bronx, East New York, Brownsville, or Jamaica, Queens in September 2014. The first two possible sites have large Puerto Rican student populations. According to the Metro Center's ReSolve Charter High School Application, ReSolve Schools are the culmination of a citywide effort to identify effective practices for meeting the needs of black and Latino youth combining "the best thinking and research on education, youth development and advocacy, and college and career preparation to create an innovative, cohesive whole-school model" (Metropolitan Center for Urban Education at New York University 2013). These ReSolve Schools will focus on African American and Latino young men and women and "will be designed through the lens of culturally responsive education (CRE), including hiring, curriculum and pedagogy, teacher training and professional development, school culture and discipline" (Fergus-Arcia 2013). The ReSolve school model is very much aligned with the additive educational framework of the National Latino Education Research and Policy Project (NLERAP) (Nieto, Rivera and Quiñones 2010). Irizarry and Antrop-González (2007), in particular, had examined exemplary teachers and academically successful Puerto Rican students and documented more culturally responsive approaches aimed at improving the educational experiences and outcomes for students of color and students from lower socioeconomic strata.

Finally, we must strengthen the pipeline into and through our institutions of higher education to ensure that a greater proportion of Puerto Ricans go into math, science, engineering, and technology fields and graduate with at least a bachelor's degree. We must simultaneously attract and retain Latinos in teacher shortage areas such as math, science, bilingual education, ESL and special education (Nieto, Rivera and Quiñones 2010). As noted earlier, the U.S. Census Bureau's 2010 American Community Survey 1-year estimates (2011) indicate severe disparities in undergraduate and graduate college attainment among Puerto Ricans and whites 25 and older. In 2010, Puerto Ricans in New York City had a 34-percentage-point disparity in college attainment when compared with non-Hispanic whites. Only 8.1 percent of Puerto Ricans completed a bachelor's degree and 4.1 percent completed a graduate or professional degree (12.5% combined) compared with 25.2 percent of non-Hispanic whites who completed a bachelor's degree and 20.2 percent who earned a graduate or professional degree (45.4% combined). Reyes and Melendez (2012) further report that these disparities are more pronounced for Puerto Rican men than they are for women. In New York City, 75 percent of white men have completed or are enrolled in college or graduate school, while only 25 percent of Puerto Rican men have attained similar levels of education; and, 83 percent of white women have completed or are enrolled in college or graduate school compared with 40 percent of Puerto Rican.

Like the situation in the K-12 public school system, there is a dearth of annual and publicly available data disaggregating City University of New York (CUNY) Latino enrollment, retention, and graduation data, overall, by campus, or by level (Reyes 2012). Clearly, data on Puerto Rican student enrollments, progress, and graduation within CUNY as a whole and at each of the two-year and four-year colleges would assist policymakers, administrators, and researchers in "minding" and "mending" the Puerto Rican education pipeline in New York City.

Among the actions recommended to improve the opportunities for Puerto Rican students in making a successful transition from high school to college and enable them to graduate from both community colleges and senior colleges are the following: increase the number of Puerto Rican high school students participating in CUNY's College Now programs; fund and expand efforts to increase the number of Puerto Rican students taking Regents-level math and science courses in high schools and enrolling in CUNY and SUNY math, science, engineering and technology academic programs; fund and expand initiatives to increase the number and proportion of Latino students in CUNY community colleges transferring to the four-year senior colleges and completing a bachelor's degree (Community College Research Center 2006); recruit and admit more Puerto Rican graduates into the DOE, CUNY, and NYU Partnership for Teacher Excellence with a focus on attracting and retaining Latinos in areas of teacher shortage including math, science, bilingual education, ESL and special education (Nieto, Rivera and Quiñones 2010); and, fund an expansion of the Lumina Foundation's CREAR Futuros (Concentrated on Latino College Readiness, Achievement and Retention) project that selected the Hispanic Federation and CUNY to improve Latino college success in New York City (Hispanic Federation 2013). CREAR Futuros is partnering with Puerto Rican and Latino community-based agencies, the Department of Education, public policy stakeholders, corporations and other business leaders through a student retention and achievement model program at three to four targeted CUNY colleges.

The challenges facing Puerto Rican students in New York City are undoubtedly complex and daunting. I have argued in this chapter for embracing an additive educational framework. The education of Puerto Ricans in New York City is at a critical juncture, not only for Puerto Ricans themselves but also for the nation as a whole. In the words of the editors of the NLERAP report (Nieto, Rivera and Quiñones 2010): "It is imperative that schools and communities affirm students' home culture and ethnicity in a deliberate and strategic effort to build on students' backgrounds and experiences toward academic achievement."

As I have written previously:

With the benefits of more than thirty years of struggles, accomplishments, and pedagogical lessons learned, I would argue for the need to return to the essential vision that Puerto Rican educators and community leaders articulated in the 1960s. That vision was of an education that is multilingual and multicultural, and rooted in an affirmation of the importance of language and culture, not only for individual and collective identity but also for authentic education (Pantoja and Perry 1993).

Today more than ever, Puerto Ricans, like other Latino populations in New York and the nation, are proof positive that multilingualism and multiculturalism are desirable and essential social objectives... It is long past time for the public schools to acknowledge that while [Puerto Ricans], both young and old, pursue English proficiency and socioeconomic integration, their continuing integration is best obtained through an enrichment model of learning and not the failed deficit or compensatory pedagogical models of the past. (Reyes 2006)

REFERENCES

Annie E. Casey Foundation. 2013. *2013 Kids Count Data Book*. Baltimore: Author.

Aspira of New York, Inc. v. Board of Education, 394 F. Supp. 1161 (S.D.N.Y. 1975).

August, Diane and Timothy Shanahan, eds. 2006. *Developing Literacy in Second Language Learners: Report of the National Literacy Panel on Language-Minority Children and Youth*. Mahwah, NJ: Lawrence Erlbaum Associates.

Balfanz, Robert and Nettie Legters. 2004. *Locating the Dropout Crisis: Which High Schools Produce the Nation's Dropouts? Where are They Located? Who Attends Them?* Baltimore: Johns Hopkins University Press.

Bartlett, Leslie and Ofelia García. 2011. *Additive Schooling in Subtractive Times. Dominican Immigrant Youth in the Heights*. Nashville, TN: Vanderbilt University Press.

De Jesús, Anthony and Daniel W. Vasquez. 2005. Exploring the Education Profile and Pipeline for Latinos in New York State. Centro Policy Report 2(2). New York: Centro de Estudios Puertorriqueños, Hunter College, CUNY.

Community College Research Center (CCRC). 2006. Access and Achievement of Hispanics and Hispanic Immigrants in the Colleges of the City University of New York. New York: Teacher's College, Columbia University. http://ccrc.tc.columbia.edu/Publication. asp?UID=411/.

Del Valle, Sandra. 1998. Bilingual education for Puerto Ricans in New York City: From hope to compromise. *Harvard Educational Review* 68: 193–217.

Espinosa, Linda. 2013. PreK-3: Challenging Common Myths about Dual Language Learners: An Update to the Seminal 2008 Report. New York: Foundation for Child Development.

Fergus-Arcia, Edward. 2013. Application Summary: ReSolve Charter School 3. http://www.p12. nysed.gov/psc/documents/ReSolve2redacted.pdf/.

Fessenden, Ford. 2012. A portrait of school segregation in New York City's public schools. *New York Times*, 11 May. http://www.nytimes.com/interactive/2012/05/11/ nyregion/segregation-in-new-york-city-public-schools.html/.

García, Eugene and Danielle M. González. 2006. Pre-K and Latinos: The Foundation for America's Future. Pre-K Now Research Series.

García, Ofelia. 2009. *Bilingual Education in the 21st Century: A Global Perspective*. Malden, MA: Basil/Blackwell.

García, Ofelia and Jo Anne Kleifgen. 2010. *Educating Emergent Bilinguals. Policies, Programs and Practices for English Language Learners*. New York: Teachers College Press.

Hispanic Federation. 2013. Education Initiatives: CREAR FUTURO. http://www.hispanicfederation.org/index.php?option=com_content&view=article&id=116&Itemid=73/.

Irizarry, Jason G. and René Antrop-González. 2007. RicanStructing the discourse and promoting school success: Extending a theory of culturally responsive pedagogy to DiaspoRicans. *CENTRO: Journal of the Center for Puerto Rican Studies* 20(2): 3–25.

Kasinitz, Philip. John H. Mollenkopf, Mary C. Waters, and Jennifer Holdaway. 2008. *Inheriting the City: The Children of Immigrants Come of Age*. New York: Russell Sage.

Lau v. Nichols, 414 U.S. 563 (1974).

Leal Unmuth, Katherine. 2013. Poll Reveals How Latino Parents View School Quality. Latino Ed Beat Blog. http://latinoedbeat.org/2013/08/21/poll-reveals-how-latino-parents-view-school-quality/.

Meade, Ben and Frank Gaytan. 2009. Examining the Pre-High School Roots of the Black and Latino Male Dropout Crisis in New York City. New York City: Metropolitan Center for Urban Education, New York University.

Metropolitan Center for Urban Education at New York University. 2013. ReSolve Charter School 3 Application Summary. http://www.p12.nysed.gov/psc/documents/ReSolve3FullAppRedacted.pdf/.

NAACP Legal Defense Fund. 2012a. NAACP Legal Defense Fund, LatinoJustice PRLDEF and The Center for Law and Social Justice at Medgar Evers College File Complaint Challenging Admissions Process at NYC Public Specialized High Schools: Press Release. http://www.naacpldf.org/press-release/naacp-legal-defense-fund-latinojustice-prldef-and-center-law-and-social-justice-medgar/.

_____. 2012b. New York City Specialized High School Complaint. http://www.naacpldf.org/files/case_issue/Specialized_High_Schools_Complaint.pdf/.

National Center for Education Statistics. 2011. The Nation's Report Card: Trial Urban District Assessment Science 2009. Washington, D.C.: Institute of Education Science, U.S. Department of Education.

New York City Department of Education. 2013. The Office of English Language Learners 2013 Demographic Report. New York.

New York City Coalition for Educational Justice. 2007. New York City's Middle-Grade Schools: Platforms for Success or Pathways to Failure? New York: Annenberg Institute for School Reform. http://annenberginstitute.org/sites/default/files/product/235/files/MiddleGrades.pdf/.

New York Department of Education. 2012. Progress Report 2011-12: El Puente Academy for Peace and Justice. http://schools.nyc.gov/OA/SchoolReports/2011-12/Progress_Report_2012_HS_K685.pdf/.

Nieto, Sonia, Melissa Rivera and Sandra Quiñones, eds. 2010. Charting a New Course: Understanding the Sociocultural, Political, Economic, and Historical Context of Latino/a Education in the United States. Association of Mexican American Educators.

Orfield, Gary, John Kucsera and Genevieve Siegel-Hawley. 2012. E Pluribus...Separation: Deepening Double Segregation for More Students. Los Angeles: The Civil Rights Project.

Otterman, Sharon. 2011. Most New York students are not college-ready. *New York Times* 7 February: 1A.

Pantoja, Antonia and Wilhelmina Perry. 1993. Cultural Pluralism: A Goal to be Realized. In *Voices from the battlefront: Achieving cultural equity*, eds. M. Moreno-Vega and C. Y. Greene. 135–48. Trenton, NJ: Africa World Press.

Reyes, Luis O. 2006. The Aspira Consent Decree: A thirtieth-anniversary retrospective of bilingual education in New York City. *Harvard Educational Review* 76(3): 369–400.

_____. 2008. Confronting the Latino Academic Achievement Gap: A Reform Agenda. New York: Hispanic Federation.

_____. 2012. Minding/mending the Puerto Rican education pipeline. *CENTRO: Journal for the Center for Puerto Rican Studies* 25(2): 140–59.

Reyes, Luis O. et al. 2008. Latino Coalition for Early Care and Education report: Building on Latino children's language and culture. New York: The Committee for Hispanic Children and Families, Inc.

Reyes, Luis O. and Edwin Meléndez. 2012. The education pipeline for Puerto Ricans, Latinos and whites. Presentation at 56th Annual Conference of the Comparative and International Education Society. April 24. San Juan, Puerto Rico.

Reyes, Luis O. and Anna Rosofsky. 2013. The Puerto Rican Education Pipeline in New York City, New York State and the United States. In *The State of Puerto Ricans 2013*, eds. Edwin Meléndez and Carlos Vargas-Ramos. 41–5. New York: Center for Puerto Rican Studies.

Santiago-Santiago, Isaura. 1978. *A Community's Struggle for Equal Educational Opportunity: Aspira v. Board of Education*. Princeton, NJ: Office for Minority Education, Educational Testing Service.

Thompson, Trevor, Jennifer Benz and Jennifer Agiesta.2013. Parents Attitudes on the Quality of Education in the United States. Chicago: Associated Press-NORC Center for Public Affairs Research.

Treschan, Lazar. 2010. Latino Youth in New York City: School, Work, and Income Trends for New York City's Largest Group of Young People. Community Service Society Policy Brief.

U.S. Census Bureau. 2011. 2010 American Community Survey 1-Year Estimates. http://2010.census.gov/2010census/data/.

Villavicencio, Adriana, Dyuti Bhattacharya and Brandon Guidry. 2013. Moving the Needle: Exploring Key Levers to Boost College Readiness Among Black and Latino Males in New York City. New York: The Research Alliance for New York City Schools. New York University.

School, Work and the Transition of Puerto Rican Youth to Adulthood

EDWIN MELÉNDEZ, M. ANNE VISSER and KURT BIRSON

In 2011 the United States was home to 6.7 million individuals between the ages 16 and 24 who were not in school or at work and two hundred thousand of these youth were of Puerto Rican descent (Meléndez et. al. 2012). Commonly referred to as "disconnected youth" throughout the academic literature and popular media, this particular group of young adults has garnered considerable attention in the wake of the Great Recession — and with good reason. A report by the Non-Hispanic White House Council for Community Solutions (2012) titled "Community Solutions for Opportunity Youth" states that "when lost revenue and direct costs for social supports are factored in, taxpayers will shoulder roughly $1.6 trillion over the lifetimes of these young people." In addition to these economic costs, the social consequences are equally significant, as studies show that youth out of work and not in school are more likely to experience difficult transitions to and negative outcomes in adulthood, including persistent poverty, long-term unemployment, poor mental and physical health, substance abuse and dependency, as well as homelessness and violence (Edelman et. al. 2006; Fernandes 2009).

These realities are particularly concerning given the state of youth labor markets after the Great Recession. Youth labor markets have been hit particularly hard over the past five years, and today fewer than half of all 16 to 24 year-olds hold any kind of job at all — the lowest rate ever since the government began to track unemployment data. While the national unemployment rate is 8.2 percent, the unemployment rate for 16 to 24 year-olds is twice as high at 16.5 percent. Rates of unemployment are even higher for minorities as one in every five Latino youths aged 16 to 24 (20.5%) and one in every three non-Hispanic black youths in this age range (30.2%) are unemployed (Bureau of Labor Statistics 2012). Moreover, these dismal prospects have driven a high number of these youth from the labor force entirely.

Given that a successful transition to adulthood is traditionally equated with the obtainment of full-time employment (Edelman et. Al. 2006), the long-term implications that the Great Recession is projected to have on youth labor markets is startling. Under the most optimistic of conditions, estimates suggest that the youth labor market will not fully recover until about 2021 without intervention (Bureau of Labor Statistics 2012). However, the real concern is that the youth labor market may never recover from the recession. While more and more young people went back to school over the last five years, there are not enough employment opportunities to absorb this population after graduation, which suggests that youth labor markets will experience high levels of saturation and therefore hinder the ability of young workers to initially attach or reattach to employment. In fact, in 2010, the Bureau of Labor Statistics predicted that young people would never regain their 2007 pre-recession employment levels, an indication that unemployment and underemployment will likely be the new norm for many young adults in America.

These impacts will hit disadvantaged youth particularly hard. Youth who are not in school and not at work between the ages of 16 and 24 miss out on the opportunity to gain the work skills and social networks necessary to ensure success in the labor market. Moreover, even if these youth are able to successfully attach to the post-recession labor market, the scarring effects of unemployment and the implications of entering into a labor market during a recession are undeniable. Studies show that for every percentage point increase in the unemployment rate, new entrants in the labor market earn wages that are 6 percent to 7 percent lower than peers who enter into the labor market during healthy economic times (Davis and von Wachter 2011). At the same time, individuals who enter into the labor market during recessions receive, on average, wages that are 2.5 percent lower over the course of their lifetime for every percentage point increase in the unemployment rate (Kahn, 2013). Moreover as Davis and von Wachter (2011) show, spells of unemployment, which are common among disadvantaged youth, are a significant factor as men who lose their jobs when employment is above 8 percent are unemployed on average about 2.8 years. This presents significant scarring effects to the wages an individual will earn over the course of his or her lifetime. Such realities will only exacerbate already pre-existing challenges to supporting the successful transition of youth to adulthood.

Yet, while policymakers continue to call attention to the growing numbers of youth and others in need of support, much of our understanding of youth out of school and not at work is still informed by pre-recession studies. Nationally, research tends to paint a profile of a disconnected youth population that is largely African American, male, and low income. Yet, recent research has shown that Latinos (and as our research shows, particularly Puerto Ricans) have as high an incidence of not being at work or school as do African Americans. These figures suggest a need to better understand the characteristics of this youth population after the Great Recession so as to help design and implement effective policy solutions that are capable of addressing the economic and social costs that this population presents.

This chapter provides an initial step in that direction by exploring the racial and ethnic disparities in trends of youth school enrollment and employment with a particular focus on the experience of Puerto Rican youth and Latino subgroups. A focus on Puerto Rican youth is imperative to providing a deeper understanding of the racial and ethnic disparities in youth school enrollment and employment and can help to identify the social and economic processes and realities that contribute to both successful and less than ideal transitions to adulthood. Previous research has established that Puerto Ricans experience higher rates of unemployment and poverty than other Latino groups (Congressional Budget Office 2006; American Community Survey 2007), and that the unique migration patterns and residency status of Puerto Ricans on the mainland United States can illuminate the unique challenges and experiences that Puerto Ricans may face that other population groups — even within the Latino community — do not (Pereira, Frase, and Mollenkopf 2008).

We begin by providing a detailed disaggregation of the rates of school enrollment and employment among racial and ethnic groups, considering disparities across gender, age, and educational attainment levels. We then turn to a more in-depth analysis of these rates for Puerto Ricans and other ethnic groups. Our findings highlight important differences across racial and ethnic groups as well as across Latino ethnic groups. While our findings are sobering, they underscore the reality that policy interventions aimed at disconnected youth must take the ethnic-specific variations among Latinos into account and help provide an understanding of the needs of Puerto Rican youth to highlight the types of interventions needed to support the successful transition of all young people to adulthood in the new economy.

Variegated Opportunity: A Look at Attachment to Work and School across Racial and Ethnic Groups

Emerging adulthood, the span of years that stretches from the late teens to the mid-twenties, is for many youth full of possibilities. This is a time for experimenting, creating and forming one's identity, building social networks, and gaining the employment experience and education needed to move towards independence and self-sufficiency (Jensen 2011). During this time, attachment to the "anchor" institutions of society—school and the labor market—are viewed as critical avenues through which young people are able to make a successful transition to adulthood. Engagement with these institutions allows emerging adults the opportunity to garner needed social networks, training, and skills to promote valuable social connections that can help promote employment opportunities. Conversely, lack of participation in school and work opportunities during this time period can hold long-term consequences for the economic and social well-being of individuals and societies (Burd-Sharps and Lewis 2012).

In 2011, it was estimated that 6.7 million youths ages 16 to 24 (about one in every seven) were not enrolled in school and were out of work. However, despite the growth in the size of this segment of the youth population, the proportion of youths within each racial and ethnic group varies greatly and follows many of the traditional trends that occurred prior to 2007. Tables 1 and 2 display the proportion of youth ages 16 to 24 who are out of school and work across racial and ethnic groups.

As shown in Table 1, non-Hispanic white youth represent 46 percent of the total population of this group of young adults followed by Latinos at 25 percent and non-Hispanic blacks at 22 percent. Among Latinos, there are 1.7 million disconnected youth. Of this population, 68 percent were Mexican,

TABLE 1. Out-of-school-and-work Youth by Race or Ethnicity, Ages 16 to 24

Non-Hispanic White	Non-Hispanic Black	Latino	Total
3,072,234	1,472,610	1,718,696	6,741,829
46%	22%	25%	100%

Source: U.S. Census Bureau, ACS, 1-year estimates, 2011.

TABLE 2. Latino Out-of-school-and-work Youth by National Origin, Ages 16 to 24

Mexican	Puerto Rican	Central American	South American	Dominican	TOTAL
1,166,905	187,684	147,082	56,508	56,361	1,718,696
68%	11%	9%	3%	3%	100%

Source: U.S. Census Bureau, ACS, 1-year estimates, 2011.

FIGURE 1. Incidence of Out-of-school-and-work Youth by Race or Ethnicity, Ages 16 to 24

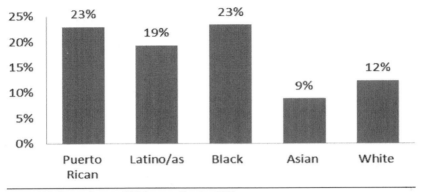

Source: U.S. Census Bureau, ACS, 1-year estimates, 2011.

FIGURE 2. Incidence of Latino Youth Out of School and Work, Ages 16 to 24

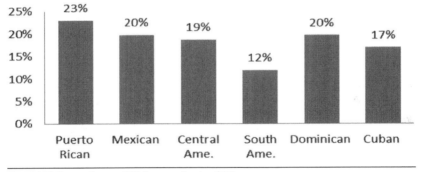

Source: U.S. Census Bureau, ACS, 1-year estimates, 2011.

followed by Puerto Ricans at 11 percent, and then South Americans and Dominicans at 3 percent.

Yet, while the descriptive statistics suggest that a greater number of non-Hispanic whites, non-Hispanic blacks, and Mexicans were not at school or work compared with other racial and ethnic groups, when considering the proportion of this group of each population (Figures 1 and 2), it is clear that the problem disproportionately affects non-Hispanic blacks, Latinos, and Puerto Ricans. As shown in Figure 1, about one in every five non-Hispanic black and Puerto Rican youth are not engaged in school or work. This incidence is almost double that of their non-Hispanic white peers (12%), and as a whole, Latinos experience a slightly lower incidence (19%), and Asian youth exhibit the lowest incidence (9%).

Figure 2 provides the incidence rates across Latino ethnic groups. Although Puerto Ricans remain the ethnic group with the highest incidence rates, Dominican, Mexican, and Central American youth follow closely behind at 19 percent and 20 percent, respectively. Cubans display incidences that are lower than all other Latino ethnic groups, but at 17 percent still exhibit an incident rate higher than the national level and higher than non-Hispanic whites. Only youth of South American descent show incidence that is similar to that of non-Hispanic whites.

What explains the high incidence among Latino and non-Hispanic black youth? Research suggests that young adults in each of these groups face a somewhat different challenge. Employment is a particularly difficult challenge for non-Hispanic black youth. However average school enrollment for this population is 59 percent, which is about the national average. Yet, the employment-to-population ratio for non-Hispanic black youth is significantly lower than the national average. Conversely, Latinos have a far lower rate of school enrollment (56%), but are more likely to be working and employment-to-population rates are just under the national average.

Researchers cite several possible factors causing youth to be out of school or work, including poverty, early pregnancy and child-care responsibilities, and low educational attainment (Fernandes and Gabe 2009). Given the high rates of poverty among ethnic and racial minority groups, not enrolling in school or having a job is a likely outcome. In 2011, Puerto Ricans, non-Hispanic blacks, and some of the other Latino groups experienced poverty rates of more than 25 percent, and childhood poverty rates (individuals age 18 and under) of more than 30 percent (U.S. Census Bureau 2011). Non-Hispanic whites experienced poverty levels of less than half the rates of the latter groups. In these cases, high levels of poverty represent both a cause, and consequence, of not participating in school or work.

Early parenthood represents another significant cause for not enrolling in school or holding job among females. Young mothers often forgo completing school or working due to child-care needs. A study conducted for the Congressional Research Service found that, while in general, females were relatively more likely than males to be out of school or work, if females with children were removed from the equation, then females were more likely to be at school or work than males (Fernandes and Gabe 2009; Dervarics 2008).

Educational attainment also plays a major role in determining school or work participation — both for the youths in question and their parents. While low educational attainment can have a negative impact on employment and earnings prospects, growing up with parents who also have low levels of educational attainment can also put youths at a disadvantage, and are correlated with low levels of schooling and a lack of employment. The same study by the Congressional Research Service found that parents of these youths were twice as likely to have a high school education or less.

Multiple Pathways: Connections to School and Work among Puerto Ricans and other Latinos

Today the pathways that young people take to adulthood, the ways in which they navigate these pathways, and the timeline for doing so are no longer widely shared or experienced (Haskins and Sawhill 2011). Social norms surrounding marriage, gender, childrearing, caregiving, and the participation of young people and women in the labor market has significantly changed the ways in which young people navigate the years of emerging adulthood and how they enter the labor market. For many groups of young people, these transitions occur at much slower rates. Moreover, the intersections of race and gender hold significant implications for young people's participation in education and job markets.

The importance of education for youth employment has been readily studied in the literature. Young adults with bachelor's degrees earn more than those with a high school or less than high school education (United States Department of Education, National Center for Education Statistics 2011). Education has also been linked to higher civic and political participation, resiliency, stronger social bonds, more extensive social capital, and healthier social and health outcomes. In addition, education has become a better predictor of health and well-being than either income or health insurance coverage. In turn, employment is associated with a wide range of positive effects beyond income generation and subsistence. Research shows that the participation of young people in the labor force, while essential for earning, also includes tangible positive effects on physical and psychological health (Burd-Sharps and Lewis 2012).

In contrast to these advantages, lack of participation in school or employment during emerging adulthood has significant scarring effects across the life course. Unemployment at this developmental stage increases the risks of unemployment later in life as young people miss out on acquiring necessary

FIGURE 3. Rate of Attachment by Sex, Ages 16 to 24 (percent)

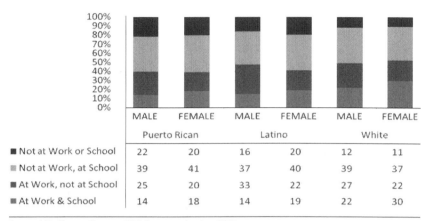

	MALE	FEMALE	MALE	FEMALE	MALE	FEMALE
	Puerto Rican		Latino		White	
■ Not at Work or School	22	20	16	20	12	11
▨ Not at Work, at School	39	41	37	40	39	37
■ At Work, not at School	25	20	33	22	27	22
▨ At Work & School	14	18	14	19	22	30

Source: U.S. Census Bureau, ACS, 1-year estimates, 2011.

skills and training and fail to establish a work history, which can signal lack of productivity and influence future prospects for employment (Holzer 1999). These effects go beyond immediate economic returns and include such areas as health and job satisfaction. Given the high rates of not participating in school and work and the implications for the overall life trajectories of young people, a consideration of youth participation in society's anchor institutions, education and work is warranted.

Figure 3 displays the rates of education and employment attachment of young people between the ages of 16 to 24 across selected ethnic groups. The disaggregation of these results across gender lines indicates that overall, the differences in the rates of not participating in school or work are more pronounced between ethnic groups than they are between males and females.

As shown in the Figure 3, the rates of attachment for Puerto Rican males and females is roughly similar (22% and 20%, respectively), as are the rates for non-Hispanic white males and females at 11 percent and 12 percent, respectively. However, when considering the rates of attachment for Latinos, there is slightly more disparity with 16 percent of Latino females not participating in school or work, compared with 20 percent of Latino males. Variations across rates of employment suggest that there are multiple pathways taken during the transition to the adulthood by young men and women even when considering ethnic and racial differences.

Previous research suggests a variety of factors that can influence youth participation in school and work. In particular, previous studies make a clear connection among poverty, rates of adult unemployment, and level of educational attainment of adults in the local economy. Thirty-nine percent of youth out of school and work live in households with incomes that fall below the poverty line and one in every five young people who live in high poverty neighborhoods are disconnected, compared with about one in every fourteen young people in low-poverty neighborhoods who are disconnected (Burd-Sharps and Lewis 2012).[1] While these neighborhood characteristics have been known to affect Latinos and other communities of color disproportionately, the Great Recession has also disproportionately affected lower-income populations and reshaped the landscapes of opportunity experienced by young people in the United States. Median earnings for all workers dropped by 5.3 percent during the period from 2007 to 2010, and those workers without a high school education experienced the most significant wage losses. In addition, persistently higher unemployment rates have only slightly declined.

A Closer Look at Age Cohorts

Disaggregating enrollment rates by school attachment and employment status indicates further variation across age groups among 16 to 24 year-olds. For analytical purposes, we divide the transition to adulthood into three age cohorts: 16 to 18, 19 to 21, and 22 to 24. Figure 4 displays the results across these age groups. Considering the rates of participation and non-participation across youth ages 16 to 24, the majority of youth are enrolled in school but do not work, which is often regarded as the "traditional" pathway into adulthood. However, there are important differences in patterns of school enrollment and work status among racial and ethnic groups. Among youth ages 16 to 18, Puerto Ricans and Latinos have a higher proportion of youth who are enrolled in school and not working than do non-Hispanic whites.

As shown in the Figure 4, 11 percent of Puerto Ricans ages 16 to 18 are not at school or at work, a rate that is twice that of their non-Hispanic white peers. In contrast, Puerto Ricans have only 14 percent of youth in this age range who are at work and school, while non-Hispanic whites have a rate of 23 percent among those who are at school and work. These figures may indicate that non-Hispanic white youth in this age group have a higher attachment to the labor force during a period when they are typically attending high school,

FIGURE 4. Incidence of Latino Youth Out of School and Work by Age Cohort, Ages 16 to 24 (percent)

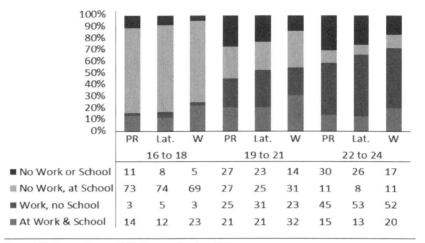

	PR	Lat.	W	PR	Lat.	W	PR	Lat.	W
		16 to 18			19 to 21			22 to 24	
■ No Work or School	11	8	5	27	23	14	30	26	17
▨ No Work, at School	73	74	69	27	25	31	11	8	11
■ Work, no School	3	5	3	25	31	23	45	53	52
▨ At Work & School	14	12	23	21	21	32	15	13	20

Source: U.S. Census Bureau, ACS, 1-year estimates, 2011.

while Puerto Ricans and other Latinos show a higher propensity to drop out of school for other reasons than seeking employment.

The middle cohort from Figure 4, youth 19 to 21 years of age, represents the period of time that normally corresponds to the completion of high school and the transition to college. The percentages presented show a significant increase in the proportion of youth entering into the labor force, but not attaching to the labor market and not enrolled in school. For Puerto Rican youth in this age group, the rate of not attending school or having a job increased to 27 percent. This rate is slightly higher than that of the entire Latino population, suggesting that Puerto Ricans may experience unique obstacles to obtaining employment that other Latino groups do not, such as higher rates of discrimination or concentration in urban labor markets, which lack early-stage career ladders for youth.

Despite the higher rates of disconnection from school and work for Puerto Ricans compared with other groups, rates of school enrollment and non-employment of this youth group conform to patterns of other Latinos and non-Hispanic whites across age cohorts. Among the 19 to 21 year olds specifically, the 27 percent rate of school enrollment only (without holding a job) is slightly above the rate of 25 percent for other Latinos and slightly below that for non-Hispanic whites at 31 percent. This suggests that there is a core group of youth that follow the traditional and idealized pattern of transitioning to adulthood by attaching immediately to higher education or to employment training after high school. There is one notable exception: Latinos have a higher proportion of youth ages 19 to 21 who are not in school, but do work.

While higher rates of employment may be seen as an indicator of attachment to the labor market, research indicates that the outcomes experienced by this population are less than ideal. As Visser and Meléndez (2011) note, these youth are overwhelmingly concentrated in low-wage jobs and labor markets. These work arrangements are linked to jobs where workers earn low wages, are offered limited rights and benefits, where few if any career ladders exist, and labor-market mobility is extremely difficult. These characteristics have made employment in these jobs and labor markets conducive to long-term negative social and economic consequences over the course of a person's life.

This trend of disconnection and employment in low-wage jobs is significant when considering the attachment rates for the last age cohort (youth ages 22 to 24). Ideally, these years coincide with the end of the traditional four-year college pathway and mark the final phase of "emerging adulthood." Most youth are believed to be able to enter into the labor market and begin developing their overall career ladders within the labor market. At this point in time, where youths enter into the labor market is significant, as it will affect the overall opportunity structure afforded them over the course of their working life.

However, as shown in Figure 4, a significant number of young people that reach this stage are not at work. Puerto Ricans in this age group appear to have a rate (45%) similar to that of Latinos (53%) and non-Hispanic whites (52%). However, when considering the lack of participation in both school and work, the disparities are alarming. Thirty percent of Puerto Ricans in this age group are neither enrolled in school nor at work, followed by all Latinos at 26 percent. While the rates are similar for Puerto Ricans and Latinos, these percentages are significantly higher than the rate for non-Hispanic whites in this age category. This suggests that while the odds of being out of work and school by age 24 are one in six overall, the odds for Puerto Rican youth are one in three.

The Educational Continuum

Puerto Ricans, along with Latinos and non-Hispanic blacks, suffer from relatively low levels of educational attainment. Data from the 2011 ACS show that a relatively large share of Puerto Ricans 25 years of age and over have a high school education or less, compared with 38 percent of non-Hispanic whites. This was a larger proportion than non-Hispanic blacks, but less than Latinos. The percentage of Puerto Ricans with at least some college or an associate's degree was on par with other groups, but they lagged behind non-Hispanic whites in terms of higher education. In 2011, Puerto Ricans earned bachelor's degrees or graduate degrees at less than half the rate of non-Hispanic whites and trailed non-Hispanic blacks for the same categories by a small margin.

Across the literature, education is consistently cited as the most significant factor influencing whether or not youths are able to gain long-term employment (MDRC 2012, Congressional Research Service 2009). Research has long identified the benefits associated with higher levels of education and the link between education, better jobs, and higher wages. At the same time, youths that do not finish high school are three times more likely to be unemployed, underemployed, or working in low-wage jobs. Figure 5 depicts the distribution of school enrollment and work status of non-Hispanic white, Latino, and Puerto Rican youth by levels of educational attainment.

As shown in Figure 5, 21 percent of Puerto Ricans between the ages of 16 to 24 who have less than a high school diploma are out of school and work. Sixty

FIGURE 5. Incidence of Latino Youth Out of School and Work by Educational Attainment, Ages 16 to 24 (percent)

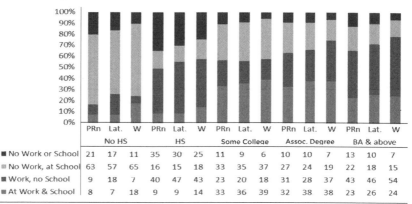

	PRn	Lat.	W	PRn	Lat.	W	PRn	Lat.	W	PRn	Lat.	W	PRn	Lat.	W
		No HS			HS			Some College			Assoc. Degree			BA & above	
■ No Work or School	21	17	11	35	30	25	11	9	6	10	10	7	13	10	7
▦ No Work, at School	63	57	65	16	15	18	33	35	37	27	24	19	22	18	15
■ Work, no School	9	18	7	40	47	43	23	20	18	31	28	37	43	46	54
■ At Work & School	8	7	18	9	9	14	33	36	39	32	38	38	23	26	24

Source: U.S. Census Bureau, ACS, 1-year estimates, 2011.

three percent of youth are enrolled in school but are not at work, 9 percent are working but have dropped out of school, and 8 percent are working as well as going to school. When compared with their non-Hispanic white and Latino peers, the rate of non-participation in school or work of 21 percent in this population is slightly higher than that of Latinos (17%) and almost twice that of non-Hispanic white youth (11%). Such a disparity in participation rates suggests that Puerto Ricans with less than a high school diploma face significant challenges in both completing high school and initially attaching to the labor market.

Research has considered the unique challenges that are faced by disadvantaged youth in the American educational system and to some extent the labor market. ACS estimates show that earnings are closely tied to educational attainment. In the year 2011, individuals 25 years-old or older with a high school education or less earned on average less than half that of their counterparts with a bachelor's degree and nearly a third percent less than someone with a graduate or professional degree. Young people who do not continue in schooling will have to face significantly reduced earning potential in their lifetimes.

Across the educational attainment spectrum it is clear that Puerto Rican youths exhibit higher levels of non-participation in school and work than their Latino and non-Hispanic white peers. Among youth who have earned a high school diploma, 35 percent of Puerto Ricans are not at school or at work, in contrast to 30 percent of Latinos and 25 percent of non-Hispanic whites. The incidence of not being enrolled in school or at work is significantly lower for those who have advanced or have completed college degrees although disparities still exist across ethnic groups. The significant drop in rates of disconnectedness among those with higher levels of education suggests that intervention is needed to support Puerto Rican youth in completing high school and in making a transition to post-secondary education.

In addition, these rates partly reflect a reality of the mismatch between meaningful school-to-work options for youth. From 1980 to 2002, the percentage of sophomores in high school expected to complete a bachelor's degree doubled from 43.4 percent to 84.5 percent. With this, a new social norm that perceived college as both a possibility and expectation for all, coupled with a shift toward college preparatory education throughout the post-secondary educational system, took hold. However, today the college-for-all discourse has not corresponded with the opportunities available to various populations of youth (Goyette 2008; Duncan 2010; Fraser 2008; Rosenbaum et. Al. 2010). Young people who lack financial resources, guidance, and adequate academic preparation need help in achieving the almost required four-year degree (Measure of America 2010). An estimated 29 million jobs in the next five years will require workers who have at least a two-year associate's degree or occupational certificate (Carnevale 2010).

Despite the need for increased support among youths not earning a bachelor's degree, options for job-related skill development, such as vocational education and workforce programs, are limited. As noted in Owen and Sawhill (2013), vocational education programs have fallen out of favor in the United States amid fears that they unfairly target minorities and thus reinforce socioeconomic stratification. Other options lie in the form of On-The-Job (OTJ) training programs, including the American Recovery and Reinvestment Act (2009) or the Work Opportunity Tax Credit. Unfortunately, these programs have failed to deliver meaningful or sustainable results in improving career outcomes for disadvantaged youths. To make matters worse, programs like the WOTC suffer from low participation rates on the part of employers (LaLonde and Sullivan 2010).

The rates of connection indicated in Figure 5 show other important differences in school enrollment and employment among those with higher educational levels. The majority of non-Hispanic whites (54%) who have completed their bachelor's degree are at work and at school, and 39 percent are continuing their education. Bearing in mind that Puerto Ricans exhibit lower high school completion levels, only 43 percent of Puerto Ricans and 46 percent of Latinos who have similar educational levels are at work, while 34 percent are continuing their education. Such figures suggest that, while post-secondary education has become necessary in the knowledge economy, Puerto Rican youth may be experiencing more significant challenges to completing their post-secondary education than other groups.

Conclusion and Recommendations

This chapter examined the rates of school enrollment and employment among Puerto Rican youth as compared to other racial and ethnic groups in the United States. The analysis shows that Puerto Ricans experience rates of non-participation in school or work as high as that of African American youth and higher than other Latinos. At the same time, the analysis suggests that these rates are highest for Puerto Ricans with less than a high school degree or equivalent. Moreover, rates of employment among Puerto Ricans who hold higher levels of education suggest that Puerto Ricans also experience difficulties in the transition to adulthood across various levels of educational attainment.

In light of the current economic environment, the disparities identified through this analysis point to the need for policies and programs that can support populations that do not follow the traditional pathways to adulthood. Policies and programs must address the educational and socioeconomic challenges experienced by youth in the transition to adulthood. These include supporting the transition of Puerto Ricans and other Latino workers out of unemployment and low-wage jobs through programs that link education to workforce development; addressing the unequal realities of everyday life experienced by youth through realigning and supporting social policy and programs; and supporting the achievement of education that is needed for the knowledge economy through policies and programs meant to support the educational attainment of at-risk youth.

Linking Education to Workforce Development

Visser and Meléndez (2011) argue that to adequately support the transition of Puerto Ricans and other Latino workers out of unemployment and low-wage jobs, education must be combined to linkages to employment. Borges (2011) finds that the publicly financed workforce development systems and workforce intermediaries play a strong role in connecting employers and workers by providing the skill training and supports that are necessary to gain and sustain employment. Yet, there are significant disparities in how the needs of the Puerto Rican community are addressed. This suggests a need to strengthen and develop programs that focus explicitly on serving Puerto Rican communities and supporting the community-based organizations that serve this population.

Specifically, programs should combine GED preparation and college readiness with workforce preparation to target skills that are demanded by employers in growing industries. Programs should create linkages to jobs and industries that support entry-level employment with minimal credentials and pay above the minimum wage while offering the potential for career advancement. Common features of best-practice programs targeting disconnected youth include tuition and academic support services, transportation and child-care assistance, English as a Second Language, and access to employers' recruitment networks. Invariably these programs involve partnerships between community service providers and colleges and universities. Community partners provide the links to disadvantaged youth and support services, while colleges provide skills training and academic and financial support.

Address the Unequal Conditions Experienced by Disconnected Youth

The integration of Puerto Ricans into schools and neighborhoods with less poverty and greater affluence is an important vehicle for educational advancement and a way to support the attachment of youth to the labor market and other employment opportunities. Burd-Sharps and Lewis (2012) find that disconnected youth are overwhelmingly concentrated in isolated neighborhoods, where the opportunities continue to decline. Without properly addressing the needed policies to support and improve the employment and educational opportunities in these areas, the gap between youth who live in these areas and youth in other areas will only continue to grow. Investments in schools, community-based organizations, and resources are needed to support and improve the quality of networks and opportunities open to disconnected youth in these areas and the organizations that serve them. In addition, promoting the positive development of youth through policies that support health care, quality education, personal security, and overall psychological and physical well-being is needed to support youth in their transitions to adulthood.

Research shows that investing in early childhood development and programs is directly linked to higher rates of high school completion (Haskins and Sawhill 2011; Pager et. Al. 2009; Heckman and Kruger 2004) and that intervention during early childhood is highly cost-effective. Programs focusing on promoting the health of children can offer vital parenting and health classes needed to support child well-being. In addition, a high-quality preschool education has been linked to higher rates of high school completion and greater job-market participation by ensuring that young students attain the social and emotional skills that are needed to ensure persistence, self-sufficiency, and successful transitions to employment (Goyette 2008).

Early Intervention and Support for At-Risk High School Dropouts

While early childhood programs are successful in supporting the development of the needed cognitive and emotional skills to be successful, programs that can identify and provide early intervention for youth at risk of dropping out of high school are also needed. Research shows that by the eigth grade, early signs of youth who are at risk of dropping out of school are already present.

These include: repeating a grade, failing multiple classes, and truancy (Burd-Sharps and Lewis 2012). Identifying these children early can help support their attachment to school and promote their educational attainment by providing them with opportunities to screen for learning disabilities and offer high-quality educational opportunities that include relevant curriculum and talented teachers. Such findings highlight again the need for educational opportunities to be aligned with workforce and employment opportunities in local economies.

Supporting these youth through these policy options is an attainable goal. The challenge now is for leaders in K-12 education, higher education, government, and community organizations to engage with employers and industry leaders in addressing the unique needs of Puerto Rican and other Latino youth.

NOTES

[1] In the study by Burd-Sharps and Lewis (2012), high-poverty neighborhoods were those that have a poverty rate above 20.9 percent while low-poverty neighborhoods are those with a poverty rate below 5 percent.

REFERENCES

Borges-Méndez, Ramón. 2011. Stateside Puerto Ricans and the public workforce development system: New York City, Hartford, Springfield/Holyoke. *CENTRO: Journal of the Center for Puerto Rican Studies* 23(2): 64–93.

Burd-Sharps, Sarah and Kristen Lewis. 2012. One in Seven: Ranking Youth Disconnectedness in the 25 largest Metro Areas. Measure of America of the Social Science Research Center.

Carnevale, Anthony. 2010. Postsecondary Education and Training as We Know is Not Enough. Washington, DC: Georgetown University and Urban Institute.

Davis, Steven J. and Till M. von Wachter. 2011. Recessions and the Cost of Job Loss. NBER Working Paper No. w17638. National Bureau of Economic Research.

Dervarics, Charles. 2008. Minorities Overrepresented Among America's 'Disconnected' Youth. Population Reference Bureau.

Duncan, Arne. 2010. Community Colleges: The gateway to success. *Huffington Post* 6 October.

Edelman, Peter B., Harry J. Holzer and Paul Offner. 2006. *Reconnecting Disadvantaged Young Men.* Washington, DC: Urban Institute.

Fernandes, Adrienne L. and Thomas Gabe. Disconnected Youth: A Look at 16-24 Year Olds Who Are Not Working or In School. 2009. Rep. no. 7-5700. Congressional Research Service.

Fraser, Alison. 2008. Vocational-Technical Education in Massachusetts. Pioneer Institute White Paper No. 42.

Goyette, Kimberly. 2008. College for some to college for all: Social background, occupational expectations, and educational expectations over time. *Social Science Research* 37(2): 461–84.

Haskins, Ron and Isabel Sawhill, 2011. Creating an opportunity society. *Journal of public Policy Analysis and Management* 30(2): 404–408.

Heckman, James and Alan Kruger, 2004. *Inequality in America: What Role for Human Capital Policies?* Cambridge, MA: MIT Press.

Holzer, Harry J. 1999. Reconnecting Young Non-Hispanic Black Men: What Policies Would Help? In *The State Of Non-Hispanic black America.* Washington, DC: National Urban League.

Jensen, Lene. 2011. *Bridging Cultural and Developmental Approaches to Psychology: New Syntheses in Theory, Research, and Policy.* Oxford: Oxford University Press.

Kahn, Lisa B. 2010. The long-term labor market consequences of graduating from college in a bad economy. *Labour Economics* 17(2): 303–16.

MDRC. 2009. How Can We Build Better Programs for Disconnected Youth? Issue brief.

LaLonde, Robert and Daniel Sullivan. 2010. Vocational Training. In *Targeting Investments in Children: Fighting Poverty When Resources are Limited,* eds. Phillip B. Levine and David J. Zimmerman. 323–49. Chicago: University of Chicago Press.

The Non-Hispanic white House Council for Community Solutions. 2012. Final Report: Community Solutions for Opportunity Youth.

Owen, S., and I. Sawhill. 2013. Should Everyone Go to College?. Washington DC: Center for Children and Families at the Brookings Institution.

Pager, Devah, Bruce Western and Naomi Sugie. 2009. Sequencing disadvantage: Barriers to employment facing young non-Hispanic black and non-Hispanic white men with criminal records. *Annals of the American Academy of Political and Social Science* 623(1): 195–213.

Pereira. Joseph, Peter Frase, and John Mollenkopf. 2008. The Future of Low-Wage Work in Metropolitan America. New York City Labor Market Information Service. New York: Center for Urban Research, Graduate Center, CUNY

Rosenbaum, James et. al. 2010. Beyond one-size fits all college dreams: Alternative pathways to desirable careers. *American Educator* 34(3): 2–13.

Visser, M. Anne and Edwin Melendez. 2011. Puerto Ricans in the U.S. low-wage labor market: Introduction to the issues, trends and policies. *CENTRO: Journal of the Center for Puerto Rican Studies* 23(2): 1–19.

U.S. Department of Education, National Center for Education Statistics. 2011. *The Condition of Education 2011.* (NCES 20111-03).

The Asset Profile of Puerto Ricans and Other Latinos after the Great Recession: 2008–2010

KURT BIRSON, RAMÓN BORGES-MÉNDEZ and KOFI AMPAABENG

Much of the research and literature on poverty among Latinos in the United States has focused on income and wages and often overlooked the importance of the non-income assets of poor households. A further concern has been that even for the studies that do consider asset wealth, Latinos have been bundled into one group, thus obscuring any individual observations or effects for distinct Latino groups.

Using the Consumer Expenditures Survey (CES) for 2008 and 2010, we examine the relative asset wealth of Puerto Rican households compared with that of other Latino groups and non-Latinos in the United States, building on previous research by Borges-Méndez (Forthcoming 2014). In addition, these two recent surveys allow us to observe the differences in the composition of these asset portfolios at the very early stages of the recession and a year after its official end.[1]

Moreover, the CES, which is produced by the U.S. Bureau of Labor Statistics, provides a unique ability to measure the wealth of specific Latino groups. Other available federal surveys, such as the American Community Survey (ACS), the Survey on Income and Program Participation (SIPP), or the Survey of Consumer Finances (SCF), do not provide the same level of detail on assets and racial or ethnic groups as the CES.

We find a broad range of differences in the net (non-income) wealth of Latinos and non-Latinos, as well as in the relative impact of the Great Recession on that wealth. Notably, there were also marked differences in asset holdings within the different Latino subgroups studied. Puerto Ricans consistently had the lowest values for net worth and assets of all Latinos in both periods considered, but also lost relatively little in terms of asset value as a result of the recession. South and Central Americans had the highest asset values for the groups considered in 2010, while Mexicans stood out for having the highest net wealth in 2008 and the second highest in 2010, despite major losses in housing values following the recession. These differences among the different Latino groups merit further scrutiny and reinforce the value in disaggregating Latinos as a general research practice.

Background

Most poverty studies focus on income, however non-income assets are just as relevant in discussing poverty. Assets are an important store of wealth, serving as both a short-term hedge against emergencies, as well as a longer-term means of achieving financial security and generating savings for retirement. This is especially critical for poor families who are dependent on less stable low-wage employment (Mckernan et al. 2012). As discussed elsewhere in this volume, a relatively high percentage of Puerto Ricans (41%) are in this category (Birson and Meléndez, in this volume). Among all groups in the United States, increasing the size of asset holdings has the largest impact on those in the bottom two-thirds of the income distribution and less of an impact on the upper-third of income groups (Mckernan et al. 2009).

Households with few or no assets are vulnerable to asset poverty—a situation in which a household's net worth is not sufficient to live at the federal poverty level for at least three months. In 2010, this value was $5,580 for a family of four (Ratcliffe 2012). Recent trends in longterm unemployment may suggest that even three months of assets may not provide a sufficient safety net for families, especially if they live in an area where the cost of living is high (Birson and Meléndez 2014).

Several studies identify a significant *wealth gap* among non-Hispanic whites, non-Hispanic blacks, and Latinos in the United States, which has grown steadily since the Great Recession (Lui 2009; Taylor 2011; Mckernan et al. 2013). The fact that this racial wealth gap has been identified as being three times greater than the racial *income gap* is cause for concern and highlights the importance of asset-building strategies for reducing household vulnerability to asset poverty.[2] Recent strategies come in the form of such federal programs as Individual Development Accounts (IDAs), the Earned Income Tax Credit, the Head Start program, and the Self-Help Homeownership Opportunity Program. Though a step in the right direction, these programs are limited in scope and in many ways have failed to fully address the problem. More efficient programmatic targeting of the most vulnerable groups would ensure the greatest impact (McKernan et al. 2009). Unfortunately, spending on most federal asset-building programs has primarily favored higher-income households by channeling benefits mostly through tax incentives. As many low-income families have relatively small or no tax liability, such programs have a limited impact on the poorest segments of the population (Woo et al. 2010). Other studies have demonstrated that with enough support and the right approach, asset-poor families can generate positive savings over time and avoid poverty re-entry (Leonard 2013; McKernan et al. 2012).[3]

Several studies on wealth, as well as the CES data used in this analysis, show that Latinos lag behind non-Latinos in terms of asset wealth. However use of the umbrella category "Latino" or "Hispanic" obscures important observations about the wealth profile of individual Latino groups and backgrounds. Further, as Mexicans constitute the vast majority of individuals of Latino origin (near 60% of Latinos in 2010), any statistics on Latinos tend to be heavily skewed towards this group (Ennis et al. 2011).[4]

The following analysis compares the wealth data of several different Latino groups with that of non-Latinos in the United States for 2008, at the beginning of the Great Recession, and 2010, a year after the recession ended.[5]

Assets

Total assets were determined by adding the mean dollar value of six major sources of assets provided in the CES — housing, pension, savings and checking accounts, bonds and securities, other financial income, and vehicles.[6]

For all groups, housing assets comprised the largest source of value by far, between 85 percent and 92 percent for all Latino groups. This lack of diversification leads to greater vulnerability to economic shocks, which became especially evident after the housing crisis that led to the Great Recession (see Table 1).

Among Latinos, Central and South Americans had the highest average housing values ($95,858), and Puerto Ricans had the lowest ($46,506) in 2010 (see Table 2). Non-Latinos had the highest average housing values of all the groups compared ($102,333). Cars represented the second-most valuable asset among Latinos. Again, the value of this asset was highest for Central and South Americans. Puerto Ricans had the second-lowest car-asset value. Although cars do not serve as a reliable source of asset wealth (as their value depreciates over time), they are important for offering a form of reliable transportation to and from work and greater flexibility in choosing where to live.[7] On average, cars represented from 5 percent to 12 percent of the total assets of Latinos. Because Puerto Ricans had the lowest housing-asset value, car-asset value formed a bigger proportion of their total wealth portfolio than

TABLE 1. Share of asset holdings by Latino origin

	Mexican		Puerto Rican	
	2008	2010	2008	2011
Housing	89.8	87.5	87.7	85.3
Pension	0.4	1.3	1.4	2.1
Savings and Checking	0.7	1.0	0.7	0.7
Bonds and Securities	0.1	0.8	1.6	0.0
Financial Income*	0.2	0.0	0.1	0.1
Cars	8.8	9.3	8.6	11.7

	Central/South American		Other Latino		Non Latino	
	2008	2010	2008	2010	2008	2010
Housing	93.3	91.5	92.4	89.8	85.6	81.9
Pension	0.1	0.2	0.4	1.4	1.9	1.9
Savings and Checking	0.5	0.7	0.5	1.7	2.2	2.8
Bonds and Securities	0.0	0.0	1.2	1.7	4.4	8.3
Financial Income*	0.1	0.2	0.3	0.4	0.9	0.5
Cars	6.1	7.4	5.2	5.0	4.9	4.7

Source: U.S. Bureau of Labor Statistics Consumer Expenditures Survey, Microdata Sample 2008 and 2010.
*Financial Income includes interest and dividends, welfare receipts, unemployment benefits, pension, social security, farm and non-farm income, and scholarships or fellowships.

it did for all the other groups studied. Non-Latinos had a more diversified asset portfolio and were the only group in 2010 for which average holdings in securities and bonds exceeded $10,000.

The devastating impact of the Great Recession, however, is clearly evident when comparing 2010 assets to their levels in 2008. In particular, plummeting housing values resulting from the housing and credit crisis eroded the foundation of asset wealth for all groups. For the most part, the magnitude of the loss in total asset value depended on the value of housing assets before the recession; those groups with the highest average housing values lost the most in terms of total assets during this time. This lack of a diversified asset portfolio increased vulnerability to asset losses during the recession (Leonard 2013). Among Latinos, Central and South Americans lost the most (25% of value), while Puerto Ricans lost the least (5% of value). Mexicans also lost a significant

TABLE 2. Mean value of asset holdings by Latino origin

	Mexican		Puerto Rican	
	2008	2010	2008	2011
Housing	$80,277	$63,680	$50,374	$46,506
Pension	$390	$933	$809	$1,166
Savings and Checking	$643	$757	$396	$390
Bonds and Securities	$96	$599	$919	$0
Financial Income*	$146	$32	$43	$54
Cars	$7,825	$6,799	$4,926	$6,379
Total	$89,377	$72,800	$57,467	$54,495
Percent Lost		-23%		-5%

	Central/South American		Other Latino		Non Latino	
	2008	2010	2008	2010	2008	2010
Housing	$122,114	$95,858	$99,709	$91,042	$137,013	$102,333
Pension	$88	$247	$430	$1,365	$3,097	$2,353
Savings and Checking	$613	$718	$549	$1,763	$3,593	$3,455
Bonds and Securities	$0	$0	$1,304	$1,726	$7,098	$10,406
Financial Income*	$149	$200	$268	$370	$1,441	$578
Cars	$7,925	$7,742	$5,669	$5,103	$7,794	$5,872
Total	$130,890	$104,765	$107,929	$101,369	$160,035	$124,997
Percent Lost		-25%		-6%		-28%

All values presented in 2008 dollars.
Source: U.S. Bureau of Labor Statistics Consumer Expenditures Survey, Microdata Sample 2008 and 2010.

value in housing and, as a result, experienced a decline in total asset value of 23 percent, as they tend to reside in states that were most impacted by the housing crisis, such as California, Arizona, and Nevada (Taylor 2011; Brown and Lopez 2013). Non-Latinos lost the highest percent of value (28%), but still had by far the highest average asset value of any group even after the recession.

The rate of homeownership has fallen in concert with the decline in value of housing assets. Table 3 shows the evolution of homeownership rates among several racial and ethnic groups in the United States. Since 2007, there has been a clear downward trend in the rate of homeownership as a direct result of the Great Recession and the credit and foreclosure crisis, where subprime lending

TABLE 3. Homeownership rates by racial/ethnic group (percent)

	Mexican	Puerto Rican	South American	Central American	Total Latinos	Non-Latino White	Non-Latino Black	Total U.S.
2007	51.2	40.3	50.2	42.7	49.9	73.8	46.7	67.2
2008	50.6	40.2	50.7	42.3	49.1	73.4	45.8	66.6
2009	49.7	38.2	49.5	40.2	48.0	72.8	44.7	65.9
2010	49.2	38.1	48.6	38.0	47.1	73.9	44.4	65.4
2011	48.5	37.0	47.8	37.5	46.5	72.0	43.7	64.6
2012	48.0	36.6	47.1	36.6	45.7	71.5	42.8	63.9

Source: U.S. Census Bureau American Fact Finder, Table S0201 Selected Population Profile (1-year estimates) 2007–2012.

FIGURE1. Homeownership rates by ethnicity/race (percent)

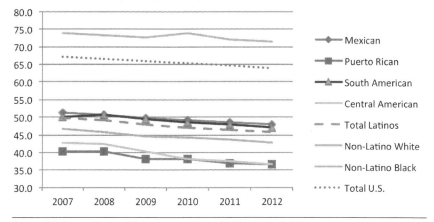

Source: U.S. Census Bureau, ACS, 1-year estimates, 2010.

in minority communities represented a key factor in the decline (Shapiro 2006; Keubler and Rugh 2013). Nonetheless, Puerto Ricans have consistently had the the lowest rate of homeownership (36.6% in 2012) compared with both the average for the United States and the average for all Latinos. This is likely due to the high concentration of Puerto Ricans in urban areas where there is a high cost of real estate, such as New York City, Philadelphia, Chicago, or Boston (U.S. Census Bureau 2012).[8] Mexicans and South Americans were the most likely to own a home rather than rent, but of the groups shown, non-Latino whites had by far the highest rate of homeownership at 73 percent. Among

Latinos, Mexican homeownership rates have exceeded the total for all Latinos since 2007, possibly due in part to their high concentration in the southern and western States, where it is more common to own a home than rent (Taylor 2011; Brown and Lopez 2013; Keubler and Rugh 2013).

Such low rates of homeownership account for a significant portion of the wealth gap. Given that housing assets are often the largest source of household asset wealth, renting families face a sizeable opportunity cost of building assets in the form of housing. Latinos and non-Latino blacks have had homeownership rates below 50 percent since 2007, placing them at a distinct disadvantage compared with non-Latino whites. Moreover, the decline in homeownership was higher among these groups than it was for non-Latino whites; the rate decreased 4.2 percent for Latinos and 3.9 percent for non-Latino blacks compared with 2.3 percent for non-Latino whites. A study by the Corporation For Enterprise Development (CFED) expressed the trend in terms of median family income. "In 2009, the homeownership rate for households making at least $57,175 (the median family income) was 81 percent, while for those earning up to $25,000 it was 32 percent" (Woo et al. 2010: 6).

In assessing the wealth gap vis-à-vis homeownership disparities, Keubler and Rugh (2013) make important observations about the Latino population, but specifically about Puerto Ricans. In their analysis they find:

> ...there were no significant differences between whites, Asians, Mexicans, or Cubans. Conversely, blacks and Puerto Ricans remain substantially disadvantaged... the persistent disparities in homeownership faced by blacks and Puerto Ricans relative to whites combined with incipient divergence of Puerto Ricans from blacks during the crisis also remain important trends worthy of future research. (Keubler and Rugh 2013: 1357, 1372)

These findings reiterate the importance of disaggregating Latinos into distinct and detailed subgroups. In fact, the authors' model shows that spatial settlement is a key determinant of homeownership; those living in the South and West were more likely to own a home (Mexicans and Cubans), while the concentration of Puerto Ricans and blacks in the Northeast limit these opportunities. However, as Puerto Ricans increasingly move to southern states (especially Florida), these trends could change, as the authors observed a divergent pattern for blacks and Puerto Ricans where the latter improved relative to non-Latino whites (Keubler and Rugh 2013; García-Ellín 2013).

TABLE 4. Asset ownership category by Latino origin (percent)

	Mexican		Puerto Rican		Central/ South American		Other Latino		Non Latino	
	2008	2010	2008	2010	2008	2010	2008	2008	2010	2008
Income Dependent	35.9	38.0	52.5	51.2	40.7	38.4	49.6	52.6	22.2	24.5
Propertied	61.3	58.5	37.4	44.1	53.8	55.8	47.0	44.9	70.1	68.5
Investors	2.8	3.5	10.1	4.8	5.5	5.8	3.5	2.6	7.7	6.9

Source: U.S. Bureau of Labor Statistics Consumer Expenditures Survey, Microdata Sample 2008 and 2010.

To further decompose asset holdings among the groups, we created the following three asset categories: the *Income Dependent* group, who held zero or negative non-income assets, the *Propertied* group, who owned a car, house, and had a pension, and the *Investors* group, who held additional liquid financial assets (i.e., stocks, bonds, and dividends) as well as a car, house, and pension. Note that those in the Income Dependent group rely on not just wage and salary income, but also on government transfers and savings. The results are shown in Table 4.

Among the groups reporting zero assets in 2010, Puerto Ricans ranked second at 51.2 percent, a slight decrease from the 2008 level of 52.5 percent and just behind other Latinos, who were ranked highest at 52.6 percent. Mexicans and Central and South Americans ranked lowest among the groups, with 38 percent and 38.4 percent, respectively, in 2010. These rates for the *Income Dependent* group, however, were still significantly higher than the rates for non-Latinos, which averaged nearly 25 percent in 2010. Most Mexicans were concentrated in the *Propertied* group, where they and Central and South Americans formed the highest percentage of households. Puerto Ricans had the lowest representation in this group. Among Latinos, Puerto Ricans actually had the second-highest percentage of households in the *Investor* group (4.8%), while Other Latinos had the lowest (2.6%). The percent of Puerto Ricans in the *Investor* group fell sharply, dropping from 10.1 in 2008 to 4.8 percent in 2010. This was the largest decrease among any of the groups in the category. Many of these Puerto Rican households moved down to the Propertied group, where their percentage rose 6.7 percent representing the highest change of any group in the category.

The data shows that by 2010 asset wealth for Puerto Ricans became more concentrated towards the bottom two asset categories, and the losses in the *Investors* category may represent losses of value in retirement holdings.

Liabilities

Total liabilities were based on four types of liabilities — mortgage, vehicle, credit card debts, and other debts.[9]

As with assets, the value of total liabilities is closely tied to housing. As seen in Table 5, differences between Latino and non-Latino groups in the value of average mortgage liabilities were similar to the differences in housing assets. Central and South Americans had the highest average mortgage liability ($72,214), and Mexicans, by a small margin, had the lowest mortgage liability ($38,669) in 2010 following the sizeable decreases that resulted from the Great Recession. The mortgage liability of Puerto Ricans was slightly higher ($39,712). Interestingly, the data shows that non-Latinos actually had the third-lowest mortgage liabilities of the groups. Vehicle and credit card liabilities represented similar proportions of value to each other.

TABLE 5. Mean value of liabilities holdings by Latino origin

	Mexican		Puerto Rican	
	2008	2010	2008	2011
Mortgage	$48,337	$38,669	$44,545	$39,712
Vehicle	$4,612	$3,382	$2,904	$3,512
Credit Card	$2,492	$3,156	$2,747	$3,016
Other	$228	$390	$81	$410
Total	$55,670	$45,596	$50,277	$46,649

	Central/South American		Other Latino		Non Latino	
	2008	2010	2008	2010	2008	2010
Mortgage	$95,006	$72,214	$72,331	$56,896	$64,705	$58,558
Vehicle	$4,819	$4,443	$3,124	$1,278	$4,231	$3,068
Credit Card	$4,218	$4,154	$3,473	$5,083	$4,956	$3,989
Other	$186	$609	$115	$724	$765	$698
Total	$104,228	$81,420	$79,043	$63,982	$74,658	$66,312

Source: U.S. Bureau of Labor Statistics Consumer Expenditures Survey, Microdata Sample 2008 and 2010. All values presented in 2008 dollars.

While lower debt values are considered by most to be a good thing, lower levels of mortgage liability may signify a lack of investment in housing, a key source of longterm asset wealth. Mortgage liability levels dropped greatly after the recession, having fallen the most for those groups with the highest liabilities in 2008. By 2010, liabilities decreased $22,729 for Central and South Americans, compared with a drop of $4,833 for Puerto Ricans. This suggests that the loss of value in housing assets and the increased rate of foreclosure that stalled the growth of the housing market had a significant impact on investment in housing.

As losses in wealth due to the recession put pressure on personal finances, many relied on credit card debt. Nearly all Latino groups increased their credit card liabilities between 2008 and 2010 (credit card debt fell on average $64 for Central and South Americans). Investment in vehicles also fell for most Latinos with the exception of Puerto Ricans, whose vehicle-related liabilities rose $608 on average. For non-Latinos all forms of liability decreased.

Net Wealth

Combining the data for assets and liabilities, we determine the value for net assets (or net wealth). Table 6 provides the results.

In 2010, the subgroup "other Latinos" had the highest net wealth of all Latinos at $37,387. This actually increased substantially from its 2008 value of $28,887, but the increase was due to the fact that they did not lose as much on average in mean housing-asset values as the other Latino groups. This increase led them to overtake Mexicans as the Latino group with the highest net wealth by 2010. Mexicans experienced a decrease in net wealth from their 2008 level of $33,707, falling to $27,203. Central and South Americans also experienced a

TABLE 6. Net Wealth

	2008	2010
Total Latino	$29,292	$25,558
Mexican	$33,707	$27,203
Puerto Rican	$7,191	$7,847
Central/South American	$26,661	$23,345
Other Latino	$28,887	$37,387
Non Latino	$85,377	$58,685

Source: Source: U.S. Bureau of Labor Statistics Consumer Expenditures Survey, Microdata Sample 2008 and 2010.

TABLE 7. Net Wealth Quintiles (percent)

	Mexican		Puerto Rican		Central/South American		Other Latino		Non Latino	
	2008	2010	2008	2010	2008	2010	2008	2008	2010	2008
Q1	8.8	9.9	2.6	6.1	14.5	14.6	9.4	10.5	20.8	21.4
Q2	22.0	17.1	10.3	6.1	10.5	6.9	22.3	14.5	19.7	20.8
Q3	15.4	25.0	20.5	21.2	18.4	18.5	12.1	10.5	25.7	19.7
Q4	27.5	29.8	30.8	45.5	35.5	30.8	35.8	43.4	15.4	19.7
Q5	26.4	18.2	35.9	21.2	21.1	29.2	20.3	21.1	18.5	18.5

Source: U.S. Bureau of Labor Statistics Consumer Expenditures Survey, Microdata Sample 2008 and 2010.

decline from $26,661 to $23,345. The figure for Puerto Ricans was eye opening, as they averaged just $7,847 in net wealth in 2010. This, despite a modest increase from the 2008 level, was far below the average for Latinos as a whole. All Latinos lagged behind non-Latinos, who, despite having experienced a large decline in net wealth during the period, led all groups with $58,685.

We arranged the overall net worth of Latinos and non-Latinos into quintiles. Figures 2a and 2b, as well as Table 8 present the data for the groups. Quintile 1 represents the group with the highest net wealth value while quintile 5 represents the group with the lowest.[10]

Among Latino groups, Central and South Americans had the highest percentage of individuals belonging to Quintile 1 (almost 15%), and Puerto Ricans had the lowest in 2008 and 2010 (2.6% and 6.1%, respectively). Non-Latinos had the highest percentage overall at over 20 percent. Puerto Ricans had the highest share of the population in Q5 in 2008 (36%), but were supplanted by Central and South Americans (29%) in 2010. Notably, the number of Puerto Ricans in Quintile 5 dropped to 21.2 percent by 2010, which was a significant improvement over 2008 levels. Still, approximately two-thirds of Puerto Ricans were concentrated in the bottom two quintiles in 2010, virtually the same as in 2008. The jump from 2.6 to 6.1 in the first quintile for Puerto Ricans was also notable, but most remained concentrated towards the bottom of the distribution. This supports the idea advanced in Borges-Méndez (forthcoming) that the Puerto Rican community is strongly divided in terms of non-income assets, having a "thin" middle class and a number of more affluent households.

From the perspective of changes in net-asset wealth, the impact of the recession was mixed, with varying effects on wealth distribution within different groups. Both Central and South Americans and Other Latinos experienced decreased shares in the top two quintiles over the period, while the bottom two quintiles grew, signifying a general shift towards the bottom and an overall negative effect from the Great Recession. Mexicans saw a simultaneous drop in both the top and bottom quintiles, and thus a shift towards the center of the distribution at Quintile 3. In terms of net wealth, Puerto Ricans experienced a shift in the bottom quintiles with little change in the top and middle. On a positive note, the share of individuals in Quintile 5 decreased greatly, with much of the share moving to Quintile 4. The movements within the non-Latino population were especially interesting. The share of the top quintiles, Quintile 1 and Quintile 2 increased, while the bottom quintiles, Quintile 4 and Quintile 5, also increased, and Quintile 3 fell. This movement reflects a movement away from the middle and outward towards the extremes of higher and lower asset wealth. Viewed individually, in 2010, each quintile for non-Latinos was virtually the same — near 20 percent, with more stability across quintiles between 2008 and 2010. This, however, seems to be an anomaly from having aggregated non-Latinos — a group that includes a broad array of racial and ethnic groups, such as whites, blacks, Asians, Pacific Islanders, and native Americans. Nevertheless, there appears to

TABLE 8. Index of Wealth Disparity (percent)

	Mexican		Puerto Rican		Central/South American		Other Latino		Non Latino	
	2008	2010	2008	2010	2008	2010	2008	2008	2010	2008
Q1	8.8	9.9	2.6	6.1	14.5	14.6	9.4	10.5	20.8	21.4
Q2	22.0	17.1	10.3	6.1	10.5	6.9	22.3	14.5	19.7	20.8
Q3	15.4	25.0	20.5	21.2	18.4	18.5	12.1	10.5	25.7	19.7
Q4	27.5	29.8	30.8	45.5	35.5	30.8	35.8	43.4	15.4	19.7
Q5	26.4	18.2	35.9	21.2	21.1	29.2	20.3	21.1	18.5	18.5
Index of Wealth Disparity	27.5	15.4	36.2	30.1	32.2	21.9	36.1	26.4	18.5	18.5

Source: U.S. Bureau of Labor Statistics Consumer Expenditures Survey, Microdata Sample 2008 and 2010.

be a large degree of inequality among Latinos according to subgroup. It remains to be seen if this trend will have continued beyond 2012.

Finally, we constructed an index of wealth disparity comparing the non-Latino and Latino populations of the United States to better illustrate the asset wealth gap. Similar in construction and use to the Gini index, the wealth index we created is a measure of inequality. However, while the Gini index measures overall (or within-group) inequality, the wealth disparity index measures the degree to which a group would need to move from quintile to quintile to achieve parity with non-Latinos.[11]

The closer the index value is to 0 (i.e., the lower the value), the closer they are in terms of the distribution of net wealth to non-Latinos (i.e., less disparity). According to the results shown in Table 8, a relatively large difference in wealth and assets exists between Latinos and non-Latinos, but Latinos experienced a favorable redistribution of wealth relative to non-Latinos following the recession. To varying degrees, all groups experienced reduced asset-wealth disparity over the period, perhaps more a function of simply having lost less compared with non-Latinos in the wake of the recession rather than improved their standing. Mexicans made the most progress in this sense, having reduced the asset-wealth disparity with non-Latino whites by 12 points on the index. Puerto Ricans reduced the difference by the lowest amount, which was still still sizeable (6 points).

Conclusion

The results from the CES offer some unique insights into the panorama of asset holdings of Latinos and non-Latinos in the United States, as well as how these asset holdings were affected by the Great Recession. Moreover, they underscore the importance of asset-building and financial-education strategies in creating anti-poverty policies and improving financial security.

The overall net wealth of Latinos was severely impacted by the Great Recession, leading to large losses in the mean value of housing assets. Central and South Americans and Mexicans lost the most in terms of percentage of their 2008 value, while Puerto Ricans lost the least. This, however, was more a result of their relatively weak position in terms of housing value, which was the case before the recession as well. Central and South Americans had the highest total asset value in both years, followed by Other Latinos, Mexicans, and then Puerto Ricans. In terms of net wealth, Other Latinos had the highest value and Mexicans the second highest — a change from 2008 when Mexicans surpassed Other Latinos. Puerto Ricans again had the lowest average net wealth of all groups considered and had the highest percentage of households with zero or negative assets. Their tenuous asset base places Puerto Ricans in an extremely vulnerable position in instances of sudden economic hardship and prevents the leveraging of assets for further growth.

Given that housing holds such a crucial position in the asset portfolio of households in the United States, policymakers should look to create programs that would encourage and support levels of homeownership. At the same time, however, the Great Recession and housing and foreclosure crisis exposed the lack of diversification in the asset portfolios of many households. Latinos tended to be less diversified than non-Latinos in terms of their asset holdings and were especially vulnerable to shocks and asset poverty.

Moreover, the sharp inter-group differences in terms of assets and net wealth give further justification to disaggregating Latinos when doing research. Doing so not only increases our understanding of the unique characteristics and patterns among the distinct subgroups, but in this case allows us to make more informed policy choices about which populations are most vulnerable and especially how regional differences can impact the cultivation of these assets. This also allows for improved targeting of asset-building programs supporting housing, education, and debt reduction to help the most vulnerable low-income households according to the individual needs of diverse communities. For instance, this could mean that programs to support housing would likely be more effective for groups like Mexicans, who tend to be concentrated in southern or western regions of the United States, while programs involving improved access to Individual Development Accounts (IDAs), the Earned Income Tax Credit (EITC), or Volunteer Income Tax Assistance (VITA) might have more impact for groups like Puerto Ricans, who live in the densely populated Northeast. The expansion of financial education programs could serve most communities, focusing on savings, budgeting, and debt reduction. These methods can serve as an effective complementary means used in conjunction with traditional income-support programs to achieve a more sustainable reduction of poverty households in the United States. Such policies are perhaps most critical in the wake of the Great Recession, where high unemployment and poverty persist. The results also call for an increased attention to the asset-development of Puerto Ricans, who lag far behind their Latino counterparts in net wealth.

NOTES

[1] According to the National Bureau of Economic Research, the "Great Recession" began in December of 2007 and ended in June of 2009.

[2] The size of the racial gap depends on whether the mean or median is used to measure net wealth. Because of the large number of households with zero or negative net wealth (nearly half of the sample for Latinos), this study uses mean values.

[3] Two such examples include the $aveNYC program and a similar pilot in St. Louis, Missouri. These programs were able to increase savings by offering matching funds to low- and middle-income families when filing their taxes.

[4] According to the 2010 Decennial Census, of the more than 35 million Latinos identified in the census, more than 20 million (58.5%) were of Mexican origin. The next largest group (just over 10 million or 28.4%) identified as "Other," which included any Latino that was not Mexican, Puerto Rican, or Cuban.

[5] The groupings used for this analysis reflected those used in the Consumer Expenditure Survey and include Mexican, Puerto Rican, Central and South American, and Other Latino. For this paper Cubans were moved to the "Other Latino" due to their relatively small sample size. Other Latinos also includes Dominicans.

[6] "Other Financial Income" includes interest and dividends, welfare receipts, unemployment benefits, pension, social security, farm and non-farm income, and scholarships or fellowships.

[7] This last point is especially important – studies have observed that by living in neighborhoods with high levels of minority concentration, non-Latino blacks and Latinos face limited appreciation of their housing values.

[8] According to Kuebler and Rugh (2013) The overall homeownership rate in New York City averaged just 32 percent between 2007 and 2011.

[9] "Other Debts" include medical debts.

[10] Quintiles were generated automatically by the R statistical software package. For these quintiles, Q5 included households that had either 0 or negative net wealth, while Q4 represented households with net wealth between 0 and 1.

[11] The formula used for constructing the index of disparity is as follows:

$$D = \frac{1}{2} \sum_{i=1}^{n} \left| \frac{w_i}{W_T} - \frac{b_i}{B_T} \right|$$

Where n=number of quintiles
w_i = number of whites (or other racial/ethnic group) in quintile
W_T = Total number of whites (or other racial/ethnic group)
b_i = number of blacks in (or other racial/ethnic group) quintile
B_T = Total number of blacks (or other racial/ethnic group)

REFERENCES

Beverly, Sondra G., Amanda M. McBride, and Mark Schneider. 2003. A Framework of asset accumulation stages and strategies. *Journal of Family and Economic Issues* 24(2): 143–56.

Birson, Kurt and Edwin Meléndez. 2014. Puerto Rican Economic Resiliency after the Great Recession. In *Puerto Ricans at the Dawn of the New Millennium*, eds. Edwin Meléndez and Carlos Vargas-Ramos. 98–116. New York: Center for Puerto Rican Studies.

Borges-Méndez, Ramón. Forthcoming. Asset-based development and the wealth profile of stateside Puerto Rican households. *CENTRO: Journal of the Center for Puerto Rican Studies.*

Brown, Anna and Mark Hugo Lopez. 2013. Mapping the Latino Population, By State, County and City. Washington D.C.: Pew Latino Center

Corporation For Enterprise Development. 2013. Family Strengthening Through Integration and Scaling of Asset-Building Strategies: The Asset Initiative Partnership Environmental Field Scan Report. Washington, DC: Corporation For Enterprise Development.

Cordero-Guzmán, Héctor and Victoria Quiroz-Becerra. 2007. Cracking the Safety-Net: Latina/o Access to Health and Social Programs in the Post-Welfare Era. In *Latinos in a Changing Society*, eds. Edwin Melendez and Martha Montero-Sieburth. 200–26. Westport, CT: Praeger.

Dawkins, Casey J. 2005. Racial gaps in the transition to first-time homeownership: The role of residential location. *Journal of Urban Economics* 58: 537–54.

Ennis, Sharon R., Merarys Rios-Vargas and Nora G. Albert. 2011. The Latino Population: 2010. 2010 Census Briefs. Washington D.C.: U.S. Census Bureau.

Flippen, Chenoa. 2004. Unequal returns to housing investments? A study of real housing appreciation among Black, White, and Latino households. *Social Science Research* 82(4): 1523–51.

García-Ellín, Juan Carlos. 2013. Internal Migration of Puerto Ricans in the United States. In *The State of Puerto Ricans, 2013*, eds. Edwin Meléndez and Carlos Vargas-Ramos. 33–7. New York: Center for Puerto Rican Studies.

Kuebler, Meghan and Jacob S. Rugh. 2013. New evidence on racial and ethnic disparities in homeownership in the United States from 2001 to 2010. *Social Science Research* 42: 1357–74.

Leonard, Tammy and Wenhua Di. 2013. Is household wealth sustainable? An examination of asset poverty reentry after an exit. *Journal of Family Economic Issues* DOI: 10.1007/s10834-013-9357-0.

Lui, Meizhu. 2009. Laying the Foundation for National Prosperity: the Imperative of Closing the Racial Wealth Gap. Oakland, CA: Insight Center for Community Economic Development.

Mckernan, Signe-Mary, Caroline Ratcliffe, and Katie Vinopal. 2009. Do Assets Help Families Cope with Adverse Events? Brief 10. Urban Institute.

Mckernan, Signe-Mary, Caroline Ratcliffe, Eugene Steuerle, and Sisi Zhang. 2013. Less Than Equal: Racial Disparities in Wealth Accumulation. Urban Institute.

Rank, Mark R., and Thomas A. Hirschl. 2010. Estimating the Life Course Dynamics of Asset Poverty. Center for Social Development Working Papers. Ann Arbor: University of Michigan.

Ratcliffe, Caroline and Sisi Zhang. 2012).U.S. Asset Poverty and the Great Recession. Urban Institute.

Shapiro, Thomas M. 2006. Race, homeownership and wealth. *Washington University Journal of Law & Policy* 20: 53–74.

Taylor, Paul, Rakesh Kochhar, Richard Fry, Gabriel Velasco, and Seth Motel. 2011. Wealth Gaps Rise to Record Highs Between Whites, Blacks and Latinos. Washington, DC: Pew Research Center.

Wolff, E. N. 2012. The Asset Price Meltdown and the Wealth of the Middle Class. NBER Working Paper No. w18559. National Bureau of Economic Research.

Woo, Beadsie, Rademacher, Ida, and Jillien Meier. 2010. Upside Down: The $400 Billion Federal Asset-Building Budget. Baltimore, MD and Washington DC: Annie E. Case Foundation and CFED.

The Well-being of Puerto Rican Veterans and Service Members and Their Place within the Diaspora

HARRY FRANQUI-RIVERA

A common saying I heard growing up in Puerto Rico was that every Puerto Rican living on the island knew a Puerto Rican in "the states." The same can be said of military veterans and service members as it is likely that every island- and state-based Puerto Rican knows one. In 2011, the America Community Survey (ACS) estimated that there were over 221,000 state-based Puerto Rican veterans along with roughly 24,000 in active service in the United States alone in addition to some 107,000 veterans residing on the island (U.S. Census Bureau 2011).

Despite representing a significant sector of the state-based population, the condition of Puerto Rican veterans and service members and their socio-economic impact have been largely ignored by the academic community. Furthermore, whereas service members may not represent a large percentage of the state-based Puerto Rican labor force in numerical terms, they bring substantial educational, social, and economic capital to their communities. Additionally, service in the armed forces also contributes to the dispersion of the Puerto Rican population through the United States.

Service in the armed forces of the United States has directly and simultaneously contributed to both the growth and expansion of the Puerto Rican diaspora and the increase in traffic between the island and the mainland. Since the closing of basic and advance training facilities in Puerto Rico during the 1950s and 1960s, island-based Puerto Ricans drafted into or enlisting in the military have had to travel to the continental United States for training.[1] Moreover, since the deactivation of the 65th Infantry Regiment in 1954 (the active army unit based in Puerto Rico known as *el sesenta y cinco*), new island-based recruits joining the active army have remained in the United States or were sent overseas to fulfill their service. Even those who join the reserves (such as the Air/Army National Guard and Reserve) and serve in units stationed in Puerto Rico must complete their initial training on the mainland.[2] Furthermore, most Reserve and National Guard units from

Puerto Rico travel yearly to the mainland for annual training purposes. Thus, military service instantly creates two related phenomena. First, it contributes to a significant transit of Puerto Ricans between the island and the mainland. Second, it contributes to the growing numbers of the Puerto Rican diaspora. Island-based Puerto Ricans joining the active military immediately become part of the diaspora of the mainland United States and throughout the world— even if not permanently. This point is hard to miss as there are over twice the number of veterans living in the continental United States than there are living on the island, despite the similarity of the state- and island-based population of Puerto Ricans who are eighteen years of age and older and that there are no indications that the state-based population joins the military in greater numbers than its island-based counterpart.

A third consequence of military service is the dissemination of the diaspora. As new recruits do not choose the units to which they will be assigned, Puerto Rican service members are stationed mostly in the southern United States, where most military bases are located. Patricia Silver (in this volume) has found that the growth in the Puerto Rican population of Orlando is connected to military service, with Puerto Rican housing settlement spreading east and south from areas originally located near military posts. Moreover, it seems that Puerto Rican veterans return and settle near the posts in which they served (Silver 2010; Firpo 2012). Similarly, Carlos Vargas-Ramos (also in this volume) has found a link between the growth of the Puerto Rican populations in Texas and Georgia and the location of military bases. Additionally, Silver has also found that a larger percentage of Puerto Ricans in the southern United States are employed in the armed forces than in the country as a whole. Moreover, Puerto Ricans were also found to have much higher rates of employment in the armed forces than were non-Hispanic whites in Georgia, North Carolina, South Carolina, Tennessee, Texas and Virginia (Silver 2012). Silver's and Vargas-Ramos' findings show that military service is both a factor behind the dispersion of the diaspora and a source of employment. Military service thus appears to have contributed to the growing numbers of Puerto Ricans in the United States moving beyond the traditional centers of Puerto Rican migration, and to the establishment of new communities.[3] The significance of these trends is magnified by the fact that young Puerto Ricans are enlisting in the military at higher rates than in the previous decade, and as this study will show, Puerto Ricans are almost twice as likely to be in the military as the general population.

In spite of the obvious importance of military service for the state-based Puerto Rican community, there is a dearth of studies directly examining the roles and condition of veterans and service members within Puerto Rican communities. As military service has become a facilitator for the growth and spread of the diaspora and as Puerto Rican military participation in the armed forces is likely to increase or at least remain at current levels in the future, a study of the present condition of the Puerto Rican service members and veterans is much needed. This study will examine the relation between the increasing percentage of Puerto Rican military personnel in the United States and employment and unemployment rates. Moreover, it will demonstrate that the state-based veteran population of the United States is growing rapidly due to the combination of higher enrollment rates in the military (by younger Puerto Ricans) and the exodus of island-based Puerto Ricans veterans. Finally, this study will show that in terms of measurable well-being, the island-based veteran population (and probably the state-based too) enjoys a higher quality of life overall than its non-veteran counterparts. In sum, the questions and discussion in this study point to the historical role of military service as an economic escape valve, a path towards middle-class status for a disadvantaged population, a facilitator of migration. Finally, I would like to propose areas for further inquiry related to both the Puerto Rican service members and the veteran population.

For this study, I relied mostly on data and reports from the U.S. Department of Veterans Affairs, the U.S. Department of Defense, and the U.S. Census Bureau-American Community Survey (ACS). Most of the data and the analysis cover the period between 2005 and 2011. Data for island-based and for Latino/Hispanic military personnel and veterans are included to provide a point of reference and for a better understanding of the state of Puerto Rican service members and veterans in the United States.[4]

Historical Background of Puerto Rican Service in the Military
Although Puerto Ricans have served in the military since 1899, only a few hundred served at any one time, and most were confined to the island before World War I. During World War I, some 18,000 Puerto Ricans served in the military. Then again, with the exclusion of a few thousand service members, most served with Puerto Rican units on the island and were quickly disbanded after the war ended. Nonetheless, this war created the first sizable group of Puerto Rican veterans under United States sovereignty. Much work still needs

to be done to gauge the impact of the World War I veteran population on the diaspora—although there are indications that during this period veterans from the island started to join the state-based community.[5]

The second wave of Puerto Rican military participation occured during World War II. Between those serving in units trained on the island and on the mainland, it is estimated that some 58,000 Puerto Ricans served during this conflict during the period of 1940 to 1945. (NARA, Center for Electronic Records). Puerto Rican veterans from this period could count on a generous package of benefits through the Servicemen's Readjustment Act of 1944 (known as the G.I. Bill), which was designed to ease the soldier's re-entry into civil life. Their salaries and federal benefits, in fact, boosted the local economy, and military service became a permanent means of alleviating unemployment in the island (Franqui 2010). Military service seems to have eased migration to the mainland United States as well.

Altogether, the World War I and World War II veteran population residing in Puerto Rico in 1947 totaled 70,426 men and 210 Women Army Corps (WACs) veterans. Roughly 13,000 World War II Puerto Rican veterans were not living in the island by 1954 and had presumably moved to the mainland. This is evidence that Puerto Rican veterans were joining the post-war exodus to the mainland United States.[6] Furthermore, Silver has found evidence through oral history projects indicating that as early as the 1940s Puerto Rican service members assigned to bases in central Florida returned and settled in the area after fulfilling their service (Silver 2010). This also appears to be the case for veterans of the Korean and Vietnam Wars. Some 61,000 Puerto Ricans participated in the Korean War and roughly 48,000 served during the Vietnam War.[7] After the Vietnam War, Puerto Rican yearly participation in the "All Volunteer Force" (AVF) has ranged from 14,000 to 30,000 service members. In view of the lack of specific data for the post-Korean War period—and based on the experience of the previous generations of veterans—we can presume that service members who were originally island-based have added to the growth of the Puerto Rican diaspora between the end of the Vietnam War in 1972 and 2005.

2005-2011 American Community Survey Data

The focus of this study is the period 2005–2011, which is also the period covered by the majority of data collected from the ACS. Since the ACS data used for this study takes into account only those military personnel in active service and stationed in the United States, some 400,000 service members deployed overseas are unaccounted for. If we add that number to the total military population, the percentage of people in uniform compared with the total United States population age sixteen years and older jumps from 0.4 to 0.6. The significant increase in the proportion of the population in the armed forces when oversees deployments are considered suggests two questions for further, more in-depth study. First, would the representation of Puerto Ricans in the military compared with the Puerto Rican state-based population (0.7% using the ACS 1-year estimate for 2011) also increase if we sampled troops stationed overseas? Second, are Puerto Ricans more likely than other groups to be deployed overseas?

Some factors point to the possibility of Puerto Rican service members being overrepresented among military personnel deployed overseas. Military occupational skills (MOS) influence a service member's chances of deployment. For instance, generally speaking, combat troops are more likely to be deployed overseas than non-combat troops. The MOS assigned to new recruits is based on both the needs of the military and, since 1968, on the recruit's initial score on the Armed Services Vocational Aptitude Battery test (ASVAB).[8] Studies have shown that state-based Puerto Ricans have low graduation rates and academic achievement.[9] If Puerto Ricans joining the military are underprepared academically, this may result in lower ASVAB scores. The lower the recruit's scores, the fewer options for choosing an MOS requiring high technical skills. It is then very likely that a disproportionate number of Puerto Ricans are being assigned to combat roles—such as the infantry in the Army— a factor that would increase their chances for overseas deployment. But as mentioned above, further in-depth studies are necessary to explore this matter. Hence, for the purpose of this study we will focus on the military personnel currently stationed in the United States as reported by ACS.

Armed Forces, Population Growth, and Employment
In 2005, some 15,861 Puerto Ricans were serving in the armed forces representing 0.6 percent of the state-based Puerto Rican population sixteen years of age and older (see Table 1). The following year, 22,588 or 0.8 percent of the sampled population was in uniform. It is interesting to note that in 2006 the number of Puerto Ricans in the armed forces augmented 6,727 or 42 percent while the correspondent civilian population grew by only 180,027 or roughly 6.7 percent. This disparity likely affected the unemployment rate among state-based Puerto Ricans. Even though employment fell 0.2 percent

among the civilian labor force in 2006, unemployment also saw a reduction of 0.6 percent. The next year (2007) shows similar patterns.

The fact that unemployment and employment can fall simultaneously is explained by a reduction of the civilian labor force, which might be caused by an increase of the actual number of Puerto Ricans in the armed forces. That is, the number of Puerto Ricans in the armed forces in the United States increases at the same time the number employed in the total labor force and in the civilian labor force decreases.[10] Members of the armed forces do not count as "employed." However, by being in the armed forces they help to reduce the unemployment rate. Because most military personnel range in age from seventeen to fifty, if the thousands of Puerto Ricans in the military were to abruptly stop serving, they would be added to the civilian labor force, thereby potentially driving unemployment upwards. We can actually observe a relation between the increasing percentage of Puerto Rican military personnel in the United States and decreasing unemployment from 2005 to 2008.

The percentage of Puerto Rican military personnel in the United States in relation to its correspondent civilian population begins to steadily decrease in 2009. However, the number of Puerto Ricans in the military remained relatively high compared with previous years. Even though that

TABLE 1. Puerto Rican Population in the U.S. by Employment Status, 2005-2011

	2005	2006	2007	2008	2009	2010	2011
Population 16 years +	2,643,529	2,823,556	2,942,009	2,973,757	3,090,805	3,307,199	3,464,953
Change in Population (%)		6.8	4.1	0.1	3.9	7	4.7
Total Labor Force (%)	62.7	62.1	61.8	64	63	62.2	61.9
Civilian Labor Force (%)	62.1	61.4	61	62.9	62	61.3	61.3
Employed (%)	55.3	55.1	54.9	56.6	52.9	51.3	51.4
Unemployed (%)	6.9	6.3	6.1	6.3	9.2	10	9.8
Armed Forces (%)	0.6	0.8	0.8	1.1	1	0.9	0.7
Armed Forces Number	15,861	22,588	23,536	32,711	30,908	29,765	24,255
Unemployed	6,799	4,926	6,379	7,825	6,799	4,926	6,379

Source: U.S. Census Bureau, ACS, 1-year estimates, 2005-2011.

TABLE 2. U.S. Puerto Rican Veteran Population Compared to Puerto Rican Population 18 Years and Older

Year	2005	2006	2007	2008	2009	2010	2011
Civilian Population 18 years +	2,494,071	2,662,253	2,762,003	2,794,741	2,908,862	3,104,183	3,263,485
Civilian Veteran	199,526	204,993	207,150	198,426	200,711	211,084	221,917
Veteran Population (%)	8	7.7	7.5	7.1	6.9	6.8	6.8

Source: U.S. Census Bureau, ACS, 1-year estimates, 2005-2011.

number begins to drop after 2008, it is not until 2011 that there is a dramatic decrease of both the number and the percentage of Puerto Rican military personnel in the United States (but as it will be further discussed- that may be a function of greater number of Puerto Ricans serving outside the United States). In 2011, the percentage of military personnel among the corresponding state-based Puerto Rican population drops to 0.7 percent, which seems to be a usual rate for this population (see Table 1).[11]

Patterns in Selected Years

ACS data for the years 2005–2011 show a steady increase in the number of both Puerto Rican veterans and active armed forces personnel among the state-based population. Between 2005 and 2006, the state-based Puerto Rican population in the armed forces as a percentage of the Puerto Rican population sixteen and older increased by 0.2 percent. In 2007, the percentage remained unchanged. It increased by 0.3 percent in 2008 when it reached a high of 1.1 percent. It started to decrease in 2009 when it dipped to 1 percent, followed by decreases of 0.9 percent in 2010, and 0.7 percent in 2011.[12] As shown in Figure 1, the normal rate for Puerto Ricans in the military as a percentage of the Puerto Rican population sixteen years and older in the United States ranges from 0.6 percent to 0.8 percent.

In real numbers, however, the Puerto Rican military population in the United States has increased steadily from 15,861 in 2005 to 22,588 in 2006 and 23,536 in 2007. In 2008, the number grew sharply to 32,711, representing a 39 percent increase over the previous year. The following year, the number of Puerto Rican military personnel in the United States dropped to 30,908. These fluctuating numbers are most likely the result of military situations and the Great Recession of 2007–2009.

The Impact of Iraq-Afghanistan Troop Surges
on Puerto Rican Veteran and Military Populations

The 2008 and 2009 population numbers were also affected by the *surge* of troops in Iraq and Afghanistan and the *stop-loss* order employed by the military to retain military personnel during the worst periods of both wars.[13] The troop surge in Iraq, which started in 2007 and continued until late 2008, consisted of some 27,000 additional troops. The United States began to reduce its personnel in Iraq in 2009, and by August 2010, the last two American combat brigades had left Iraq. On October 2011, after failing to reach a status of forces agreement with Iraq, the White House announced a full troop withdrawal, which was completed on December 18 of the same year. The Iraq troop surge affected the numbers of both veterans and service members during the 2007–2009 period.

A quiet surge ordered by President George W. Bush sent another 4,500 troops to Afghanistan in September 2008. It was followed by President Barack Obama's surge that ordered another 33,000 service members sent to Afghanistan in 2009. By September 2012, the 33,000 additional troops of the Afghanistan troop surge had been withdrawn, but roughly 70,000 American troops will remain in Afghanistan until at least the end of 2014. We thus have two overlapping troop surges, which should help to explain the sharp increase of numbers and percentage of Puerto Rican military personnel in relation to the total Puerto Rican population age sixteen years and older in the United States.

As two sequenced administrations opted for troop surges in two different theaters of war, the military increased stop-loss orders to involuntarily retain service members beyond their contract obligation. In April 2007, the Department of Defense decided to increase the combat tour from twelve to fifteen months. To keep up with the extension and maintain the troop levels necessary for the surge, thousands of stop-loss orders were issued to keep soldiers from leaving the service immediately before a combat tour or in the middle of a deployment (Barnes 2008). The Stop Loss program had started in 2005 previous to the surge in Iraq.

The military had to recur to other measures to keep up with manpower demands. It seems that many civilian veterans serving the inactive reserve portion of their military obligation were called into active service. ACS data show 23,536 Puerto Rican service members in 2007 and 32,711 in 2008 for an increment of 9,175 (See Figure 1). For the same years, there is a sharp decrease of the total number of Puerto Rican veterans in the United States from 207,150

FIGURE 1. Puerto Rican Service Members and Veterans in the U.S., 2005-2011

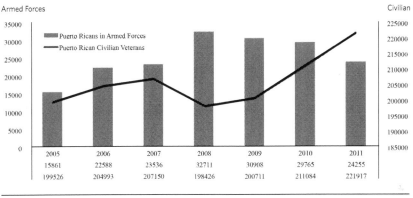

Source: U.S. Census Bureau, ACS, 1-year estimates, 2005-2011.

in 2007 to 198,426 in 2008. The year 2008 is the only one in which the Puerto Rican veteran population diminished in real numbers. More importantly, the combined totals of Puerto Rican veterans and service members in the United States for 2008 and 2009 only differs by an additional 271 in 2009. This suggests that Puerto Rican veterans were called in great numbers into active service from the "inactive reserve." This trend started to reverse during the next years as the Iraq and Afghanistan surges ended.

Veterans and Military Personnel

The Puerto Rican civilian veteran population of the United States seems to have been greatly affected by the surge in Iraq. ACS data show there were some 8,724 less veterans in 2008 than there were in 2007 (see Table 3)—and as mentioned above, that is the only year during which there was a reduction in the state-based Puerto Rican veteran populations. However, from that point onwards, the population of state-based Puerto Rican veterans has grown considerably. From 198,426, or 7.1 percent of the population 18 years of age and over in 2008, the veteran population grew to 221,917 in 2011 (an 11.8% increase), although representing just 6.8 percent of the population 18 years and over for that year.

The decrease in the actual numbers and percentage of Puerto Rican military personnel in 2011 in the United States (compared with the 2008–2009 period) coupled with the simultaneous growth of the veteran population seem to confirm the theory that the missing veterans from the

ACS 2008 data had been called into active service. Other questions remain unanswered. As returning soldiers become civilian veterans, what is their impact on the total labor force? Do veterans fare better or worse in terms of finding employment? Are they joining the pool of unemployed Puerto Ricans? Are they making use of such benefits package as the G.I. Bill and the veteran's mortgage program? Unfortunately, the data collected for this report do not allow us to directly answer these questions. This study includes a section on the condition of island-based veterans compared with the general veteran population in the United States, which may serve to address, if only briefly and indirectly, some of these questions.

A New Normal for State-based Puerto Rican Veterans and Service Members?

The percentages of Puerto Rican veterans and active service members seem to have stabilized in 2010 and 2011. During those years, service members made up 0.9 percent and 0.7 percent, or an average of 0.8 percent, of the total Puerto Rican population over 16, while the percentage of veterans remained steady at 6.8 percent of the Puerto Rican population over 18 in the United States. These percentages, however, don't tell the whole story. The percentage of Puerto Ricans in the armed forces was 0.6 percent of the corresponding civilian population in 2005 and grew to 0.7 percent in 2011. However, in real numbers there were 15,861 Puerto Ricans in uniform in 2005 compared with 24,255 in 2011. That is an increment of over 50 percent. On the other hand, the number of state-based Puerto Ricans 16 years and older went from 2,643,529 in 2005 to 3,464,953 in 2011, a 32 percent increment. This seems to indicate

TABLE 3. State-based Puerto Ricans, Armed Forces, and Veterans

Year	2005	2006	2007	2008	2009	2010	2011
Puerto Ricans in Armed Forces	15,861	22,588	23,536	32,711	30,908	29,765	24,255
Change		6,727	948	9,175	-1,803	-1,143	-5,510
Puerto Rican Civilian Veterans	199,526	204,993	207,150	198,426	200,711	211,084	221,917
Change		5,467	2,157	-8,724	2,285	10,373	10,833
Total	215,387	227,581	230,866	231,137	231,619	240,849	246,172

Source: U.S. Census Bureau, ACS, 1-year estimates, 2005–2011.

that Puerto Rican youth are enlisting in the military at higher rates than in the previous decade, a trend that should eventually lead to an increase of both the number of veterans and their percentage of the corresponding Puerto Rican population in the United States.

This theory is also supported by the fact that between 2005 and 2011 there was an increase of only 11 percent among the Puerto Rican veteran population in the United States (from 199,526 in 2005 to 221,917 in 2011). But the corresponding civilian population increased by roughly 30 percent (from 2,494,071 in 2005 to 3,263,485 in 2011). If the growth of Puerto Rican military personnel exceeds that of its corresponding civilian population by almost 20 percent, and the growth of state-based Puerto Rican veterans is exceeded by almost 20 percent by the population 18 years and over, then one may conclude that the Puerto Rican veteran population will grow dramatically in the near future. This could also be indicative of a higher percentage of Puerto Ricans serving overseas rather than in the United States.

The assertion that Puerto Ricans are overrepresented overseas compared with the general population is supported by the fact that even as the number of state-based Puerto Ricans in the military began to drop in 2009 and continued to drop until 2011, the reduction of military personnel in the mainland United States was not enough to cover the growth in the veteran population. For example, there were some 24,255 Puerto Rican service members in 2011 representing a decrease of roughly 5,510. However, the veteran population grew by almost twice that number, 10,833. In 2010, there was an even greater, more dramatic disparity in the small decrease of roughly 1,143 service members on active duty in the United States compared with an increase of 10,373 over 2009 numbers, another year in which the number of new veterans outpaced the reduction of Puerto Rican military personnel in the United States. These numbers may indicate a high percentage of Puerto Ricans in the military deployed overseas and a growing veteran population in the United States due to higher enrollment rates in the military by younger Puerto Ricans combined with the exodus of island-based Puerto Ricans veterans. The Puerto Rican military population is thus younger and remaining in the military, which points to a sustained percentage of Puerto Ricans in the military and a steady growth of new veterans in the near future. The Department of Veterans Affairs has made similar predictions for "Hispanics" as a whole.[14]

TABLE 4. Change in Puerto Rico's Veteran Populations, 2007–2011

Year	2007	2008	2009	2010	2011
Civilian Population 18 years +	2,938,517	2,967,963	3,001,482	2,822,640	2,828,365
Change		29,446	33,519	-178,842	5,725
Civilian Veterans	120,479	121,686	120,592	112,905	107,478
Change		1,207	-1,094	-7,687	-5,477
Percentage of Population	4.1	4.1	4	4	3.8

Source: U.S. Census Bureau, ACS, 1-year estimates, 2007–2011.

Puerto Rican Island- and State-based Veteran Population

If the growth of the Puerto Rican veteran population in the United States has been affected by an influx of veterans from Puerto Rico, then the island-based veteran population should be decreasing. And that is exactly the case. The percentage and number of island-based Puerto Rican veterans compared with the total population of the island 18 years and over decreased steadily during the 2009–2011 period, while the number of state-based Puerto Rican veterans has increased (though not the percentage) within the same group. It is likely that this signifies that island-based Puerto Rican veterans are moving to the mainland United States.

The island-based veteran population has decreased as a percentage of its corresponding civilian population from 4.1 percent in 2007 to 3.8 percent in 2011 (see Table 4). Since the percentages are based on the total Puerto Rican population over 18 at a time when this population had been decreasing, they don't show the actual dramatic reduction of the island-based veteran population. The most significant change occurred between 2009 and 2010, when the percentage of veterans in relation to their corresponding civilian population group remained stable at 4 percent, but 7,687 veterans were not present on the island (representing a 6.4 percent decrease in the actual number of veterans). From 2010 to 2011, there was a further 4.8 percent reduction of the veteran population (5,427 fewer veterans in 2011), although in relation to the civilian population the decrease was only 0.2 percent. That the island-based veteran population has diminished both in number and as a percentage of the total population over 18 at a time when that segment of the population is also decreasing seems to indicate that island-based Puerto Rican veterans are joining the state-based Puerto Rican community.

While mortality rates among veterans may account for a portion of the reduction of the veteran population in Puerto Rico, a few factors suggest

TABLE 5. Island- and State-Based Puerto Rican Veterans by Age Group

Age Group	State-Based Veterans	Island-Based Veterans	Total Veterans	State-Based Veterans (%)	Island-Based Veterans (%)	Total Puerto Rican Veterans (%)
18 to 34	36,630	7,267	43,897	17.3	6.7	13.7
35 to 54	88,312	22,343	110,665	41.8	20.6	34.6
55 to 64	43,606	21,801	65,407	20.6	20.1	20.5
65 to 74	22,411	22,994	45,405	10.6	21.2	14.2
75 +	17,332	34,057	51,389	8.2	31.4	16
Total	211,381	108,412	319,793	66.1	33.9	

Source: U.S. Census Bureau, ACS, 1-year estimate, 2011; ACS, 5-year estimates, Puerto Rican Veterans in U.S., 2006-2011.

that the reduction is mostly due to migration. For once, there is no indication that mortality rates among Puerto Ricans veterans differ due to geographical location. Hence, any reduction of island-based veterans due to mortality should be similar in scale to that of state-based veterans. Furthermore, the Department of Veterans Affairs has recently revised its veteran population projections due to increased longevity among veterans.[15] Island-based Puerto Rican veterans, in particular, seem to enjoy much greater longevity compared with the general population. Almost 73 percent of the island-based veteran population are in the age brackets og 55 to 64, 65 to 74, and 75 years and over, while only 32 percent of the non-veteran population is in those age brackets (see Table 5).[16]

Hence, besides greater enrollment in the military during a decade of constant war, it seems that increase in the number of Puerto Rican veterans in the United States is directly related to veterans moving from the island to the continental United States. As mentioned above, as both the Iraq and Afghan surges started to wind down, we witnessed an increase in the state-based Puerto Rican veteran population and a decrease in active-duty personnel. As fewer active troops were needed, the veterans recalled into active service returned to civilian life thereby inflating the number of civilian veterans. The case of island-based Puerto Rican veterans seems to be different. Their numbers actually increased in 2007 and 2008, remained stable in 2009 (the most intense years in relation to both the Iraq and Afghanistan surges) but decreased in 2010 and 2011.

Notably, the increase of the state-based veteran population parallels the decrease of the island-based veteran population. For the years 2009, 2010, and 2011 the number of veterans "missing" in Puerto Rico almost exactly matches the difference between the decrease of active military personnel and the increase of veterans in the United States. For example, in 2009, roughly 500 more veterans were added in the United States while there was a decrease of active-duty personnel, over 9,000 in 2010 and over 5,000 in 2011. Coincidentally, there is a reduction of roughly 800 veterans in Puerto Rico in 2009; 8,000 in 2010; and 5,000 in 2011. These numbers strongly indicate that the island-based veteran population is joining the state-based community.

Age Group of Island- and State-based Veterans and Its Relation to Migration

A look at the age brackets to which state and island-based Puerto Rican veterans belong shows parallels to historical processes and supports the argument that island-based Puerto Rican veterans are joining the diaspora. The younger the age bracket, the higher the percentage of Puerto Rican veterans living in the United states compared with those living in Puerto Rico. Even though the civilian populations are basically the same in terms of total numbers, there are marked differences when it comes to age groups. The general population on the island surpasses, and at times doubles, the state-based Puerto Rican population for the age groups 55 to 64, 65 to 74, and 75 years and over. The inverse is true for the general population in the age brackets 35 to 54 and 18 to 34 years. Coincidentally, in the group 75 and over, Puerto Rican veterans living on the island is double the number living on the mainland. The numbers are practically equal for the group 65 to 74 years old. In the group age 55 to 64, Puerto Rican state-based veterans are double the number of those living on the island, and the ratio is quadrupled for the group 35 to 54 years old and quintupled for the population 18 to 34 years of age.

That the Puerto Rican island-based veteran population is much older than its state-based counterpart seems to be related to historical processes. The bulk of island-based veterans served during World War II and the Korean War. During this period, as I have discussed elsewhere, the government of the island was bent on using every veteran's benefit to create the native know-how for the socioeconomic reconstruction of the island. Education, housing, and employment opportunities, as well as rapid socioeconomic mobility were available for World War II and Korean War veterans, which helps to explain why such a high percentage of these veterans remained on the island (Franqui 2010). Service members continue to enjoy these benefits today, however, there are no island-based initiatives to match those of the period from 1940 to the 1960s. It is more than likely that high unemployment rates in Puerto Rico combined with the absence of state programs supporting returning veterans compels younger island-based veterans to migrate to the continental United States.

Puerto Rican Veterans and Service Members in 2011: Under- and Overrepresentation

ACS data show that Puerto Ricans are overrepresented in the military. In 2011, state-based Puerto Ricans 16 years old and over, represent 2.46 percent of the total armed forces personnel in the United States but only 1.4 percent of the total population in this age category. These numbers are clear evidence of Puerto Rican overrepresentation in the military. This trend is more than remarkable, because Latinos (counted as "Hispanics" by the military) are traditionally underrepresented in the military.[17] Furthermore, ACS estimates that only 0.4 percent of the total population 16 and over is in the military compared with 0.7 percent of the Puerto Rican population in the United States (see Figure 2). Puerto Ricans are almost twice as likely to be in the military than the total population.

Those numbers are more compelling when compared with the Puerto Rican veteran population. As stated previously, in 2011, the Puerto Rican state-based veteran population represented 6.8 percent of its corresponding civilian counterpart (see Figure 3). In comparison, 9.1 percent of the total population of the United Sates in the same group are veterans (U.S. Census Bureau 2011). Thus, even though Puerto Ricans are overrepresented in the military, they seem to be underrepresented within the larger veteran population.

In 2011, the Puerto Rican population in the 18 years and over age bracket represented only 1.37 percent of the total population of the United States in that same age group (see Figure 3). But state-based Puerto Rican veterans represent only 1 percent of the total veteran population. That percentage changes when the island-based veteran population is included, increasing to 1.52 percent. But, on the other hand, if we include the island-based population over 18 years old in the total U.S. population, its percentage also rises to 2.54 percent. So, then again we see an underrepresentation of Puerto Rican veterans compared with corresponding civilian groups.

The overrepresentation of Puerto Ricans in the military and their underrepresentation within the veteran population also reinforces the finding that Puerto Rican service members belong to the younger age brackets, which should transform into a rapidly increasing Puerto Rican veteran population in future years. This is also indicative of the continuing role of the military

FIGURE 2. Puerto Ricans in Active Military

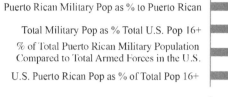
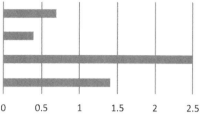

Puerto Rican Military Pop as % to Puerto Rican

Total Military Pop as % Total U.S. Pop 16+

% of Total Puerto Rican Military Population
Compared to Total Armed Forces in the U.S.

U.S. Puerto Rican Pop as % of Total Pop 16+

Source: U.S. Census Bureau, ACS, 1-year estimate, 2011.

as an escape valve alleviating unemployment among Puerto Rican youth. Not only is the Puerto Rican veteran population growing, but the Hispanic veteran population is also growing as well. The Department of Veteran Affairs projects that the percentage of Hispanic veterans will practically double by 2040 from representing roughly 6 percent to 12 percent of the total veteran population. That is at the same time when the Gulf War I-era (August 1990 to August 2001) veterans and beyond are projected to become the biggest group, representing more than 55 percent of the total veteran population from about 25 percent in 2010 (Department of Veterans Affairs 2013).[18]

The Department of Veterans Affairs estimates that 19 percent of Hispanic veterans fall in the age bracket of 17 to 34 years old.[19] Hispanics also represent 11.9 percent of the veterans from the Gulf War II period (September 2001 or later) and beyond. Currently, Puerto Rican veterans (both state- and island-based) constitute 25.85 percent of the total Hispanic veteran population (329,395 out of 1,274,220). Puerto Rican veterans are indeed overrepresented within the Hispanic veteran population. Will Puerto Ricans continue to represent a quarter of the total Hispanic veteran population? If the current enrollment patterns continue it seems likely. Another indicator is the fact that for the period of the Gulf War II, the percentage of island-based Puerto Rican veterans surpasses the percentage of the total state-based Puerto Rican veteran population (13% and 10.3%, respectively) (see Figure 4). This is significant, not just because it also surpasses the percentage of Hispanics for this period but because the state-based Puerto Rican veteran population is much younger than its island-based counterpart. More than likely, the Puerto Rican veteran population will increase or at least remain the same as a percentage of the Hispanic veteran population at a time of rapid growth for the latter.

FIGURE 3. Puerto Rican Veteran Population, 2011

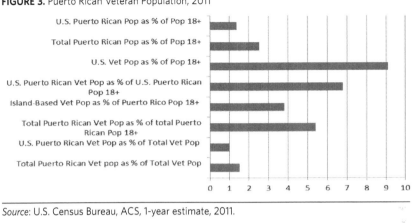

Source: U.S. Census Bureau, ACS, 1-year estimate, 2011.

Well-being and Quality of Life of the Puerto Rican Veteran

By looking at the veteran population of Puerto Rico and the general and Hispanic veteran populations in the United States, we can extrapolate the condition of the state-based Puerto Rican veteran population for which there is little available data. According to ACS data, the non-veteran population in Puerto Rico with any kind of disability (AKD) surpasses both the general and Puerto Rican state-based counterpart populations by roughly 10 percent. There is virtually no statistical difference between the general population and the Puerto Rican population in the United States when it comes to disability. However, 39.9 percent of island-based Puerto Rican veterans have AKD, surpassing the general veteran population in the United States by roughly 14 percent (see Figure 5).

Such disparities may be explained by the fact that over 73 percent of the veteran population in Puerto Rico falls in the three oldest age brackets compared with only 66 percent of the veteran population in the United States. Only 32 percent of the state-based Puerto Rican veteran population falls into the three oldest age groups. Moreover, 31 percent of veterans in the island are over 75 years old compared with only 22 percent of all veterans in the United States, and only 8.19 percent of state-based Puerto Rican veterans. This is significant because the older the veteran, the higher the chances of having any kind of disability. In any case, it is obvious that the disability rate for the veteran and non-veteran populations on the island is much higher than the rate for the corresponding populations in the United States. Even more disconcerting is

FIGURE 4. Island-based Puerto Rican Veterans Compared to Total Veteran Population In the U.S. by War Period (percent)

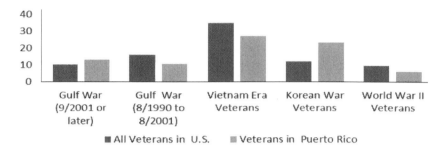

Source: U.S. Census Bureau, ACS, 3-year estimates, 2008–2011; ACS 1-year estimates, PR, 2011.

the fact that non-veteran, island-based Puerto Ricans have a disability rate almost identical to that of the general veteran population in the United States. In short, both the island-based veteran and non-veteran populations have much higher disability rates than their state-based counterparts.

Educational Attainment

In other measures of well-being, island-based veterans seem to hold certain advantages over their non-veteran counterparts. This is particularly true for women veterans. Island-based non-veterans are three times more likely to not having completed high school than are island-based veterans. This is striking, considering that the veteran population on the island is much older than its mainland counterpart and that almost 30 percent of these veterans joined the military during World War II and the Korean War, when a fourth-grade education was the standard for being inducted or joining the service. When it comes to higher education, the island-based veteran population has a clear advantage over the non-veteran population and the state-based total Puerto Rican population. Moreover, island-based veterans surpass the general veteran population in the United States in terms of higher education and are on a par with the total non-veteran population. It is clear that there is a connection between military service and education. An in-depth longitudinal study measuring the role of the G.I. Bill among Puerto Rican service members and veterans is much needed.

FIGURE 5. Disability, Any Kind, in U.S. and Puerto Rico (percentage)

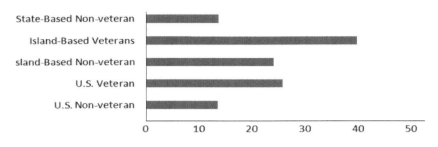

Source: U.S. Census Bureau, ACS, 1-year estimate, PR, 2011; ACS, 3-year estimates, U.S. Veteran Status, 2009–2011; ACS, 5-year estimates, Puerto Rican Veterans in U.S., 2006–2011.

Economic Situation

The percentage of island-based non-veterans living under the poverty line is more than double that of the island-based veteran population (see Figure 6). The same is true for the total non-veteran and veteran population in the United States, although the percentage of those living under the poverty line is much lower than on the island. The percentage of island-based veterans leaving under the poverty line is three times higher than that of the general veteran population in the United States. Hispanic veterans have a poverty rate of 9.7 percent (whereas 23.4% of Hispanic non-veterans fall below the poverty line), which it is higher than the total veteran population but lower than the total non-veteran population (NCVAS May 2013). There is no reason to believe that state-based Puerto Rican veterans should have a higher poverty rate than the total Hispanic veteran population.

In terms of median income, male island-based veterans have a clear advantage over male island-based non-veterans, although half the median income of all veterans in the United States (see Figure 7). Island-based female veterans, on the other hand, have almost double the median income of island-based non-veteran females and have close to the same income as non-veteran females in the United States. The total Hispanic veteran population has a median personal income three times that of its civilian counterpart. (NCVAS 2013).[20]

A look at unemployment rates reveals that there is no much difference between the veteran and non-veteran total population in the United States, but there is a striking difference between those same populations on the island (see

Figure 8). The unemployment rate for the island-based non-veteran population is eight percentage points higher than it is for the island-based veteran population. The island-based veteran unemployment rate is similar to that of the veteran and non-veteran population in the United States.

Together, these well-being measures indicate that the island-based veteran population enjoys a higher quality of life than its non-veteran counterparts. When we consider that the state-based Puerto Rican veteran population is younger than its island-based counterpart and that Hispanic veterans as a whole are doing much better than non-veteran Hispanics, it is safe to say that both island- and state-based Puerto Rican veterans enjoy socioeconomic advantages over the non-veteran population. Has this socioeconomic empowerment served as a path towards attaining middle-class status? Has it translated into political enfranchisement and engagement? These are areas for further study that should paint a more complex picture of the Puerto Rican diaspora.

It would be unwise to ignore that all of these well-being measures, in which Puerto Rican service members and veterans seem to have the advantage over the non-veteran population, are more affected by the structural disadvantages faced by the Puerto Rican population, both state- and island-based, than the general population. In short, as the previous data and discussion show, Puerto Rican veterans and service members make socioeconomic gains as a result of their military service that put them more

FIGURE 6. Poverty Status, 2011 (percent)

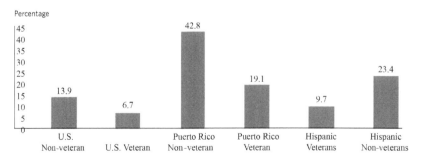

Source: U.S. Census Bureau, ACS, 1-year estimates, PR, 2011; ACS, 3-year estimates,
U.S. Veteran Status, 2009–2011; National Center for Veterans Analysis and Statistics (NCVAS),
U.S. Department of Veterans Affairs, Profile of Veterans, 2011.

FIGURE 7. Median Income

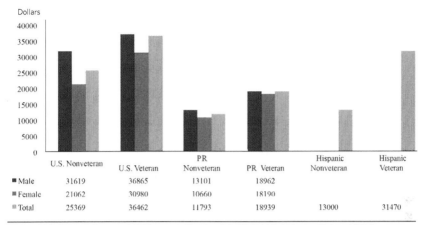

	U.S. Nonveteran	U.S. Veteran	PR Nonveteran	PR Veteran	Hispanic Nonveteran	Hispanic Veteran
■ Male	31619	36865	13101	18962		
■ Female	21062	30980	10660	18190		
■ Total	25369	36462	11793	18939	13000	31470

Source: U.S. Census Bureau, ACS 1-year estimates, PR, 2011; U.S. Veteran Status ACS, 3-year estimates, 2009–2011; National Center for Veterans Analysis and Statistics (NCVAS), United States Department of Veterans Affairs, Profile of Veterans, 2011.

TABLE 6. Educational Attainment of Veterans in U.S. and PR, Population 25 Years and Older

	U.S Non-Veteran	U.S. Veteran	Island-based Non-Veteran	Island-based Veteran	Total State-based Puerto Ricans
Less than high school graduate	15.2	8.1	29.7	11.3	25.6
High school graduate (includes equivalency)	28.3	29.8	26.3	30.6	29.6
Some college or associate's degree	28	36.2	20.9	29	28.8
Bachelor's degree or higher	28.5	26	23	29.1	16.1

Source: U.S. Census Bureau, ACS, 1-year estimate, 2011.

or less on a par with the average civilian. The military is still very attractive to Puerto Rican youth in part because of limited choices and opportunities and the poverty and unemployment rates among this population. Moreover, Puerto Rican youth entering the military is also facilitated by their political status as United States citizens and by a tradition of voluntary service (the latter also being related to socioeconomic conditions and structural disadvantages) dating back to World War I.

FIGURE 8. Civilian Population Employment Rate, 18-64 years

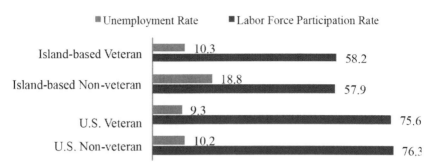

Source: U.S. Census Bureau, ACS, 1-year estimates, PR, 2011; ACS, 3-year estimates, U.S. Veteran Status, 2009-2011.

Conclusion

Historically, economic hardships have provided an incentive for racial, ethnic, cultural, and religious minorities to join the military. But one cannot ignore that such service has also been used as tool for improving the social and political standing these communities.[21] Some scholars have debated the role of the military for socioeconomic advancement and improved social status, while others have emphasized its relationship to obtaining full citizenship and enfranchisement. Even as military service came to be somewhat disregarded as requisite for full citizenship and social standing during the 1960–1980 period, minority groups continued to depend on it as a means of improving their social status. Furthermore, as David Leal has shown, there is a link between military service and active political participation among Latinos that cannot be ignored (Leal 1999).

The first Gulf War and the subsequent wars after 9/11 have brought back the ethos of heroism, patriotism, and the citizen-soldier at a time when minorities are increasingly participating in the military. A general positive perception of military service may place minorities in general, and Puerto Ricans in particular, in an influential position to effect change. As the Latino and Puerto Rican military population continues to grow, especially among those 18 to 34 years of age, one has to wonder about the kind of societal changes it will bring about within the civilian society. As Hispanics in general and Puerto Ricans in particular enroll in greater numbers in the military and come to represent a larger percentage of the veteran population, how will they affect current debates on greater political participation and equality and bilingual education and immigration reform? Will these veterans and service members and their families be more engaged politically, and if so, what will be their position? Will their service lead to more acceptance of what is perceived as Latino culture, and will that in turn lead to a more inclusive "Americanism"?

From the data obtained for this study it is safe to say that military service continues to be a way to alleviate unemployment among Puerto Rican youth. Second, Puerto Rican youth are enlisting in the military at higher rates than in the previous decades. Third, high rates of enlistment among Puerto Rican youth (during a period of constant war) will lead to a dramatic increase of both the number of veterans and their percentage of the corresponding Puerto Rican population in the United States. Fourth, the high number of Puerto Rican veterans currently living in the United States is influenced by a combination of higher enrollment rates in the military and island-based Puerto Ricans veterans joining the state-based community in great numbers. Finally, these trends indicate that service in the armed forces will continue to influence the growth of the state-based Puerto Rican community while also stimulating the transit between the island and the mainland. Furthermore, military service will continue to disperse the Puerto Rican diaspora beyond traditional centers of Puerto Rican migration in the United States and throughout the world. What these changes will signify for the Puerto Rican, Latino, and overall population of the United States and society in general has yet to be seen and demands further study.

NOTES

[1] The military draft ended in 1972 and the United States switched to an all voluntary force (AVF).

[2] Initial pre-basic training for Puerto Ricans (and other individuals) whose first language is other than English may include a few months of English as second language instruction in Lackland Air force Base in San Antonio, Texas.

[3] Silver found that Puerto Rican veterans have been relocating particularly in Central Florida after finishing their service. Also, North American who served and married to Puerto Ricans in the island have contributed to the growing of the diaspora near military bases. Firpo has discussed how military posts attract industries which in turn attract Puerto Rican workers and also veterans who chose to return to Central Florida or to other places near the bases where they served. (Silver 2010; Firpo 2012)

[4] "Military Forces" includes all the active military branches as well as reserve components activated into federal service. National Guard and Reserve components for all branches of the military are not included as "Military Forces" if at the time they are not serving on active duty.

To calculate the percentage of service members in relation to the general population ACS looks at the population 16 years old and over. (ACS Definitions 2010: 54–6) ACS defines "Civilian Veterans" as a person "who served (even for a short time), but is not now serving on active duty in the U.S. Army, Navy, Air Force, Marine Corps, or the Coast Guard, or who served in the U.S. Merchant Marine during World War II. People who served in the National Guard or Reserves are classified as veterans only if they were ever called or ordered to active duty, not counting the 4-6 months for initial training or yearly summer camps. All other civilians are classified as nonveterans." ACS uses the term "Civilian Veteran" and restricts its veteran data products' sample to the population 18 years and older. (ACS Definitions 2010: 119–21).

[5] A local newspaper in Puerto Rico, *Diluvio* argued that in Puerto Rico there were over 200,000 *cuerdas* of public lands- and hundreds of thousands more in private absentee idle hands that could very well be put to good use by the more than 15,000 soldiers whom in their majority were peasants. *Diluvio's* editorial argued that providing training for the Puerto Rican veterans, along with farmland legislation should help to create the necessary conditions so the labor exodus would become unnecessary. *Diluvio* (2 November 1918, 16 November 1918).

[6] Of those residing in the Island in 1947, 13,271 served in WWI and 52,586 in WWII. (U.S. Department of War 1948). The Military Aide to the Governor of Puerto Rico, Teodoro Vidal, prepared a report which stated that between November 20, 1940 and March 31, 1947, 65,034 Puerto Ricans served in the U.S. military of which 368 lost their lives (combat, training, and accidents). Over 12,000 WWII Puerto Rican veterans (counted as 1940-47 period) were not living in the Island by 1954 (Vidal 1954).

[7] About 61,000 Puerto Ricans served in the U.S. Armed Forces during the Korean War (NARA, Center for Electronic Records).

[8] Scores from four of the ASVAB' sections; Word Knowledge (WK), Paragraph Comprehension (PC), Arithmetic Reasoning (AR), and Mathematics Knowledge (MK) — are combined to calculate a prospective recruit's Armed Forces Qualification Test score (AFQT). Scores on the AFQT are used to determine eligibility for enlistment in any of the branches of the U.S. Armed Forces. The scores for all ASVAB sections are used to determine the military occupational skills (MOS) best suited for a recruit. See, http://official-asvab.com/index.htm accessed 7/15/2013/.

[9] See Meléndez, Plaza and Segura (2012).

[10] The combined numbers for "Employed" and "Unemployed" make the total "Civilian Labor Force". "Civilian Labor Force" plus "Armed Forces" equals "Total Labor Force". (ACS Definitions 2010: 56).

[11] See ACS 2005-2011.

[12] See Table Puerto Rican Population in the Armed Forces as a Percentage of the Puerto Rican Population 16 and over 2005-2011.

[13] The military delineates "different types of services, such as active duty, active reserves, and inactive reserves. The common misconception of the minimum length of service in the military is four years, but in fact the minimum commitment which must be made is eight years." The military requires new recruits to spend between two to four years on active duty while the remainder may be spent in the inactive reserves. Inactive reserves are not required to train periodically unlike the active reserves. A service member who fulfilled his/her "active duty" phase of the contract (and served during a time of conflict) and moved into either "active" or "inactive reserve" phase will be

count as a "Civilian Veteran" by ACS. "However, without cause, members in the inactive reserves may also be called into active duty to serve out the remainder of their contract. In the event of war or special emergency, the military may also lengthen the commitment period as long as necessary." The latter is usually called "Stop Loss". These policies may significantly alter the number of veterans and military personnel in a given year and need to be accounted for. http://faircontracts. org/issues/military-recruiting, accessed 5/2/13.

[14] See Department of Veterans Affairs, March 2013, April 2013.

[15] "VetPop2011 projected lower mortality rate for older age Veterans due to longevity improvement. As a result of the longevity improvement, VetPop2011 projected a relatively larger Veteran population in the future than earlier generations of VetPop models (Department of Veterans Affairs , April 2013).

[16] S2101 Veterans Status 2011 American Community Survey 1-Year.

[17] The Department of Defense's data and analysis shows "Hispanics" underrepresented across all sectors of military but the navy for the year 2008. They represent 11.6 percent of the enlisted ranks throughout the military while representing 18 percent of the population in the relevant comparison group. They were 5 percent of the officers whereas their counterpart civilian group accounted for 7 percent (Department of Veterans Affairs 2013). The DoD considers individuals between the ages of 18-44 in the civilian work force as the comparison group for enlisted members. For officers the comparison group considers college graduates between the ages of 21 and 49 in the civilian workforce. Hispanics seem to be joining the military in greater numbers recently. When the DoD counts "accessions" or new recruits only, the level of Hispanics rises to 15 percent (compared to 18% of Hispanics in the relevant civilian population). In the Navy they make up 21 percent of new accessions (FY2008) and in the Marine Corps, the representation of Hispanics is very close to their representation in the correspondent civilian population (Department of Defense 2008).

[18] Gina Pérez has argued that the military has recently targeted the Latino population with a public relations campaign that appeals to "Hispanic values" being compatible with "Army values". Pérez's work problematizes Latino military service especially with regard to "the good" and the "bad" Latino, the denigration of other non-white groups who are thus represented as unpatriotic when compared to Latinos, the lack of opportunities within the Latino community, and the high price Latino service members may have to pay to enjoy some acceptance into the nation (Pérez 2010).

[19] Asians follow up close with 18.2 percent of all veterans in the 17-31 years old bracket. Those belonging to "some other race" represent 16.9 percent, Blacks 11 percent and Whites 6.7 percent. NCVAS, Minority Veterans: 2011, May 2013, 8-10.

[20] Hispanic veterans have surpassed the African American population in this category but they still earn some 3,000 dollars less than White veterans. Asian veterans have the highest Median Personal Income of all races and ethnicities (NCVAS 2013).

[21] Building on previous work by Morris Janowitz on the erosion of patriotism and Judith Shklar's work on American citizenship, James Burk, has explained how minority groups have tried to attain full citizenship by participating in the military even as avoiding military service has become less of a negative determinant of social standing. This citizenship, he argues, is sought more on the basis of social recognition and standing than in economic improvement (Burk 1995).

REFERENCES

Barnes, Julian E. 2008. Army 'stop-loss' orders up dramatically over last year. The jump coincides with the extension of combat tours. *Los Angeles Times* 9 May. http://articles.latimes.com/2008/may/09/nation/na-stoploss9/.

Burk, James. 1995. Citizenship status and military service: The quest for inclusion by minorities and conscientious objectors. *Armed Forces and Society* 21(4): 503–29.

El Diluvio. 2 November 1918; 6 November 1918.

Fair Contracts.Org http://faircontracts.org/issues/military-recruiting/.

Firpo, Julio R. 2012. Forming a Puerto Rican Identity in Orlando: the Puerto Rican Migration to Central Florida, 1960–2000. Master's thesis, University of Central Florida.

Franqui, Harry. 2010. Fighting For the Nation: Military Service, Popular Political Mobilization and the Creation of Modern Puerto Rican National Identities: 1868–1952. 2010. Open Access Dissertations. http://scholarworks.umass.edu/open_access_dissertations/229/.

Harold-Lee, Jason and Julia B. Beckhusen. 2012. Veteran's Racial and Ethnic Composition and Place of Birth: 2011 American Community Survey Briefs. United States Census Bureau, ACS, December.

Leal, David L. 1999. It's not just a job: Military service and Latino political participation. *Political Behavior* 21(2): 153–74.

Meléndez, Edwin, Roseni Plaza, and Raúl Segura. 2012. School, Work and the Transition of Puerto Rican Youth to Adulthood. Research Brief. New York: Center for Puerto Rican Studies, Hunter College, CUNY.

National Archives and Records Administration, Center for Electronic Records. n.d. State-level Lists of Casualties from the Korean and Vietnam Conflicts. Accessed 1 December 2001. http://www.nara.gov/nara/electronic/homensx.htm/.

National Center for Veterans Analysis and Statistics (NCVAS), United States Department of Veterans Affairs. 2013. Profile of Veterans: 2011 Data from the American Community Survey. March. _____. Minority Veterans: 2011, May 2013.

Office of the Actuary, United States Department of Veterans Affairs. 2013. Veteran Population Projections: FY2010 to FY2040. http://www.va.gov/VETDATA/docs/Demographics/New_Vetpop_Model/VetPop2011_ExSum_Final_123112.pdf/.

Pérez, Gina, M. 2010. Hispanic Values, Military Values: Gender, Culture, and the Militarization of Latina/o Youth. In *Beyond El Barrio: Everyday Life in Latina/o America*, eds. Gina Pérez, Frank Guridy, and Adrian Burgos. 168–85. New York: New York University Press.

Puerto Rico National Guard. https://www.pr.ngb.army.mil/.

Silver, Patricia. 2010. "Culture is more than bingo and salsa": Making *puertorriqueñidad* in Central Florida. *CENTRO: Journal of the Center for Puerto Rican Studies* 22(1): 57-78.

U.S. Census Bureau, American Community Survey. *Puerto Rico Community Survey 2010.* Subject Definitions. _____. Hispanic or Latino, Sex by Age by Veterans Status for the Civilian Population 18 Years and Over, 3-Year Estimate, 2009-2011. B21001I. _____. 2011. Puerto Rican, Sex by Age by Veterans Status for the Civilian Population 18 Years and Over, 5-Year Estimate, 2006-2010. B21001.

_____. Selected Population Profile in Puerto Rico, 3-Year Estimates 2008-2010, S0201PR.

_____. Selected Population Profiles in the United States 1-Year Estimates 2005-2011, S0201.

_____. Selected Population Profile in the United States (Puerto Rican) 3-Year Estimate 2009-2011, S0201.

_____. Selected Population Profile in the United States (Puerto Rican) 1-Year Estimates (2005-2011) S0201

_____. Selected Social Characteristics in Puerto Rico 1-Year Estimates (Includes 2007, 2008, 2009, 2010 and 2011) 2011, CP02PR.

_____. Selected Social Characteristics in the United States, 1-Year Estimate, 2011, DP02.

_____. Service-Connected Disability-Rating Status for Civilian Veterans 18 Years and Over, 3-Year Estimate 2009-2011, C21100.

_____. Veteran Status by Educational Attainment for the Civilian Population 25 Years and Over 3-Year Estimate 2009-2011, B21003.

_____. Veteran Status, Puerto Rico, 1-Year Estimates 2011, S2101.

_____. Veteran Status United States, 3-Year Estimate, 2009-2011, S2101.

U.S. Department of Defense. Representation of Racial and Ethnic Groups in the U.S. Military Fiscal year 2008. http://prhome.defense.gov/rfm/MPP/ACCESSION%20POLICY/ PopRep2008/summary/chap5.pdf/.

U.S. Department of War. Estimated Veteran Population, Puerto Rico and Virgin Islands, 1947. Archivo Luis Muñoz Marín, Sección IV Serie 1 Subsección 1: Datos y Estadísticas Sub-serie 33 Cartapacio 29 Documento 2ª.

Vidal, Teodoro. 1954. Participación Puertorriqueña en la Segunda Guerra Mundial y en el Conflicto de Corea. Archivo Luis Muñoz Marín, Sección V Serie 9: Artículos, Discursos, Mensajes, Declaraciones Luis Muñoz Marín Gobernador de Puerto Rico 1949-1964, Noviembre-Diciembre. Cartapacio 7 Documento 9.

Lessons from the European Demographic Winter for Puerto Rico

ALEJANDRO MACARRÓN LARUMBE

> *Puerto Rico,*
> *my heart's devotion,*
> *let it sink back in the ocean.*
> *Always the hurricanes blowing,*
> *always the population growing...*
> (*West Side Story* 1961)

This paper is about the potential effects of modern demographic changes on the economy and society of Puerto Rico and the key lessons that Puerto Rico could learn from studying current demographic changes in Europe. The relevant demographic changes for this paper include very low fertility rates—well below the replacement rates of many other countries—and very long life expectancy and migration patterns, which have particular relevancy to Puerto Rico.

This is not the first period of reduced fertility to be experienced in Europe. What is different now is the concomitant increased life expectancy. While birth rates have decreased, people are now living to be 80 years old on average, which is the case in developed countries now and will be the case relatively soon, given current trends, all over the world. We still do not know the upper limit to the extension of human life expectancy because it continues to grow.

Initially, as life spans increase faster than birth rates drop, the net result is population growth (births minus deaths), which has occurred in Europe and North America and is still occurring in some parts of the world. But as growth in life span continues among the elderly, sooner or later the population becomes too skewed toward the elderly and mortality rates exceed birth rates and the population drops.

In many countries, where fertility levels are below 2.1 children per woman, native populations tend to shrink, in some cases heavily, at astounding speed. This phenomenon has been dubbed "demographic winter" by many, as the winter in Nordic latitudes of Eurasia and America is a season in which nature seems close to dead. Others, like the author of this paper, refer to it as "demographic *suicide*" (Macarrón Larumbe 2011), because indefinite voluntary sub-replacement fertility will eventually lead to extinction of the population.

In some countries, such an unpleasant demographic season is already well under way. In Russia, for example, between 1991 and 2011, deaths outnumbered births by 13 million. In the core historic region of Spain, Castilla y León, one in eleven citizens is 80 years of age or older. In Japan, more diapers are now sold for the elderly than for babies. In Germany, where deaths have exceeded births by 4.5 million for the past forty years, one half of the population is 45 years old or older. In the case of Puerto Rico, when the third variable of migration rate is taken into account, the threat of a demographic winter is accelerated.

In this chapter we will look at the main economic, social, and political implications of this new demographic situation for Puerto Rico and, examine ways of coping with any major challenges they pose.

As we are in unchartered demographic territory, we cannot know with full certainty the future dynamics of the three main demographic variables (fertility rates, life expectancy/mortality rates, and migration flows). But, we believe, and we will try to argue objectively, that this new demographic scenario is very challenging to the economic welfare, quality of democracy, and richness of private lives. We also believe that since Europe is a few decades ahead of Puerto Rico in its demographic winter season, there are useful lessons to to be learned from the Old World.

Unchartered Demographic Territory: Few Babies and Very Long Lives

Life expectancy at birth has grown substantially to about 80 years old or older in developed countries and 68 years old for the world as a whole. Life expectancy is increasing steadily everywhere. Initially, life extension came mostly from reductions in infant and youth mortality. For example, in 1870 in Spain (and almost everywhere), more than half the population lived less than 16 years. Nowadays in Spain, more than 50 percent of those who die are at least 82 years old.

In our time, in developed countries, the increase in life span is now mostly due to modern medicine, health care, enhanced hygiene, more and better food, jobs that are less dangerous to health, the virtual suppression of maternal mortality, and reduced death tolls by wars in most countries. If life expectancy progression keeps the same pace of the past decades of one more year of life every four or five years in developed countries, the lifetime of more than half of babies born today in developed countries would surpass one century. As emerging nations develop, they are expected to follow this trend.

In emerging nations, one in three to five newborns typically died before their first birthday, and this is still the case in very poor regions of sub-Saharan Africa. But in the more advanced emerging nations, as parents saw reductions in infant and youth mortality, the population began to feel more assured of their children having a greater life span, and women began feeling they could deliver fewer babies and still have enough survive to reach their desired family size. Thus, the birthrate has decreased in these areas.

While the main cause of the decrease in fertility rates has been widely attributed to the fall in childhood mortality, other contemporary changes—massive urbanization, more and more women working in jobs outside the home, modern public pension and health care systems lessening the importance of children as a means of support for old people, more years of education, greater emphasis on secular values—all seem to have played significant roles.

This shift from societies with high fertility and mortality to low fertility and low mortality is called the "demographic transition." First, as noted above, the net balance is an accelerated rate of population growth, since births vastly outnumber deaths. This helped spread fears of overpopulation, synthesized in books like *The Population Bomb* (Ehrlich 1968), linking the classic Malthusian concern about humankind growing faster than the resources needed and warning of mass starvation to be caused by overpopulation.

A demographic winter starts when birth rates fall below replacement levels, or 2.1 children per woman in countries where infant and youth mortality is very low.[1] Sub-replacement fertility levels are reached when each new generation is smaller than the previous one. The case of Spain illustrates this point. With the average fertility rates of the past 30 years and the current rates,[2] new generations of Spaniards are 35 percent to 40 percent smaller than their parents' generation.

In 2012, for every million fertile-aged Spanish women (age 15 to 44–49 years) there were approximately 628,000 fertile-aged women. By 2044, in the absence of positive or negative external migration flows, the figure will be about one-third lower. If still nothing changes in fertility and net migration, by 2075, the 628,000 fertile-aged females of 2012 would have decreased to just 248,000, and by 2107 to only 156,000, and so on. Demographically, long-term, this would mean a slow but clear collective population decline. The total population of Spain, according to our estimates, all things being equal, in 2100 would drop about 55 percent from 2012 figures and by 2200, it would drop 86 percent. The remaining population would be, on average, much more aged than it is today.

Recent changes in Spain started with a drop in fertility from 2.81 children per woman in 1976 to 1.16 in 1996 and an increase in average age from 33 years at the beginning of 1976 to 43 years at the beginning of 2013 (one year less when foreign–born residents of Spain are included). About 75 percent of this 10-year increase in the average age of Spaniards was caused by a drop in fertility, according to estimates from the author made by projecting to the present Spanish population pyramid at the beginning of 1975, keeping fertility rates in Spain constant at 1976 levels, and applying mortality rates each year afterwards as actually recorded for them. Another 25 percent of increased age was the result of higher life expectancy. The median age of all Spanish nationals increased from 30 years at the beginning of 1976 to about 42 years now (41 years with foreign immigrants), and it is close to 50 years in some provinces. The average age of residents in Spain should jump from 42 years to 51 years in 2050.

In 2012, according to official sources, Spain lost inhabitants for the first time since 1939, when its last civil war ended. Given its meager fertility, a drop in current population was anticipated as inevitable due to emigration prompted by the Great Recession. Unless there is net positive substantial immigration and/ or a sizeable rebound in fertility, Spain is poised to lose more population and age further every year from the second half of the current decade onwards, more or less in line with the projections presented in this chapter. Emigration then stands as the third demographic factor tipping Spain's population into a declining trend.

What Other Countries Can Teach Puerto Ricans Concerning Migration

In Puerto Rico, fertility has dropped to 1.6 children per woman in 2010–2012, according to the U.S. Census Bureau—about 25 percent lower than what is needed for replacement. That is still above the lowest-low levels, as fertility in countries with 1.3 to 1.4 children per woman or less is called.

The good news is that this trend of sub-replacement fertility is relatively recent. Only 10 years ago, the rate was least 2.1 children per woman. Life expectancy at birth in Puerto Rico was already high—79 years in 2012, according to the U.S. Census Bureau, which is 0.5 years more than it is in the United States. However, life expectancy in Puerto Rico is lower than it is in Western Europe, which averages 81 years of age. Thus, since fertility rates dropped later in Puerto Rico than they did in

FIGURE 1. Puerto Rican midyear population (thousands)

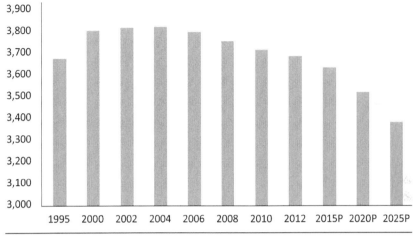

Source: U.S. Census Bureau.

Europe, the island population is not yet as aged as the population of the European continent. There are still many more births than deaths in Puerto Rico.

The bad news for Puerto Rico is that demographic decay traits (e.g., low fertility, aging) are increasing every year. And, even worse news is that the country has a substantial net external migration of a magnitude larger than the combined balance of births, deaths, and immigration to the island.

Given these findings, it is migration from Puerto Rico that is currently responsible for the reduction of the population living on the island. Migration has also accelerated age levels, as migrants are generally younger than the rest of the island's inhabitants. In this respect, the Puerto Rican case resembles that of Eastern European countries, with Boricuas going to the United States, while Poles, Romanians, Bulgarians, and Ukrainians— whose fertility rates are lower than Puerto Rico's—migrating to their more affluent Western European neighbors.

In the United States, France, the United Kingdom, and Sweden, demographic prospects are brightened because of active immigration, in part due to the higher fertility rates of immigrants living in these nations. The worst demographic winter cases are found in Eastern Europe, where a combination of very low fertility, higher mortality than in the West, and high next external migration is causing a very significant reduction in population and an accelerated aging of the remaining population. Ukraine, for instance, saw its population drop from 52 million to 46 million between 1993 and 2009.

If recent trends continue worldwide, and there are no major reasons to think otherwise, in a matter of five to ten years, world fertility would probably be at replacement levels, falling below this threshold afterwards. This means that within 25 to 35 years, the world population would cease to grow, peaking between 9 billion and 10 billion people, and then it would start to decrease, while aging intensely throughout the twenty-first century, in any case. Worldwide, the total fertility rate has fallen by approximately 50 percent in the past 25 to 30 years, from around five children per woman to fewer than half that number (2.4 in 2011, according to the U.S. Census Bureau International Database). Only in Sub-Saharan Africa and some scattered countries is there still very high fertility (five children per woman or more), and the observed pattern nearly everywhere is a tremendous drop in birth rates as the countries develop and adopt international standards of living and habits.

The Puerto Rican Migration Factor

In demographic terms, we are in historically uncharted territory. For this reason, plus the inherent difficulty of predicting the future, we cannot know with sufficient scientific certainty whether fertility rates will remain as they are now, bounce back, or decrease further in the coming years and decades. The same can be said about the pace of future changes in life expectancy, migration patterns, and the effects of combined population shrinkage and unprecedented aging. But, we can speculate about these key issues with a reasonable degree of plausibility, using facts we know.

Puerto Rico has singular traits with deep effects on its demography, like its unique political, economic, and human relationship with the United States and its location in the Caribbean region, which both spur substantial migration flows. There is a sizable net outflow of Puerto Ricans migrating to the United States and a sizable net inflow of Dominicans and other Caribbean people migrating to Puerto Rico. The net balance has been a loss of population in Puerto Rico every year since 2004, according to the U.S. Census Bureau. In 2012, net emigration was estimated to be at least 28,000 people, equivalent to 0.8 percent of the island population.

In the absence of these migration flows, the Puerto Rico population would be expected to continue growing, because for the next five to ten years, more Puerto Ricans will be born than die. But unless birth rates rebound and net emigration rates reverse, this positive natural change will tend to shrink Puerto Rico's population every year, until reaching negative numbers within the next decade. When this happens, because the number of births is already insufficient to replace the existing population, between 2020 and 2025, Puerto Rico will continue to lose population every year. Population growth among the younger cohorts of Puerto Ricans will continue to be part of the population growth among Puerto Ricans stateside.

Potential Effects of Demographic Decay

Many people in developed countries believe that the problem of aging and eventual population decline is limited to the resulting difficulty in paying for retirement pensions. What few people are aware of is the extent to which the problems caused by demographic decay might be much bigger and much more immediate. Potential trouble and damage associated with demographic decay could be of the following five major types:

- **Substantial damage to the economy.** Reduction in population implies smaller aggregate economic demand (less consumption and investment), diminished economies of scale, and depreciation of most assets, including houses and shares in companies whose growth is linked to population trends. Older consumers will mean fewer sales of almost all goods and services, except those that are specific to the elderly. Lower worker-to-retiree ratios means there will be a growing burden on the economy to fund future pensions, pensions for those who are already retired, and public services used by the elderly.
- **Distortion of democracy.** One of the theoretical tenets of sound democracy is that voters choose what they think is best for their country's general interest. As the electorate becomes older, elections will be decided by an ever-growing segment of elderly voters who have a major specific interest in their pensions and health care services, which are funded via mandatory wealth transfers from the diminished ranks of active workers. The result could be oppressively higher taxes for working citizens, which in the absence of economic growth, would damage the economy and social equity and encourage younger workers to leave their country and move to less tax-oppressive nations.
- **Affective impoverishment.** With so few children being born, more and more of the population will have few or be entirely without children, brothers, sisters, uncles, aunts, nephews, nieces, or cousins. Indeed, if

everybody had just one child, all lateral relatives would disappear, and our only family downstream would be one single child, and later on one grandchild. In countries like Germany, China, Spain, Japan, Italy, and many others, with close to an average of one child per person, a family scenario not far from this is being built.

- **Increasing danger for the elderly of being eliminated or mistreated.** If old people are perceived as a burden for society because there are so many them and they are very costly to maintain, pressure to get rid of them through "involuntary euthanasia" or to take care of them as poorly as possible could substantially increase. This is already happening in some countries, though still in a scattered way. Taro Aso, finance minister of Japan, said it bluntly at the beginning of 2013: "The elderly should be allowed to hurry up and die to relieve pressure on the State to pay for their medical care."[3]

- **Younger and wealthier residents will flee, leaving the aging poor in demographically decaying regions and countries.** This has happened other times in history, but now it can happen at a dramatic speed. Eastern Europe is being depleted of its young and middle-aged people who are attracted to the wealthier West. For instance, about 9 percent of all Romanians several years younger in average than their compatriots have emigrated since 1999 to Italy (5%) and Spain (4%). This also is happening more slowly but still steadily, with Puerto Rican migration to the United States.

Damage to the Economy from Demographic Decay

Reduced Aggregate Demand (Consumption and Investment)
Until recently, all students of economics and all the main creators and professionals of economic science, from the scholastics of Salamanca in the sixteenth and seventeenth centuries to Adam Smith, Marx, Keynes, Hayek, Friedman, or Samuelson, lived in economies with constant population growth that fueled demand. Such demographic fuel is starting to sputter now. Until very recently, economists have probably underestimated the importance of the demographic factor because its contribution to economic growth has always been positive. As with good health, as the saying goes, one only notices it when it is lacking. Indeed, a shrinking population means less consumption and investment for any kind of goods, services, assets, and

infrastructures. An aging population means more or less the same thing, except for products and services that are consumed by the elderly, like medication.

Asset Depreciation and Reduction of Workforce

By the same token, with fewer people demanding housing, real estate in the aggregate will tend to steadily depreciate. In countryside villages, whose younger inhabitants tend to migrate to cities in search of better opportunities, leaving mostly the elderly behind, the value of housing drops, trending eventually to zero. Indeed, according to a study made by the Swiss-based Bank for International Settlement (Takáts 2010), real estate property would heavily depreciate in all countries affected by demographic winter. In Spain, for instance, demographic decay might cause price erosions in housing, in constant money, of 75 percent between 2010 and 2050, with similar collapses in prices for other heavily aging and shrinking countries.

Additionally, if growth prospects are nil to negative due to demographics, the value of shares in companies will also tend to fall. The Nikkei stock index of Japan, the country with the most people (with 24% 65 or older in 2011), had approximately the same value at the beginning of 2013 as it had in January 1984, while the Dow Jones Industrial Average grew by a factor of twelve in the same period. The Nikkei Index, and the Japanese economy in general, has never fully recovered from the devastating effect of the housing and stock market bubbles that ended in the crash at the beginning of the 1990s. Since then, the national public debt has climbed to more than 200 percent of the country's GDP, by far the highest such ratio in the world, due to huge public budget deficits. The economic pain suffered by the population could have been substantial. But the behemoth-size debt burden is there, and nobody knows how to cope with it in the future.

The extent to which Japan's high degree of aging has contributed to such prolonged stagnation and enormous public indebtedness is something that nobody knows with certainty. But, demographics have probably played a significant role. It is clear, for instance, that with a growing and younger population the surplus of dwellings built during a real estate boom could have been absorbed by buyers much faster than when the population is flat or declining in number and aging rapidly.

If demographic decay continues as expected in Japan, and it will do so unless fertility strongly rebounds and/or there are massive inflows of foreign immigrants to Japan—two types of events that look rather unlikely right now—the long-term prospects of the Nikkei index and the Japanese economy range from mediocre to grim.

The dearth of a younger workforce to replace retiring workers can also be a major problem in countries with an advanced demographic winter. For instance, in Germany, nowadays, where every year there are nearly 200,000 more deaths than births and about 400,000 more people who are 70 or over, workforce ranks suffer a demographic loss of several hundred thousand workers per year. Either the country fills this gap with steady flows of immigrants or its economy feels the pain or wastes opportunities for growth.

(Good) Public Pensions at Risk
The problem with demographic decay for public pensions based on the prevalent model of pay-as-you-go (i.e., active workers' pay in through taxes to fund the pensions of retired people) is clear, with fewer and fewer active workers per pensioner. This is not the case for the distant future. In the parts of Europe with the most aged populations, it has already started, because more than 10 percent of the GDP is spent on pensions, putting national social security systems in danger. In the past, the cost of pensions was much smaller because the population pyramid had the classic shape, with fewer older people. Moreover, the great majority of workers died before retirement age or lived only a few more years after retiring. Now, in developed nations, the typical ratio of active workers to pensioners ranges from 2 and 3 to 1, trending to less than 2 to 1, to 1.5 to 1, and eventually to 1:1. The inevitable result, unless the retirement age is raised, is already happening in many countries.

With 50 active workers per retiree (as was the case in the United States 75 to 80 years ago), if payroll taxes for pensions were just a rather unnoticeable 2 percent of salaries, pensioners would enjoy very nice pensions—equal to the average salary in the country. With 2:1 ratios of workers to pensioners and a tax burden as high as 20 percent just to cover pensions on salaries, retirees would have a pension equal only to 40 percent of the country's average salary. This is more or less the case now in Spain, where there is a high tax burden on the economy, workers, and companies in exchange for rather meager pensions and with underlying prospects worsening every year due to demographics. In 2012, Spain spent approximately one euro out of nine on pensions, or about 11 percent of the GDP (a toll close to the 14% of Italy), while the input to social security system was close to 3 percent of the Spanish GDP. The current economic crisis is responsible for the majority of this gap, but demographic problems are contributing in a structural way to its widening and will continue to do so unless pensions are trimmed.

Increasing Health Care Costs

Spain is already spending about 9 percent of its GDP on health care. It is estimated that approximately two-thirds of this amount is public expenditure and one-third is privately paid by citizens and companies. Other developed countries spend more or less on health care, but nothing dramatically different. In 2011, it was estimated that around 50 percent of all pharmaceutical prescription expenditure in Spain was generated by people aged 75 or over— 9 percent of Spanish population. Hence, whether paid with taxpayer money—as is most of it in countries like Spain—or from private pockets, the health care toll tends to increase every year.

Migration, Productivity and Exports as Partial Solutions

The negative impacts of demographic decay may be partially compensated for with the following three factors: immigration, higher productivity, and exports.

Foreign immigration is the easiest (and traditional) way for wealthier nations with low-to-moderate fertility rates to compensate for their deficits of native workforce. However, there is a major risk for nations that rely only on immigrants for solving domestic demographic decay. In our opinion, foreign workers might not emigrate to the United States or Europe in as high numbers as they did before because their home countries are now developing and their fertility is no longer explosive. Indeed, for the first time since the Great Depression, more Mexicans are leaving the United States than are entering it (Bahrampour 2012). In Puerto Rico or Eastern Europe, because there are sizable net outflows of local people going to wealthier lands, migration flows are actually sharpening.

More realistically, productivity gains from technology evolution and innovation would help, but probably much less than needed. And, there are two aspects of productivity and innovation necessarily damaged by population shrinkage and aging:

- Economies of scale would be negative with fewer people. Part of the enormous productivity gains in the world in the last two centuries have been the result of a growing labor division and advantages of scale with a growing population. A smaller population will tend to entail the opposite due to diseconomies from smaller scales. In heavily tech-intensive industries and others where fixed costs are not so relevant, the impact of this might not be so big. But in person-to-person services that are provided locally, it could be huge. For instance, in territories with fewer children and less total population in schools and many other public facilities, either government-owned or private, unit costs per customer would tend to grow with the decrease in total number of customers due to demographic evolution.

- Innovation and entrepreneurship are typical of younger people and societies. Younger people are more willing to take risks than older people, for clear reasons like having more stamina and less skepticism about their capacity to "change the world." And, very importantly, young people have much more time to recover from failure. If you do not have time in life to recover from a possible failure, do not take the risk. When you are 35 years old, investing your pension fund in stocks is a sound bet for making good money in the long run, because you have time to recover from bear markets and you will certainly benefit from bull markets. When you are 75, you should rather invest your pension fund in government bonds and low-risk/low-return assets, because you might never be able to recover from heavy market downfalls.

- Exports and doing business abroad are both major opportunities to escape from the worst of domestic demographic decay, as is also the case in economic recessions. In fact, very aged, rich countries, like Germany or Japan, are maintaining high prosperity levels mostly through exports. What nobody knows is for how long increasingly grey-haired countries can remain competitive if they continue aging heavily and domestic workers become more and more scarce (and hence, probably more expensive and subject to higher taxes that would discourage productivity). The BMW car maker will probably continue to have its headquarters in Munich 25 years from now, but if the population in that country keeps getting older, it would not be surprising if the center of gravity of its manufacturing facilities is progressively shifted to other countries.

Finally, doing business abroad because domestic markets are structurally stagnant, is similar to exports. It is typically more difficult and costly to do business abroad, and it entails more risks in countries with populist or nationalistic governments. This problem is exacerbated in heavily regulated industries, where rules can be changed by governments in accordance with their political interest, in businesses such as energy or telecommunications or those based on intellectual property and copyrights that are technically easy to infringe upon, such as in pharmaceuticals, entertainment, and fashion clothing.

Puerto Rican Demography and What Can Be Done

Nobody would say nowadays "always the population growing" in Puerto Rico. The population of the island, as noted previously, is shrinking (see Figure 1). In 2004, the population peaked at 3.83 million, according to the government of Puerto Rico (Bezares Salinas and Cartagena Colón 2012). Since then, every year there are fewer people living on the island. In 2012, the resident population was 3.69 million.

The Puerto Rican population will continue to decrease steadily, as there will be more deaths than births, unless there is a sizable surge in the number of births or substantial net immigration. Since 1990, almost every year, fewer babies were born than the previous year, and the trend intensified in the last decade (see Figure 2). In 2012, according to the U.S. Census Bureau, there were 35 percent more Puerto Rican residents aged 22 than babies less than one year old. In 1990, 66,555 babies were born on the island, representing a fertility rate of 71.25 births per 1,000 women between 15 and 49 years of age. In 2010, births were 42,203—a drop of 37 percent in 20 years—which is a fertility rate of 46.55 babies per 1,000 women between 15 and 49 years of age. The rate for children born in 2012 was about 1.6. At that rate, for

FIGURE 2. Births in Puerto Rico

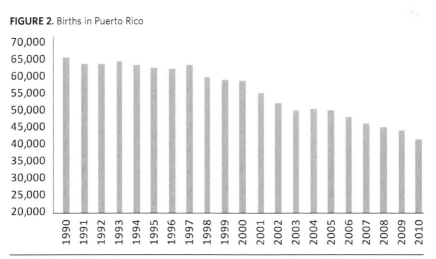

Source: Estadísticas vitales de PR 2009 y 2010-Depto. de Salud

every three babies born, one more would be needed to ensure long-term population replacement.

During the period of 2010 to 2012, there were still about 14 births for every 10 deaths. But net external emigration was about 0.8 percent of the total population per year. The result was that for every 10 births, by adding deaths to net emigrants, there were more than 13 losses. This resulted in a per-annum population loss of 0.4 percent, which should accelerate given current patterns so that some time between 2020 and 2025, deaths will exceed births. By 2025, the U.S. Census Bureau foresees a population loss of 0.9 percent per year. Additionally, the remaining population would be much more aged, with a median age of 42.9 years, up from 37.8 years in 2012, a jump of 5.1 years in just 13 years. In 2040, the median age is estimated be 48.4 years. In sum, Puerto Rico is on the verge of accelerated population decay.

Migration From and To Puerto Rico

Migratory flows, as mentioned, have been responsible for a significant net loss of population in Puerto Rico every year since the middle of the past decade. Nevertheless, for the future, structurally, low fertility might be even more worrisome. If younger people leave the island now because there are not enough good jobs, in the future, more islanders will be retiring than entering the workforce, as happens already in many European countries. If emigration does not diminish in the next decade, and there is still substantial net emigration from Puerto Rico, the country would be in an accelerated demographic death spiral, as is already the case of many Eastern European countries, like Ukraine, Romania, Hungary, or Bulgaria.

The exact itemized breakdowns per countries of current migratory flows are far from clear. If in most demographic statistics, timely accuracy is not always easy to get, in migration statistics, exactitude is even more difficult for both technical and political reasons. Anywhere in the world, it takes some time for census authorities to document the numbers of either nationals or migrants, who have left or entered to stay indefinitely. Where there is a lot of illegal immigration, as was the case in United States and Spain a few years ago, it is not easy for politicians to acknowledge this fact and promptly disclose the real numbers.

As for migration to the States according the 2010 census, 4.6 million Puerto Ricans live in the continental United States, up from 3.4 million in 2000 (see Table 1). This means that more Puerto Ricans now live in

TABLE 1. Puerto Rican midyear population (thousands)

Years	Puerto Rico migrants in the USA	Cumulative PR migrants since 1900	Puerto Rican residents in the USA, at the end of each decade	Difference between Puerto Ricans in the USA and cumulative PR migrants since 1900
1900-1910	2,000	2,000	1,513	-487
1900-1920	11,000	13,000	11,811	-1,189
1920-1930	42,000	55,000	52,774	-2,226
1930-1940	18,000	73,000	69,967	-3,033
1940-1950	151,000	224,000	226,110	2,110
1950-1960	470,000	694,000	892,513	198,513
1960-1970	214,000	908,000	1,391,463	483,463
1970-1980	65,817	973,817	2,014,000	1,040,183
1980-1990	116,571	1,090,388	2,728,000	1,637,612
1990-2000	130,185	1,220,573	3,406,178	2,185,605
2000-2010	N/A	N/A	N/A	N/A

Source: Whalen (2001); author's own analysis.

the States than live in Puerto Rico. But this view can be misleading. The census head count tells us how many residents of the United States have identified themselves as Puerto Ricans, but this figure is the sum of residents who have actually been born on the island and their descendants who were born in the United States. Those born in the United States are much more numerous than those born on the island. In the twentieth century, a total of 1.2 million Puerto Ricans emigrated to the United States (Whalen 2005). At the end of last century, there were 2 million more Puerto Ricans who had been born in the United States than had emigrated throughout the century. Also affecting the statistics are emigrants who had already died and those who returned to the island. Of the 1.2 million increase of Puerto Ricans in the United States between 2000 and 2010, according to the census, no more than 30 percent to 40 percent are island-born Boricuas who actually left the island during the past decade to live in the North. According to *El Nuevo Día*, in total, 1.5 million Puerto Rico-born Boricuas live in the United States, which represents around 31 percent of the total, compared with 69 percent who were born in the United States (Delgado 2013).

Emigration typically has an aging effect on the home country because fewer elderly than young people emigrate. According to data from the U.S. Census Bureau and the American Community Survey (ACS) 2000–2011 (Birson 2013), Puerto Ricans age 65 years represent 14 percent of the island population, but only 6.9 percent in that age range are emigrants in the States. Similarly, people within the 55–64 age bracket, again represent 12.8 percent for of the island population, but only 6.9 percent of emigrants in the States. This is similar to the situation of migrants worldwide. Romanian immigrants in Spain, for example, a country to which about 4 percent of Romanians emigrated in the past decade, are a median of six years younger than their homeland compatriots.

Economic Impact of Demographic Decay in Puerto Rico

The economic impact for Puerto Rico of population loss and aging seems clearly negative, in terms of lower GDP today and of reduced expectations for the future. This scenario, in turn, could damage the willingness of wealth managers to make long-term investments in the island unless they are directed at creating more exporting capacity and products and services for the elderly. It also poses other political and human challenges described earlier in this chapter. As for the economic damage, though, it is hard to estimate it with reasonable accuracy in the short run, without a thorough study that is not the object of this paper, for two main reasons, at least: 1) even if demographic change has much impact, the economy is also subject to many fluctuations and influences that are not linked to it, especially in the short term, and 2) the technical and political difficulties mentioned earlier in this paper concerning measuring population accurately, without too much delay.[4]

The following analysis is according to a study by Banco Popular of Puerto Rico (2012: 1):

Annual population estimates for the last decade reveal that the population decline began in 2005, shortly before the current recession began in 2006. Between 2006 and 2010, population and real GDP decreased on average 0.5 and 1.8 percent every year, respectively. A decrease in population leads to fewer income earners, fewer consumers and fewer taxpayers.
More than a quarter of the decline in real GDP can be attributed to the decline in population since the average decline in population (0.5 percent) represents about 27 percent of the average decline in real GDP (1.8

percent). The impact on economic growth could have been even larger considering that outward migration has fueled the population decline and that more productive individuals are relatively more likely to migrate.

To make things worse, Puerto Rico's economy is suffering structural problems on top of those resulting from demographic changes, which foster emigration and hence amplify the island demographic decay (Meléndez 2011).

It is even less clear how much Puerto Rican GDP per capita is affected now by demographic decay and how much will be affected in the future. Theoretically, if the decrease in the percentage of population is higher than the reduction in GDP, actual wealth per capita could even grow. But it is hard to imagine how such an increase in per-capita GDP might indeed happen in the long run.

What Are Europeans Doing to Fight Demographic Winter

In this last section of the chapter, we will try to provide possible solutions for Puerto Rico's demographic woes, in part, by looking at what is being done in Europe to fight demographic decay.

In the European Union, several major initiatives are being proposed and implemented to cope with aging and the threat of population shrinkage on two major fronts: adapting to the new demographic scenario and fostering births.

Another interesting work stream in Europe is called "active aging," trying to take advantage of the fact that not only do we live longer now, but we also enjoy more years with a healthy life. Hence, individuals should retire later in life, and by being an active worker more years and a retiree for fewer years, the economy and the pension toll for the state would both benefit. In Spain, for instance, retirement age has recently been raised from 65 to 67 years, with a transition period to that higher age. (The transition is being shortened with respect to initial government plans.)

Postponing retirement is a logical idea, but it also poses major new challenges, like higher unemployment rates for people over 50 and extra costs for companies, because senior employees in Europe, and probably most everywhere, tend to have notably higher salaries than younger workers. But if their career has stagnated since they were 50-plus or 60 (for instance, if they were promoted for the last time when they were 40, and now they are 55 years old and believe that they will not have more promotions), their motivation suffers and with it, their productivity. In such cases, they tend to have a ratio of salary to productivity much less profitable for companies than people 10 or 20 years younger, who are much more motivated, have more personal stamina, and generally require lower salaries. In the past, with a classic population pyramid, companies did not care much about this, because they were overpaying elderly people, who were not as numerous as they are now, for their experience. The result is that older workers are the main target in restructuring processes. And once unemployed between the ages of 50 and 60, they have a hard time finding a job again. Indeed, the jobless rates of people over 50 to 55 are very high in Europe, and they are also increasing in the United States.

In general, the traditionally generous welfare state in Western Europe with respect to pensions and health care benefits is being restructured and trimmed, because of the Great Recession in the short term and of the bad demographic prospects in the long run.

On top of postponing retirement age, and particularly in countries like Spain that are reconsidering formulas to calculate pensions with the goal of containing their increase in the future due to demographics, other changes include: health care co-payments by patients are increasing in diverse countries; more out-of-pocket charges are being instituted for medicines and medical services that until recently were provided cost free, or almost cost free, by the state; promoting saving through tax cuts and in private pension funds as an alternative or complement to public pensions in the future.

Finally, with respect to ways to stimulate and facilitate having more children, there is a wide array of national policies occurring in Europe, with varying results. Typically, they consist of generous paid leaves of absence for mothers, state payments to parents per child, income-tax cuts tied to the number of children, free day-care centers for working parents and other benefits, especially for larger families, and awareness campaigns. Some examples are the following:

1. *Paid leave from work per baby.* Paychecks range from 70 percent to 100 percent of the mother's salary. The most generous country in number of weeks is Sweden, with a span ranging from 55 to 68 weeks (the higher amount is if both parents share the leave for at least 12 weeks), followed by Bulgaria (55 weeks), Norway (47 weeks), Denmark (44 weeks) and United Kingdom (39 weeks).

2. *Subsidies and tax cuts per child.* In Germany, the most generous country in subsidizing family growth, regardless of their income level, families receive around 180 euros per month per child if they have one to two

children, about 190 euros per month for the third child, and over 210 euros for the fourth and successive children. This continues in all cases, until the respective children are 18 years old. In many other countries, there are state allowances per child and/or one-time bonuses per birth. For instance, in Spain, the government introduced in 2007 the so called "baby check" of 2,500 euros per newborn, a subsidy that was terminated by the end of 2010 due to Spain's huge fiscal crisis. This kind of monetary aid also can be complemented with income-tax cuts linked to the number of non-adult dependents of the taxpayer.

3. *Public pro-babies campaigns.* France, one the European countries traditionally highly worried by low fertility, in part because of its much more populated German neighbor, has made public campaigns with the slogan *La France a besoin d'enfants* (France needs kids). German Chancellor, Angela Merkel, as well, is talking more and more often about this need for Germany. Russian President Vladimir Putin is doing the same.

On top of these specific initiatives or policies, in most of Europe, the cost of medical attention for pregnant women and baby delivery is provided for free. The same applies to health care and education for children, which can be totally free or obtained at a modest co-payment. There are other kinds of legal protections for parents, generally for the mother. In Spain, pregnant and post-delivery women have a special protection against being fired. And, if they want to work part-time in order to have more time with their children, they enjoy the same anti-layoff protection as pregnant women until their youngest child is eight years old.

Are these (costly) policies aimed at fostering fertility working? Generally speaking, the answer is no, but more so in some countries than in others. Germany is dedicating enormous sums to this, with almost no results, according to official fertility rates (no more than 1.4 children per woman), as was explained in an article published in February 2013, in the prestigious German magazine *Der Spiegel*, titled "A 200-Billion-Euro Waste: Why Germany Is Failing to Boost Its Birth Rate" (Dettmer, Marcus; Hülsen, Isabell; Müller, Peter; Neubacher, Alexander; Sauga, Michael; Tietz, Janko, 2013). In other countries, highly emphasizing fertility and providing substantial state aid for people having more children, like France, Sweden, or the United Kingdom, the fertility rate recovered in the past decade to come close to replacement levels until 2010. The rate has tended to fall again since then.

In the more fertile countries, global birth rates are boosted by between 0.1 and 0.2 children per woman by the contribution in babies of foreign immigrants, who are more fertile than nationals. Russia, where President Putin has made increasing birth rates a top national priority in recent years and is now providing generous packages of state aid for parents, seems to be achieving some success in increasing birth rates, as well, but it is probably still too soon to be sure of the size and of the persistence in time of such surge in fertility.

On the other hand, in the United States, where public aid for having children is much lower than it is in Europe, fertility levels are in line with France, Sweden or the United Kingdom, close to replacement levels but below them, and going down recently, although immigrants are having more children than native citizens. The lesson to be learned from these comparisons, and from the cases of Germany or Switzerland (wealthy countries with low fertility) and many other countries, is that if people do not want to have children unless public aid is really extraordinary. And, if people view children as a wonder and a high priority in life, as in the past, they will have them, regardless of the existence of public aid.

Having few children is a core part of the blueprint of modern society. In our opinion, it is very harmful for long-term well being. But it is a fact, whether we like it or not. And it will not change solely because of more public aid. A sweeping change in mentality and prevalent values in our societies would be needed for this.

What Might Be Done In Puerto Rico to Improve Its Demographic Outlook

Unfortunately, as described in this chapter, there are substantial reasons other than low fertility and aging for the demographic problem in Puerto Rico: high emigration due to its unique links with the United States and lack of jobs linked to its internal economic and social problems. As noted, there are no easy recipes to recover fertility.

On the plus side, without considering migration flows, it is good to remember that the fertility rate in Puerto Rico (approximately 1.6 children per woman currently) is not as low as it is in countries like Japan, Germany, Spain, or Italy, which range from 1.3 to 1.4 births per woman. And since the Puerto Rican population is still relatively young as a whole—at least compared to these other countries—there will still be more births than deaths, at least for a few years. Hence, considering just births and deaths, there is still some time ahead to act before Puerto Rico demographic decay becomes much more substantial.

For Puerto Rico to adapt to a country with a growing aged population, the active aging policies of Europe and the reforms made in pension systems might provide some good ideas that government can probably adopt as well as learn from their mistakes in making public policy.

It seems clear that Puerto Rican economic difficulties, its gap in per-capita income with the United States or the crime rates in the island (now higher in murders per 100,000 people than in countries like Mexico) are good reasons for many working-age Boricuas to move to the United States and for investors to be lured by other places. Violent crime is also very bad for tourism. All this, in turn, reduces even further the availability of jobs in Puerto Rico. Improvements in such structural problems would certainly help to reduce migration rates. The long-term demographic woes of Puerto Rico, linked to low fertility and amplified by emigration, are a reason to consider such structural problems as essential priorities for the government and Puerto Rican elites, beyond their short-term importance.

An additional task for the Puerto Rican government in this regard, in order to add population and jobs to the island, would be to try to attract more retired people from the United States as occurs in Florida, or with respect to Northern Europeans retiring in Spain, especially in certain areas of its south and east coasts and the Canary and Balearic Islands. Retirees spend their pensions in a warmer and more pleasant place, and in many cases buy houses there. Unfortunately, for this purpose as well, high criminality rates in Puerto Rico act as a deterrent. Everybody likes to live in low-crime areas, but for older people this might be even more important than for the rest of us.

Given the partial success or failure of policies in Europe to increase birth rates, there are also useful lessons to be learned, but no panacea to be found. Moreover, public aid for babies is costly for taxpayers, many of whom are parents themselves.

In any case, actions that might help improve fertility and birth rates in Puerto Rico and could be an option to explore and implement, would include the following:

1. **Invest more public and private resources in demographic knowledge, prompter and more accurate demographic figures; and better understanding of the reasons for demographic decay and possible solutions.** Accurate demographic knowledge is very important for the issue that we are dealing with in this paper, but also for economic

planning for public and private agents. Official statistical information in Puerto Rico about demography and demographic phenomena, in the opinion of the author of this paper, provides less and more outdated information than in some European countries, where information is not always reliable.[5]

2. **Make of fertility a top government priority, without forgetting the local angle.** This cannot be a secondary item in the public agenda, given its importance and the difficulty that its full solution entails. This should translate into reviewing the laws with a direct or indirect impact on fertility and family. Having children and raising them must be facilitated by laws, and not obstructed. Currently, many countries have diverse regulations with negative impact on fertility. At a local level, since not all regions in any country have equally intense demographic woes, and local politicians are paid for the welfare of their respective territories, specific things can also be done, especially in those areas with the worst demographic profiles (lower fertility, higher aging, and more emigration, as in the case of Puerto Rico). In Spain, for instance, there are provinces with 50 percent more fertility than others; provinces with a population 10 years older in average than others; provinces with endemic population loss, and others where the number of inhabitants is still growing.

3. **Increase awareness by Puerto Ricans.** Puerto Ricans must become knowledgeable about how the demographic problems of low birth rate can affect the national decay of their country and about how good and satisfying it is for an integral life to have babies. And very importantly, that people try to have children not so late in life, because in our time, many women and men postpone family formation so much that, when they finally decide to do it, they are too old to have kids, or at least to have as many as they would have desired. It is good that Puerto Rico becomes aware of the problems it will face if so few babies are born, and provides more help to those who actually have them. But it is even more important that young and middle-aged people, in fertile ages, recover the sense that babies and kids widely compensate the cost and effort needed to raise them. Without this kind of positive stimulus of having babies because people believe again that they compensate by themselves, many people will continue not having kids, even if papers like this one tell them that their country will decay heavily with so few children.

There is an additional difficulty in Puerto Rico in making people understand that low fertility is a major structural problem. For so many years, the public has heard and read that there was a risk of overpopulation in Puerto Rico and in the rest of the world. So it may sound strange for many to hear the opposite warning. So, the sooner Puerto Ricans understand it, the better for eventually generating a positive reaction. Some nations, like France and Sweden, have understood better than others that a bad demographic trend is dangerous for them, and have been fostering fertility since many years now. Other countries, like Germany or Russia, seem to be reacting to this only as their demographic health has reached a point of heavy impairment. And yet there are other countries like Japan, Italy, or Spain, where, despite their advanced stage of demographic winter season, have had no clear reaction to it.

4. **Provide public assistance and benefits to families with children.** In this respect, the author favors cuts on direct income and Social Security taxes linked to the number of children of taxpayers and bonuses in pensions linked to the number of children of the pensioner. This is fair because people with more children are having extra costs and making more personal efforts in creating a benefit for society. It can be done with close to no net cost in tax revenue if the tax and public pension systems are designed to be neutral for people with, for instance, two children.

5. **Finance fertility treatments.** Finally, as science can help couples conceive and conceive later in life, public funds should be available for assisted-reproductive treatments (ART). In Spain, for instance, it is estimated that between 2 percent and 3 percent of the babies result from assisted-reproductive treatments adding 0.02 to 0.04 children per woman to the total fertility rate of the country. In Denmark, the estimates are that 6 percent of all babies, 0.1 more children per woman, are born with the use of ART. If fertility treatments where used more often in Puerto Rico, with rates of success falling between those of Spain and Denmark, the island would gain about from 0.06 to 0.07 more children per woman, more than 10 percent of the current gap in births needed to reach replacement levels, a non-negligible amount. And the good thing of ART is that its patients indeed want to have children, unlike so many people in our time.

ACKNOWLEDGMENTS

I would like to thank Carlos Vargas-Ramos and Edwin Meléndez for their help and suggestions, contributing substantially to the final shape of this essay. Moreover, their critiques and corrections are taken in the vein of Sir Winston Churchill, when he said: "Criticism may not be agreeable, but it is necessary. It fulfills the same function as pain in the human body. It calls attention to an unhealthy state of things."

NOTES

[1] Fertility replacement rate is the average number of children that women should have so that, within one generation (now around 30 years), the number of women is the same than in the previous generation. Since more men than women are born (typically, 5% - 6% more, except in countries with massive selective abortion or infanticide of female babies, like in some very populated Asian nations, where population pyramids with much higher ratios of males to females at early ages would indicate that between 6% and 12% of all baby females would be killed), and some women still die before reaching and ending their fertile years, in developed nations, replacement threshold is currently 2.1 children per woman, not just two. In the past, and in countries with still high infant and sub-adult mortality (or selective female infanticide), more children per woman are needed to ensure replacement. Two centuries ago, anywhere, no less than an average of four children per woman was needed for population replacement.

[2] These projected numbers are not a forecast, since almost certainly the values of underlying variables used for calculating them will change in time. But they are reasonably good for illustrating and understanding how fertile-aged population would tend to shrink in a country with 1.32 children per woman.

[3] See http://www.guardian.co.uk/world/2013/jan/22/elderly-hurry-up-die-japanese/.

[4] As mentioned earlier, it took two full years for a country as developed as Germany to release the figures from their 2011 census.

[5] For a glimpse of Eurostat information on demography see: http://epp.eurostat.ec.europa.eu/portal/page/portal/statistics/search_database/.

REFERENCES

Banco Popular de Puerto Rico. 2012. Población y crecimiento económico. *Progreso Económico* January and February. http://www.afppr.com/cms/images/stories/progreso.english.pdf/.

Bahrampour, Tara. 2012. For first time since Depression, more Mexicans leave U.S. than enter. Washingtonpost.com. Accessed 23 April 2012. http://articles.washingtonpost.com/2012-04-23/local/35453567_1_arrests-of-illegal-immigrants-immigrant-advocates-mexicans/.

Birson, Kurt. 2013. Puerto Rican Migration in the 21st Century: Is There a Brain Drain? In *The State of Puerto Ricans 2013*, eds. Edwin Meléndez and Carlos Vargas-Ramos. 27–31. New York: Center for Puerto Rican Studies.

Bezares Salinas, Mari Luz and Marianne Cartagena Colón. 2012. Informe Anual de Estadísticas Vitales 2009 y 2010. Nacimientos, matrimonios y divorcios. San Juan: Secretaría Auxiliar de Planificación y Desarrollo del Departamento de Salud, Gobierno de Puerto Rico.

Delgado, José A. 2013. Crece con fuerza la diáspora puertorriqueña. *El Nuevo Día* 21 June.

Destatis. 2013. Census: 80.2 million inhabitants lived in Germany on 9 May 2011. Wiesbaden (Germany): Statistisches Bundesamt

Dettmer, Marcus; Hülsen, Isabell; Müller, Peter; Neubacher, Alexander; Sauga, Michael; Tietz, Janko. 2013. A 200-Billion-Euro Waste: Why Germany Is Failing to Boost Its Birth Rate. *Spiegel Online International – Der Spiegel* 5 February. http://www.spiegel.de/international/germany/study-shows-germany-wasting-billions-on-failed-family-policy-a-881637.html/.

Ehrlich, Paul R. 1968. *The Population Bomb*. New York: Ballantine Books.

Goldman, David P. 2013. Israel's Demographic Miracle. *In Focus Quarterly* Spring. http://www.jewishpolicycenter.org/4058/israel-demographic-miracle/.

Macarrón Larumbe, Alejandro. 2011. El suicidio dpegao618@aol.comfico de España. Madrid: Homo Legens. http://www.homolegens.com/catalogo/catalogo/139-suicidio-demografico/.

Meléndez, Edwin. 2011. Understanding Puerto Rico's Economy and its Political Status. New York: Center for Puerto Rican Studies, Hunter College, CUNY.

Meléndez, Edwin and Carlos Vargas-Ramos, eds. 2013. *The State of Puerto Ricans, 2013*. New York: Center for Puerto Rican Studies.

Retiro de la Junta de Directores de la Fundación Comunitaria de Puerto Rico Humacao.

Takáts, Elöd. 2010. Aging and asset prices. BIS Working papers. Basel, Switzerland) Bank for International Settlements. http://www.bis.org/publ/work318.pdf/.

Whalen, Carmen Teresa and Víctor Vázquez-Hernández, eds. 2005. *The Puerto Rican Diaspora: Historical Perspectives*. Philadelphia: Temple University Press.

Asthma and Diabetes within the Puerto Rican Population

ANNA ROSOFSKY and JUDITH APONTE

The wellness of Puerto Ricans in the United States is challenged by a number of health conditions. According to 2001 data, Puerto Ricans had the highest rate of cancer, the highest diagnosis rate of diabetes, the highest infant mortality rate, and the highest prevalence of asthma diagnosis and hospitalizations among all Hispanic subgroups, (Pinherio et al. 2009). This chapter will focus on the two health conditions that have garnered much attention over the past decade for their prevalence among Puerto Ricans and for their particular impact on the wellness of the population: asthma and diabetes. These two health conditions are impacted by several different but interrelated factors— biologic, genetic, environmental, and socioeconomic. Due to the multifactorial nature of these diseases, it has been difficult for researchers to parse out one principal cause for either diabetes or asthma. Therefore, a curative remedy has been difficult to develop. Despite multiple approaches over the years to developing preventative measures for both diabetes and asthma, both conditions have been found to be extremely costly for families and the country's health care system.

The U.S. Census Bureau (2001) classifies Hispanics as a single ethnic group that can be classified into one of multiple race categories. Although Hispanics are classified as one ethnic group, share a common language and a similar cultural heritage, they are a heterogeneous group (Aponte, 2009a). Race, according to the U.S. Census Bureau (2001), is classified into either "one race" (i.e., White, Black or African American, Asian, American Indian or Alaska Native, Native Hawaiian or Other Pacific Islander, or some other race) or "two or more races.". The definition of race reflects how a person self-identifies. Hence, the different racial classifications for Hispanics show the complexity and difficulty of classifying the Hispanic population as a homogeneous group (Aponte, 2009a).

Given that race is a socially constructed identity with no scientific basis, it can't be used to explain the heterogeneity or genetic admixture among Hispanic subgroups (Witzig 1996). For example, studies by Centers for Disease

Control and Prevention (CDC 2003), Flegal et al. (1991), and Aponte (2009a) demonstrate that certain Hispanic subgroups, tend to be more susceptible to diabetes than others because of genetic differences, discounting the idea that all "Hispanics" are equally susceptible to the same diseases. This is also the case with asthma, where the presence of specific, identified genes impacts the phenotypic response to asthma triggers, even within the same subgroup. We will discuss health disparities between the Puerto Rican population and other races and ethnicities and the new types of research undertaken to address the role of race in health disparities within the Puerto Rican population.

Asthma

Puerto Ricans have the highest prevalence of asthma among all population groups in the United States. As of 2010, 25.1 percent of Puerto Ricans were diagnosed with asthma (U.S. Census 2010). The average rate of asthma diagnosis from 2008–2010 among mainland Puerto Ricans was 113 percent higher than non-Hispanic whites and 50 percent higher than non-Hispanic blacks (Akinbami et al. 2011). Puerto Ricans living in Puerto Rico have also seen increasing rates of asthma (Ortega et al. 2003; Perez-Perdomo et al. 2003). Among Hispanics, those of Mexican descent have the lowest (9.4%) asthma rates (see Figure 1). In addition, the rate of asthma attacks and hospitalizations are also highest among Puerto Ricans compared with all other races and ethnicities. As indicated by these data, asthma has become one of the foremost and ubiquitous health issues for the Puerto Rican population.

Asthma is a chronic lung disease characterized by periods of reversible airflow obstruction known as "asthma attacks" (NHLB Institute 2012). People with asthma have inflamed airways, whereby certain exposures will obstruct airflow through inflammation and airway hyper reactivity (contraction of the small muscles surrounding the airways). These exposures may include allergens, air pollution such as ozone, nitrogen oxides and particulate matter, airborne irritants (cigarette smoke, dust), physical activity, and viral upper respiratory infection such as colds.

Asthma is typically diagnosed via a lung function test, chest x-ray or airway sensitivity test. Currently there is no cure for asthma; however, the means to control and prevent exacerbations are well established: avoiding asthma triggers, creating a personalized action plan with a doctor based on levels of asthma severity, and taking medications for long-term control of asthma, such as steroids, or quick-relief medications that relieve asthma symptoms that might flare up.

FIGURE 1. Asthma Prevalence in the United States, 2010

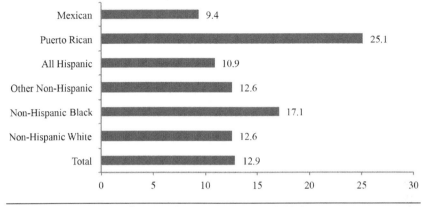

Source: Table 2-1, Lifetime Asthma Prevalence Percentages, NHIS, 2010.

Costs

Not only do the families of those with asthma suffer enormous burdens dealing with financial cost and emotional stress, but asthma has also become a huge liability for the country. As of 2007, the annual direct health care cost of asthma was approximately $50.1 billion and the indirect costs (e.g., lost productivity) added another $5.9 billion, for a staggering total cost of $56.0 billion (American Lung Association 2012).

The 2007 Great Recession was found to exacerbate the costs of asthma to families (Pearlman 2012). Due to the loss of income and/or the loss of health insurance, medications and health care visits may no longer be affordable, and families are less able to properly manage asthma (Pearlman 2012). In addition, uncertainty about future job security during a recession can create stress and depression for both unemployed and employed workers, making a parent's ability to cope with their children's asthma management more difficult both physically and mentally.

Between 2007 and 2010, the number of children with employer-based coverage fell by 3.4 million due to unemployment (Pearlman 2012). The rate of private insurance coverage during this period of time decreased across all races and ethnicities in the United States and the rate of those covered on Medicaid greatly increased (see Figure 2a). During this time, children who experienced a gap in health insurance were at increased risk of poorly controlled asthma compared with children who had continued insurance coverage (Pearlman 2012).

FIGURE 2A. Medicaid Coverage for Persons Under 65 Years of Age, 2006–2010, by Ethnicity

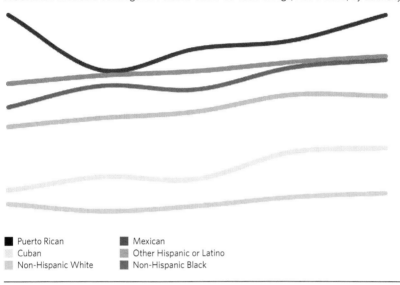

■ Puerto Rican   ■ Mexican
   Cuban   ▨ Other Hispanic or Latino
▨ Non-Hispanic White   ■ Non-Hispanic Black

Source: U.S. Census Bureau.

FIGURE 2B. Private Health Insurance Coverage for Persons under 65 Years of Age, 2006–2010, by Ethnicity

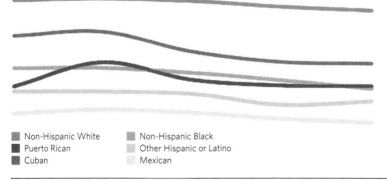

▨ Non-Hispanic White   ▨ Non-Hispanic Black
■ Puerto Rican   ▨ Other Hispanic or Latino
■ Cuban   ▨ Mexican

Source: U.S. Census Bureau.

As displayed in Figure 2b, Puerto Ricans had one of the most severe drops in private health insurance (from 54% in 2007 to 46% in 2010). Because health insurance is most often provided by an employer, this drop in private health insurance coverage may indicate high rates of unemployment. In fact, during this time, Puerto Ricans extensively increased their rate of public insurance coverage, from 28 percent to 36 percent (Figure 2a) further supporting this finding.

Disparities

Researchers have almost unanimously found that asthma is more prevalent among the Puerto Rican population than among all races and ethnicities in the United States (Akinbami 2002; Lara et al. 2006; Ledogar 2000; Schwartz 1990; Tran 2011). The disparity between Puerto Ricans and all other races and ethnicities in the United States has been heavily documented in the literature (Cagney 2007; Canino 2007; Lara et al. 2006; Ledogar 2000).

Factors that have been implicated to explain higher incidence of asthma include nativity, gene-environment interactions; access to asthma health care resources, family poverty, and genetics (Coultas et al. 1994; Findley et al. 2003; Koinis-Mitchell et al. 2011). As displayed in Figure 2a and Figure 2b, Puerto Ricans have higher rates of insurance coverage than other groups, which may account for their generally higher rates of diagnosis. There are two principal reasons for the association between being insured and higher asthma rates. First, uninsured persons with asthma who are hospitalized for asthma are often encouraged to enroll in a public insurance plan for which they qualify (Ledogar 2000). As noted by Ledogar, the finding that more Puerto Ricans have health insurance than do other Latinos would therefore be consistent with higher rates of asthma among them (Ledogar 2000 p. 934). Second, asthma among the uninsured is more likely to go undiagnosed, or conversely, there may be an over-diagnosis of asthma among the insured.

Currently, little is understood in the way of preventative measures for asthma, which partly explains the persistence of asthma among the general and Puerto Rican populations (Koinis-Mitchell 2011).

Genetics and Asthma

With the advent of genome-wide-association studies, an increasing number of suspected risk genes linked to asthma susceptibility have come to light, many of which have been identified within Puerto Rican populations (Torgerson 2011). For instance, a handful of studies have identified genetic differences that cause asthma susceptibility. In a 2011 study combining genomic data from 5,416 people with asthma, scientists found a genetic variation in a gene called PYHIN1 that was association with a 34 percent higher risk of asthma in African Americans and Afro-Caribbeans. Approximately 30 percent of those in the study who were of African ancestry inherited this genetic variant, including Puerto Ricans of African ancestry (Torgerson et al. 2011). Similarly, the epigenetic and genetic variations in the gene ADCYAP1R1 were found to be associated with asthma in Puerto Rican children in a separate study, along with chromosomal regions that may harbor genes for asthma in Puerto Ricans (Chen 2013; Choudhry 2008). A Connecticut study also found a relative risk of 2.49 among children whose mothers had been diagnosed with asthma for all races and ethnicities, indicating that asthma can be inherited (Becket et al. 1996).

Researchers have also found genetic variations between Hispanics of Puerto Rican and Mexican descent in their responses to albuterol, the most commonly prescribed treatment for asthma attacks worldwide (Burchard et al. 2004; Choudhry et al. 2004). It is known that the Puerto Rican population does not respond well to albuterol, and pharmacologists are working to create another medication. Albuterol acts as receptor to the gene that is used to mediate bronchial smooth muscle relaxation. Researchers found that genetic variation in the Albuterol-receptor-gene is present in Puerto Ricans but not Mexicans. Those possessing this genetic variation have significantly more airway obstruction and lower response to albuterol, which impacts the length and severity of asthma attacks (Choudhry et al. 2004).

Another approach to explaining asthma disparity is the study of the genetic association of ancestry to asthma. Phenotypic variations within the Hispanic population have implications for demographic data, such as U.S. Census Bureau and NHIS data. Within Hispanic subgroups, such as Mexicans, Puerto Ricans, and Cubans, there is significant genetic heterogeneity originating primarily in Europe. Many Latinos, including Puerto Ricans, often identify themselves as mixed race in self-reported surveys, which poses a challenge in studying health differences between races (Landale and Oropesa 2002; Vega et al. 2009).

Researchers have sought to overcome this obstacle in health data reporting by examining health outcomes based on ancestry, rather than self-reported race. In a recent study by Galanter et al. (2011), researchers found that those of Puerto Rican ethnicity had both European and African ancestry, while Mexicans were predominately of Native American ancestry. These differences might account for the heterogeneity in genes associated with asthma among those of the same ethnicity that makes some people more vulnerable to asthma triggers than others. Researchers also identified a higher number of genetic risk factors for asthma within the Puerto Rican population compared with the Mexican population, although heterogeneity with respect to these risks existed within the same ethnicity. In a separate study examining Puerto Rican ancestry with respect to asthma, researchers found that at low socioeconomic status, those of European ancestry had an increased risk of asthma, while African ancestry was associated with an increased risk of asthma for those of high socioeconomic status, suggesting a complex gene-environment interaction (Choudhry et al. 2006).

The field of uncovering genetic risk factors linked to disease is new and evolving. No studies have been released that have examined the removal of these asthma-linked genes to monitor asthma outcomes. However, this approach to asthma research seems to be a promising solution to a major causal factor.

Environmental Factors, Built Environment, and Allergens

Asthma is generally considered to be an immunologically mediated disease, in which abnormal immune response to inhaled agents provokes exacerbation of symptoms associated with the disease. Environmental risks factors for asthma include cigarette smoking, urban residence, outdoor air exposure (ozone, particulate matter, and hazardous air pollutants), exposure to environmental tobacco smoke (as secondhand smoke), and allergens, such as mold, insects, gas stoves and pets. Poor housing quality and disproportionate environmental pollution, burdens regularly found in low-income, minority urban neighborhoods, are consistently associated with higher exposure to the very environmental pollutants that lead to the development and exacerbation of asthma (Corburn et al. 2006).

In examining residential location as a factor contributing to asthma, Puerto Ricans have been found to live in geographic locations that have high rates of asthma hospitalizations and asthma severity relative to the rest of the population (Corburn et al. 2006; Findley et al. 2003). These typically urban neighborhoods are characteristically low income and dominated by substandard housing wrought with rodents in the home, cockroaches, peeling paint and the resulting dust, environmental tobacco smoke, and various additional sources of pollution, such as diesel exhaust and environmental particulates that tend to linger in outdoor air (Findley et al. 2003). Here is a prime example of environmental inequality, where "biases within environmental policy making and the regulatory process combine with discriminatory market forces, result in disproportionate exposures to hazardous pollution among the poor and communities of color," which plays an important role in the role in the complex and persistent patterns of disparate asthma rates (Morello-Frosch et al. 2013: 149).

New York City is a prime example of this environmental inequality, where those living in neighborhoods with elevated asthma hospitalization rates were five times more likely to be living in public housing, three times more likely to be living in housing units classified as dilapidated, and more likely overall to be concentrated in areas with a high density of polluting facilities compared with those living outside areas of elevated asthma (Corburn et al. 2006). These identified "hot spots" of asthma in New York City have some of the highest Puerto Rican populations in the United States, especially in East Harlem.

East Harlem, a neighborhood of New York City, has one of the largest Puerto Rican populations and one of the highest asthma concentrations in the United States. Researchers studying this area found that Puerto Rican children were more likely to report higher frequency of asthma exacerbations and absences from school than were children of other races and ethnicities (Diaz et al. 2000; Findley et al. 2003). Similarly, in the Williamsburg neighborhood of Brooklyn, which is home to a large Puerto Rican population and is bisected by a major urban highway, is full of idling traffic, and houses the largest bus terminal in Brooklyn and the city's only radioactive waste storage facility, toxic emissions in the air are 60 times greater per square mile than the average for the United States as a whole (Ledogar 2000). Here, Puerto Ricans made up 37 percent of the study population and Dominicans made up 52 percent, and Puerto Ricans still had higher asthma rates, despite economic, cultural and ancestral similarities between the two groups. The authors hypothesize that gene-environment interaction, such as genetically determined differences in inflammatory response among Puerto Rican children, account for the disparity in asthma incidence. Environmental inequality, such as those exemplified in New York, is the primary culprit of asthma disparities according to many community activists and researchers.

Acculturation

Asthma severity and rates of acute presentation of asthma are not just related to genetics and the environment, but also to acculturation. Acculturation is defined as "psychological and social changes that groups and individuals experience when they enter a new and different cultural context" (Lara et al. 2005: 373). These cultural influences play into symptom perception, family management practices, medication beliefs, understanding of the disease, and self-management (Bailey 2009). Cultural and language barriers of immigrants pose difficulties in being able to speak to a health care provider and acquiring knowledge about general health care access. The community thereby becomes a vital source of information and, more specifically, asthma support. In the case of Puerto Rican migrants, acculturation is an important factor to consider in understanding asthma diagnosis, risk factors, and the effectiveness of clinical and public health interventions (Lara et al. 2006).

The impact of acculturation on Latino behaviors around asthma is complex, but a new wave of research has begun to explore this issue (Lara et al. 2006; Bailey 2009; Ledogar 2000; Martin et al. 2010). Researchers have found that, in general, those assumed to be "less acculturated" have poorer access to health care, lower quality health care, and inadequate medical management by both doctors and patients (Ledogar 2000; Sze 2007). These acculturative factors have also been linked to elevated asthma morbidity, service utilization, and poor quality of life (Martin et al. 2010).

In a study by Koinis-Mitchell et al. (2011) examining acculturation-related factors between different Hispanic subgroups in asthma morbidity found that Puerto Rico-born caregivers were found to experience more acculturative stress when compared with Dominican-born caregivers, and children of Puerto Rico-born caregivers also had a higher proportion of emergency department visits. Family-based supports that alleviate stress related to acculturation and the immigration process were found to greatly contribute to a family's asthma management (Koinis-Mitchell et al. 2011). The authors hypothesize that Puerto Rican families tend to be more widely dispersed throughout the U.S. and may experience more travel back and forth to Puerto Rico, which may therefore inhibit the level of social support they receive within the community (Koinis-Mitchell et al. 2011). The importance of a community connection with respect to health care was also highlighted in a study by Cagney et al. (2007) in which collective efficacy was found to promote mutually beneficial action towards environmental justice and health.

Although there might be lack of community connectedness around health, Puerto Ricans have the highest rates of public and private health insurance. Puerto Ricans are United States citizens and, therefore, can qualify for government-sponsored health insurance, such as Medicaid, giving them more access to physician visits and information about the types and proper use of medications for asthma (see Figures 2a and 2b). Despite better access to insurance and relevant health care information, several studies have found that Puerto Ricans still face barriers in attaining anti-inflammatory medication and proper asthma care (Chang 2011; Enarson and Ait 1999; Diaz et al. 2000; McQuaid et al. 2009). Puerto Rican children were found to be 72 percent more likely to have visited an emergency department in the previous year and 38 percent less likely to have visited a doctor compared with other children (Chang 2011).

Increased access to health care might also be reflected in asthma reporting data, where Mexican or other Hispanic subgroups have less opportunity to have an asthma diagnosis made by a provider (Lara et al. 2006). Research by Lara et al. (2006) showed that being insured and having a source of care when sick were associated with higher reported asthma prevalence. Therefore, the asthma disparity between Puerto Ricans and other ethnic groups may be partly attributed to higher diagnosis rates by a physician.

Diabetes

Diabetes, a chronic disease, is a common public health concern for Hispanics, although it affects Hispanic subgroups in disproportionate rates. In 2006, diabetes was the seventh-leading cause of death in the United States overall (National Institute of Diabetes and Digestive and Kidney Diseases 2011), but the fifth-leading cause of death for Hispanics (CDC n.d.). During 2007, of the 45.5 million Hispanics living in the United States, composing 15 percent of the total population (U.S. Census Bureau n.d.), 4.7 million (10.4%) had diabetes (CDC 2008). As the Hispanic population is one of the fastest-growing in the country (Kirket al. 2007), it seems likely that diabetes will become an even greater public health concern countrywide.

Although diabetes is a growing health burden for Hispanics, it affects Hispanic subgroups differently, in particular the Puerto Rican population (see Figure 3). According to the CDC (2011), in 2010 Puerto Ricans had a higher diabetes rate (11.2%) than both Mexicans (10.2%) and Cubans (7.3%). In addition, the percentage of Hispanics at risk of being diagnosed with diabetes was higher among Puerto Ricans (94%) than it was among Mexicans (87%). The U.S. Department of Health and Human Services (DHHS) (1999), report that one in every four Mexican Americans and Puerto Ricans aged 45 or older has diabetes compared with one in every six Cuban Americans. Studies have shown that those with high diabetes rates have higher rates of mortality, amputations, and diabetes-related complications (DHHS, 1999), indicating that Puerto Ricans and Mexican Americans are at higher risk for these diabetes-related health outcomes compared with Cuban Americans.

FIGURE 3A. Diabetes Prevalence in U.S. in 2010, by percent

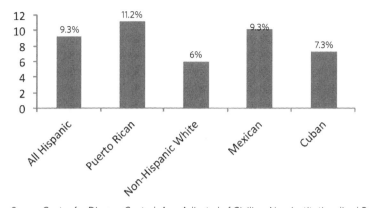

Source: Center for Disease Control. Age-Adjusted of Civilian, Non-institutionalized Population with Diagnosed Diabetes, United States, 1997–2010.

Although the reasons for diabetes-related differences among Hispanic subgroups is unclear, as Aponte (2009b) reports, diabetes-related disparities among Hispanic subgroups could potentially be due to different genetic compositions and cultural and dietary customs, thus making each subgroup unique. As with asthma, literature has emerged that examines genetic and ancestral association with diabetes in terms of linking Native American ancestry to diabetes (Hanis et al. 1991). However, the literature surrounding genetics and diabetes in Hispanic subpopulations is not well established.

As with asthma, one of the main factors that researchers attribute to diabetes disparities is a population's degree of acculturation, The literature on acculturation is mixed, showing both positive and negative associations between acculturation and the likelihood of diabetes among Latinos (Mainous et al. 2007; Perez-Escamilla and Putnik 2007). Acculturation may play a part in perceptions of breastfeeding, for instance, because research has found that those who are not breast fed are more likely to have gastrointestinal infections and be diagnosed with obesity, both risk factors for diabetes (Arenz et al. 2004; Von Kries et al. 1999). Although breastfeeding rates are typically higher among Hispanic women, they vary by acculturation status and place of birth. A recent study by Ahluwalia et al. (2012) found that Hispanic women who are more acculturated are less likely to breastfeed than those who are less acculturated. In contrast, three out of four studies reviewed by Beck (2006), showed a negative association between acculturation and breastfeeding among Latinas. In fewer than 50 percent of households in Puerto Rico, did women breastfeed compared with 90 percent of Mexican women (Pérez-Escamilla and Predrag 2007).

In addition, physical activity, dietary fat and sugar, and obesity are all impacted by acculturation and socioeconomic status (Smith et al. 2005). Higher percentages of Mexican Americans and Puerto Ricans have lower incomes and live below the poverty line than Cuban Americans, which impacts acculturation, access to health care and these risk factors (Smith et al. 2005). Research has identified that socioeconomic status, age, and movement from urban to rural areas are potential confounders when examining differences between acculturation and health-related outcomes (Perez-Escamilla, Putnik 2007). Additional research has shown that peer nutrition-education among Hispanics has a positive impact and can potentially trigger better health outcomes. Such improvements have been reported in studies utilizing peer education, which show that Hispanics have better diabetes self-management behaviors, increased breastfeeding practices, greater nutritional knowledge, and improved dietary intake behaviors as a result (Perez-Escamilla et al. 2008). The literature on acculturation of Hispanics views them as a homogenous group and has not focused on the different Hispanic subgroups. Therefore, it is essential and important to examine and identify diabetes-related disparities and acculturation among the different Hispanic subgroups.

Costs and Diabetes

As the number of people with diabetes rises, the costs for treating diabetes are also increasing at an alarming rate. Studies have shown that direct diabetes costs (e.g., medical care, medications, and supplies) are a significant burden on the United States economy. For example, the overall diabetes cost grew from $174 billion in 2007 to $245 billion in 2012, a 41 percent increase (American Diabetes Association (ADA), 2008, 2013). Of the $245 billion, $176 billion was spent on direct medical costs (e.g., inpatient care) and $69 billon on indirect costs (e.g., disability, reduced productivity). The largest component of direct medical costs attributed to diabetes is hospital inpatient care (43% of total cost), followed by diabetes medications (18%), diabetes supplies (12%), physician office visits (9%), and nursing/residential facility stays (8%) (ADA 2013).

In 2012, the indirect costs (e.g., absenteeism, reduced work performance, disability, and early mortality) related to diabetes totaled $69 billion (ADA

2013). Studies have shown that approximately 20 percent of people with diabetes incur in 80 percent of health care costs (Kahn et al. 2005). More than half (62.4%) of the diabetes costs in the United States is covered by Medicare, Medicaid and military insurances, followed by private insurance (34.4%) and uninsured (3.2%). In this time of limited financial resources and escalating health care costs, it is critical to have an understanding of the economic implications of diabetes.

Although the federal Affordable Care Act is designed to decrease the number of uninsured people in the United States, those who are insured may still have financial hardships in purchasing medications, diabetes supplies (e.g., glucometer strips), and co-payments for doctor visits. For 2012, the average diabetes medical cost incurred by a person with diabetes was $13,700 per year (ADA 2013), which impacts a person's ability to access and follow the diabetes plan of care. For example, even though Puerto Ricans have the highest rate of private and public health insurance (See Figure 2a and Figure 2b), diabetes increases a person's out-of-pocket costs, and given that Puerto Ricans have a high rate of poverty, these additional diabetes costs can potentially impact adherence to treatment and health outcomes.

Puerto Ricans and Diabetes

As the incidence of diabetes in the United States has grown at accelerated rates over the past decade, from approximately 1.2 million new cases of diagnosed diabetes cases in 2000 to 1.7 million new cases in 2010, there have been an increasing number of studies conducted on diabetes among Hispanics in the United States (NHIS 2010). The studies that examine Hispanic subpopulations all find Puerto Ricans have the highest diabetes rates (Aponte 2009a; Borrelli et al. 2009; Melnik et al. 2004; Whitman et al. 2006).

In a study by Borelli et al. (2009), the authors found that 11 percent of Puerto Ricans had diabetes, followed by Mexican Americans (10.2%), Cubans (6.2%), Dominicans (5.2%) and Central/South Americans (4%). Another study (Whitman, Silva and Shah 2006), reported that a greater percentage of Puerto Rican residents of Chicago (20.8%) had diabetes than Puerto Ricans living in New York City (11.3%) or residing in Puerto Rico (9.6%). The rate of diabetes reported in the Chicago community is the highest ever reported for Puerto Ricans and one of the highest ever reported in the United States population. The study also found a significant association of diabetes and obesity. A third study (Aponte 2009a) assessed the rate of diabetes among Puerto Ricans, Mexican

Americans, and Cuban Americans on a national scale, and the findings showed that the Hispanic subgroup with the highest rate of diabetes that also had the highest combined obese and overweight status was Puerto Ricans (82%), followed by Mexican Americans (78%) and Cuban Americans (66%). A fourth study (Melnik et al. 2004) reported that 11.3 percent of Puerto Ricans living in New York City had diabetes and that the rate of diabetes was significantly higher among those who were obese and had a family history of the disease.

Hence, this literature review gleans a lack of studies on diabetes that compare Puerto Ricans residing in Puerto Rico to those living in the United States and to other Hispanic subgroups. In addition, there is a need to examine genetic differences in Puerto Ricans with and without diabetes across Hispanic subgroups, in order to provide insight into the genetic component that make Hispanics a heterogeneous group. These studies could help health care providers with additional understanding of the uniqueness of Hispanic subgroups, allowing them to identify and effectively address each group's cultural differences.

A Call for Community Action

Asthma is multifactorial in nature, where genetics, allergens, the environment, degree of acculturation, respiratory infections, and preexisting conditions may all play a role in its incidence and severity. While there is currently no cure, especially with respect to genetics, there are various methods to control acute manifestations of asthma and to reduce exposure to the environmental factors that trigger its onset. These methods can be tailored to reduce the severity and incidence of asthma in the Puerto Rican population.

Environmental Control Methods

Environmental control practices are one of the most effective methods of managing asthma (Diette 2008). Within the Puerto Rican population, these practices are centered mostly around improvements in public housing and smoking reduction for better air quality in the indoor environment and environmental justice activism to reduce outdoor exposures to asthma triggers. Compared with non-Hispanic whites and Dominicans, Puerto Ricans appear to have more risk factors associated with smoking treatment failure, and because they are also more acculturated, they have adopted similar attitudes to non-Hispanic whites regarding smoking (Borelli et al. 2010). Culturally adapted smoking interventions must therefore be implemented to target smoking among Puerto Ricans. Additionally, improving ventilation in low-income housing to reduce particulate matter, nitrous oxide, ozone, and allergens from furred pets, dust mites, cockroaches, rodents, and molds is also necessary. These ventilation systems must be made economically feasible to residents or be provided by the public housing authorities.

National Asthma Education and Prevention Program (NAEPP) guidelines recommend that individuals with asthma avoid exertion outdoors when concentrations of certain pollutants are elevated and avoid outdoor allergens such as pollens. Avoidance decreases the likelihood of sensitization to these allergens and decreases asthma exacerbations triggered by exposure. However, there are two main problems with this recommendation. Many of the locations that have high rates of asthma also have multiple environmental pollution burdens that result in high rates of pollution year-round(Corburn 2006). Additionally, dissuading exercise in children may develop more entrenched sedentary patterns, thus encouraging the onset of obesity (Rance and O'Laughlen 2011). Obesity is very strongly associated with breathing disorders because of the effect of central body fat on the airways. Evidence also suggests that obesity may lead to the development of asthma. These guidelines should be altered so as not to encourage sedentary behaviors, especially among the Hispanic population where obesity is found at higher rates (Rance and O'Laughlen 2011).

Community outreach has therefore been the key to addressing environmental stressors on asthma. In New York City, environmental justice organizations, such as El Puente, UPROSE, South Bronx Clean Air Coalition, and West Harlem Environmental Action, have been instrumental in the environmental health movement. Their work has:

> challenged the disjuncture between the invisibility of crucial municipal service operations...and the visibility of the public perception that these neighborhoods were racially marked sites of blight, pollution and decay. The energetic nature of their challenge belied the assumption that low-income neighborhoods of color hosted compliant populations with insufficient intellectual and political resources to fight for their health and environment. (Sze 2007)

Environmental justice asthma activism also takes place in other cities with large Puerto Rican populations, such as Boston, where asthma has served as a gateway to community activism (Sze 2007). This type of work has been effective at challenging policy, increasing community empowerment and knowledge of political processes, and incorporating the precautionary principle in siting and environmental policy for potential polluters.

Acculturation-Targeted and Health Care Methods

Much of the recent literature on asthma management has focused on culturally specific programs that target acculturation and health care access. Focusing asthma prevention on genetics or controlling socioeconomic characteristics or the outdoor environment are relatively difficult objectives. However, asthma management interventions tailored to the needs of a specific community can be an important tool for clinicians and policymakers as well as highly accessible to those families most at risk for asthma (Canino et al. 2007). In a meta-analysis of data from several culturally specific programs, researchers found that these programs were superior to generic programs or standard medical care in improving quality of life in adults with asthma and knowledge about asthma in children (Bailey et al. 2009).

During the past decade, several pilot projects have been implemented to target cultural specificities of the Puerto Rican population. The core problem in the relationship between acculturation and asthma management is the gap between recommendations for physician practice, as guided by general NAEPP guidelines, and parental comfort level with administering medications for control of asthma symptoms that is dictated by certain cultural beliefs (McQuaid et al. 2009). These include thinking that asthma is caused by an untreated cold or flu, strong positive or negative emotions, or getting wet while sweating (Martin 2010). Preventative programs try to trump these cultural beliefs while also improving self-reported asthma-related quality of life (in adults), overall asthma knowledge scores for children, caregiver's asthma knowledge, and reducing emergency department visits and hospitalizations for asthma (Bailey 2009).

Most culturally specific programs involve asthma education in one or many of the following formats: face-to-face encounters, group sessions, outreach visits and home visits, asthma action plans, and education on recognition of loss of asthma control and self-management skills (Bailey 2009). One of the most widely studied programs, CALMA, was specifically tailored family management asthma management intervention for Puerto Rican children (Martin et al. 2010; Canino 2007). CALMA was a home-based intervention in which trained counselors delivered eight education modules about asthma that were culturally focused for low-income Puerto Ricans (Martin et al. 2010).

Those enrolled in the program were found to be 6.5 percent more likely to have symptom-free nights, three times more likely to have their asthma under control, and less likely to visit the emergency department than those not enrolled in the program, but the program had no impact on the occurrence of symptom-free days. In addition, caregivers were more likely to feel confident in their child's asthma management (Canino 2007). Incorporating the community into developing CALMA's specificities was also found to make the program more sustainable (Martin et al. 2010).

Asthma management is also the responsibility of the physician. The majority of physicians inadequately implement NAEPP guidelines (Rance 2010). In general, there is instruction on the overuse of acute medications such as albuterol, and only one sweeping approach to administering these guidelines is used with no culturally incorporated adaptions. These guidelines are written for the pharmaceutical industry under a "one-size-fits-all" umbrella with a tendency to overlook co-morbidities.

In order to decrease asthma prevalence and incidence within the Puerto Rican population, asthma management practices need to be tailored to Puerto Rican culture; physicians need to be better educated about using different approaches top asthma management guidelines; and the indoor and outdoor environments where Puerto Ricans reside must be improved. As better diagnosis practices become available and research works to better understand the interrelated factors that cause asthma, rates may improve. However, asthma incidence is rising at an astonishing rate and remains one of the foremost public health problems facing the Puerto Rican population.

Reducing the incidence of diabetes can also benefit from culturally competent, community-based approaches to reach Puerto Ricans and other Hispanic communities effectively. Approaches that have been successful in reducing diabetes in minority and Hispanic communities include the use of patient navigators or community health workers. A patient-navigator approach has been successful in assisting people with diabetes in finding their way around health care settings and payment systems. The incorporation of community health workers in diabetes management programs has been shown to be successful in disseminating diabetes-related health information in the preferred language of the community through community-based organizations.

These community-based approaches (i.e., patient navigator and community health care workers) can assist Hispanics with diabetes in a number of different ways, including reinforcing diabetes education, providing information on healthier lifestyle behaviors and dietary habits, providing social support, assisting with navigating through a complex health care system, and identifying health care resources within the community, while developing rapport and establishing trust with community members (Aponte 2010). To address acculturation-related factors, these community-based approaches should address perceptions based on cultural differences that inhibit proper diabetes prevention and management, much like the culturally based pilot programs described earlier that work to improve asthma management. Hence, these types of programs are essential to reaching Puerto Rican communities to reduce asthma and diabetes disparities effectively.

In addition, given that insurance coverage and access to health care services have shown to increase diabetes-related morbidity, mortality, and costs (DHHS 1999), health policy changes, such as the Affordable Care Act, are important and essential. For example, the Affordable Care Act will potentially increase access to diabetes services for those who are uninsured, providing them with the resources to better manage their diabetes, maintain continuous follow-up care, receive early treatment to reduce complications of the disease, and improve overall health outcomes.

REFERENCES

Ahluwalia, I. B., D'Angelo, D., Morrow, B., and McDonalds, J.A. 2012. Association between Hispanic women: Data from the pregnancy risk acculturation and breastfeeding among Hispanics assessment and monitoring system. *Journal of Human Lactation* 28(2): 167–73.

Akinbami, Lara J. and Kenneth C. Schoendorf. 2002. Trends in childhood asthma: prevalence, health care utilization, and mortality. *Pediatrics* 110: 315–22.

American Diabetes Association. 2008. Economic costs of diabetes in the U.S. in 2007. *Diabetes Care* 31(3): 596–615.

_____. 2013. Economic costs of diabetes in the U.S. in 2012. *Diabetes Care* doi: 10.2337/dc12-2625.

American Lung Association. 2012. Asthma and Children Facts Sheet. October 2012. Accessed 1 February 2013.

Aponte Judith. 2009a. Diabetes-related risk factors across Hispanic subgroups in the Hispanic health and nutritional examination survey (1982-1984). *Public Health Nursing* 26(1): 23–38.

_____. 2009b. Addressing cultural heterogeneity among Hispanic subgroups by using Campinha-Bacote's model of cultural competency. *Holistic Nursing Practice* 23(1): 3–12.

_____. 2010. Addressing low-density lipoprotein (LDL) in Mexican Americans with diabetes in the NHANES (1999-2000 and 2001-2002). *Holistic Nursing Practice* 24(2): 99–106.

Arenz, S., R. Rucker, B. Koletzko, et al. 2004. Breast-feeding and childhood obesity-a systematic review. *International Journal of Obesity* 28: 1247–56.

Bailey, E. J., et al. 2009. Culture-specific programs for children and adults from minority groups who have asthma. *Cochrane Database of Systematic Reviews* 2(CD006580).

Beck, C. T. 2006. Acculturation: implications for perinatal research. *MCN: The American Journal of Maternal Child Nursing* 31: 114–20.

Beckett, W. E., et al. 1996. Asthma among Puerto Rican Hispanics: A multiethnic comparison study of risk factors. *American Journal of Respiratoty Critical Care Medicine* 154: 894–9.

Borrell, Luisa N., et al. 2009. Self-reported diabetes in Hispanic subgroup, non-Hispanic black, and non-Hispanic white populations: National Health Interview Survey, 1997–2005. *Public Health* 124(5): 702–10.

Borrelli, Belinda, et al. 2010. Differences in smoking behavior and attitudes among Puerto Rican, Dominican and Non-Latino White caregivers of children with asthma. *American Journal of Health Promotion* 25(5): S91–5.

Burchard, Esteban G., et al. 2004. Lower bronchodilator responsiveness in Puerto Rican than in Mexican subjects with asthma. *American Journal of Respiratoty Critical Care Medicine* 169: 386–392.

Canino, Glorisa. 2007. 25 years of children and adult psychiatric epidemiology studies in Puerto Rico. *Puerto Rico Health Sciences Journal* 26(4): 385–94.

Centers for Disease Control and Prevention. 2011. Age-Adjusted Percentage of Civilian, Noninstitutionalized Population with Diagnosed Diabetes, Hispanics, United States, 1997–2010. Accessed 27 December 2012. http://www.cdc.gov/diabetes/statistics/prev/national/figbyhispanic.htm/.

_____. n.d. Prevalence of diabetes among Hispanics in six U.S. geographic locations. Accessed 27 December 2012. http://www.cdc.gov/diabetes/pubs/pdf/hispanic.pdf/.

_____. 2003. Prevalence of diabetes and impaired fasting glucose in adults—United States, 1999-2000. *Morbidity and Mortality Weekly Report* 52(35): 833–7.

_____. 2008. National diabetes fact sheet: General information and national estimates on diabetes in the United States, 2007. Atlanta, GA: U.S. Department of Health and Human Services, CDC.

Chen, Wei, et al. 2013. ADCYAP1R1 and asthma in Puerto Rican children. *American Journal of Respiratoty Critical Care Medicine* n187(6): 584–8.

Cloutier, M. M., et al. 2002. Childhood asthma in an urban community: Prevalence, care system and treatment. *Chest Journal* 122: 1571–9.

Coultas, D. B., et al. 1994. Respiratory diseases in minorities of the United States. *American Journal of Respiratoty Critical Care Medicine* 149(3 Pt 2): S93–131.

Corburn, Jason, Jeffrey Osleeb and Michael Porter. 2006. Urban asthma and the neighbourhood environment in New York City. *Health & Place* 12(2): 167–79.

Choudry, Shweta, et al. 2004. Pharmacogenetic differences in response to albuterol between Puerto Rican and Mexicans with asthma. *American Journal of Respiratoty Critical Care Medicine* 171(6): 563–70.

_____, et al. 2006. Ancestry-Environment interactions and asthma risk among Puerto Ricans. *American Journal of Respiratoty Critical Care Medicine* 174(10): 1088–93.

_____, Margaret Taub, Mei Rui, et al. 2008. Genome-wide screen for asthma in Puerto Ricans: Evidence for association with 5q23 region. *Human Genetics* 123: 455–68

Cohen, Robyn T., et al. 2007. Area of residence, birthplace and asthma in Puerto Rican children. *Chest Journal* 131(5): 1331–8.

Department of Health and Human Services. 1999. Testimony on Public Expectations of Health Care Quality: Role of AHCPR by John M. Eisenberg, M.D. Accessed 14 March 2013. http://www.hhs.gov/asl/testify/t990908a.html/.

Diaz, T. et al. 2000. Medication use among children with asthma in East Harlem. *Pediatrics* 105(6): 1188–93.

Diette, Gregory B., et al. 2008. Environmental issues in managing asthma. *Respiratoty Care* 53(5): 602–17.

Enarson, D. A., and N. Ait Khaled. 1999. Cultural barriers to asthma management. *Pediatric Pulmonology* 28(4): 297–300.

Escarce, J. J. and K. Kapur. 2006. Access to and Quality of Health Care. In *Hispanics and the Future of America*. National Research Council (US) Panel on Hispanics in the United States. Eds. M. Tienda and F. Mitchell. Washington, DC: National Academies Press. Accessed 14 March. http://www.ncbi.nlm.nih.gov/books/NBK19910/.

Findley, S., M. Bindra and M. Penachio. 2003. Elevated asthma and indoor environmental exposures among Puerto Rican children of East Harlem. *Journal of Asthma* 40(5): 557–69.

Flegal, Katherine M. et al. 1991. Prevalence of diabetes in Mexican Americans, Cubans, and Puerto Ricans from the Hispanic Health and Nutrition Examination Survey, 1982–84. *Diabetes Care* 14(Suppl 3): 628–38.

Galanter, Joshua M., et al. 2011. Cosmopolitan and ethnic-specific replication of genetic risk factors for asthma in 2 Latino populations. *The Journal of Allergy and Clinical Immunology* 128(1): 37–43.

Hanis, C. L. et al. 1991. Origins of U.S. Hispanics: Implications for diabetes. *Diabetes* 14(3): 618–27.

Kirk, J. K. et al. 2007. Disparities in A1C levels between Hispanic and Non-Hispanic White adults with diabetes. *Diabetes Care* 31(2): 240–46.

Koinis-Mitchell, Daphne, et al. 2011. Immigration and acculturation-related factors and asthma morbidity in Latino children. *Journal of Pediatric Psychology* 36(10): 1130–43.

Landale, Nancy S. and R.S. Oropesa. 2002. White, black or Puerto Rican? Racial self-identification among mainland and island Puerto Ricans. *Social Forces* 81 (1): 231–54.

Lara, Marielena, et al. 2006. Acculturation and Latino Health in the United States: A Review of the Literature and its Sociopolitical Context. *Annual Review of Public Health* 26: 367–97.

Mainous, Arch G., et al. 2007. Heterogeneity in management of Diabetes Mellitus among Latino ethnic subgroups in the United States. *Journal of the American Board of Family Medicine* 20(6): 598–605.

Martin, Christina G. et al. 2010. The development of a community-based family asthma management intervention for Puerto Rican children. *Progress in Community Health Partnership* 4(4): 315–24.

McQuaid, Elizabeth L., et al. 2009. Beliefs and barriers to medication use in parents with Latino children with asthma. *Pediatric Pulmonology* 44(9): 892–8.

Melnik, Thomas A., et al. 2004. Diabetes prevalence among Puerto Rican adults in New York City, NY, 2000. *American Journal of Public Health* 94(3):434-437.

Morello-Frosch, Rachel, et al. 2002. Environmental justice and regional inequality in Southern California: Implications for future research. *Environmental Health Perspectives* 110(2): 149–54.

National Diabetes Education Program. n.d. The diabetes epidemic among Hispanics/Latinos. Accessed 4 December 2012. http://www.ndep.nih.gov/media/FS_HispLatino_Eng.pdf?redirect=true/.

National Heart, Lung and Blood Institute. 2012. What Is Asthma? National Institutes of Health. Accessed 5 December 2012. http://www.nhlbi.nih.gov/health/health-topics/topics/asthma/.

National Institute of Diabetes and Digestive and Kidney Diseases. 2011. National diabetes statistics, 2007: Death among people with diabetes, United States, 2006. Accessed 4 December 2012. http://www.diabetes.niddk.nih.gov/dm/pubs/statistics/#deaths/.

Ortega, Alexander N., et al. 2002. Childhood asthma, chronic illness, and psychiatric disorders. *Journal of Nervous and Mental Disease* 190: 275–81

Pearlman, Deborah N. et al. 2012. The impact of the 2007-2009 US recession on the health of children with asthma: Evidence from the national Child Asthma Call-Back Survey. *Medicine & Health/Rhode Island* 95(12): 395–6.

Perez-Escamilla, Rafael, Amber Hromi-Fiedler, Sonia Vega-Lopez, Angela Bermudez-Millan and Sofia Segura-Perez. 2008. Impact of peer nutrition education on dietary behaviors and health outcomes among Latinos: A systematic literature review. *Journal of Nutrition Education and Behavior* 40(4): 208–25.

Pérez-Escamilla, Rafael and Predrag Putnik. 2007. The role of acculturation in nutrition, lifestyle and incidence of Type 2 Diabetes among Latinos. *The Journal of Nutrition* 137(4): 860–70.

Perez-Perdomo, Rosa, et al. 2003. Prevalence and correlates of asthma in the Puerto Rican population: Behavioral Risk Factor Surveillance System, 2000. *Journal of Asthma* 40: 465–74.

Rance, Karen and Mary O'Laughlen. 2011. Obesity and asthma: A dangerous link in children. *The Journal for Nurse Practitioners* 7(4): 287-92.

Schwartz, Joel, et al. 1990. Predictors of asthma and persistent wheeze in a national sample of children in the United States: Association with social class, perinatal events, and race. *American Review of Respiratory Disease* 142: 555–62.

Smith, Chrystal and Elizabeth Barnett. 2005. Diabetes-related mortality among Mexican Americans, Puerto Ricans and Cuban Americans in the United States. *Pan American Journal of Public Health* 18(6): 381-7.

Sze, Julie. 2007. *Noxious New York: The Racial Politics of Urban Health and Environmental Justice.* Cambridge, MA: MIT Press.

Szilagyi, Peter G. et al. 2006. Improved asthma care after enrollment in the state children's health insurance program in New York. *Pediatrics* 117(2): 486–96.

Torgerson, Dara G. et al. 2011. Meta-analysis of genome-wide association studies of asthma in ethnically diverse North American populations. *Nature Genetics* 43(9): 887–92.

U.S. Census Bureau. n.d. Hispanic Population in the United States: March 2010. Accessed 4 December 2012. http://www.census.gov/prod/cen2010/briefs/c2010br-04.pdf/.

U.S. Census Bureau. 2000. The Hispanic Population in the United States. Washington.

U.S. Census Bureau. 2001. Overview of Race and Hispanic Origin. Accessed 2 January 2013. http://www.census.gov/prod/2001pubs/c2kbr01-1.pdf/.

Von Kries, R., B. Koletzko, T. Sauerwald et al. 1999. Breast feeding and obesity: Cross sectional study. *British Medical Journal* 319(7203): 147–50.

Whitman, Steve, Abigail Silva and Ami M. Shah. 2006. Disproportionate impact of diabetes in a Puerto Rican community of Chicago. *Journal of Community Health* 31(6): 521–31.

Witzig, Ritchie. 1996. The medicalization of race: Scientific legitimization of a flawed social construct. *Annals of Internal Medicine* 125(8): 675–9.

Puerto Rican Political and Civic Engagement in the United States

CARLOS VARGAS-RAMOS

Over the past three decades of research on Puerto Ricans in the United States, the participatory profile of this population has not changed much. Their engagement in political activity, both electoral and non-electoral, is generally lower than it is for the population as a whole; lower than the involvement of non-Hispanics; and more critically, lower than the majority population of non-Hispanic whites. Consequently, their voice in the political process is largely muted (cf. De la Garza and DeSipio 2005; Verba, Schlozman and Brady 1996). Yet, in many locales and states, Puerto Ricans have achieved parity in descriptive representation and elected legislators in proportion to their numbers among the eligible voter population. They have also become elected in greater numbers to executive positions in municipal and county governments.

However, in spite of these tangible advances, Puerto Ricans have not been able to translate these representational gains into substantive changes to the social and economic conditions that mark their lives in the United States, particularly for the dispossessed segment of this group (Cruz 2006). As described elsewhere in this volume and other sources, Puerto Ricans continue to exhibit very high poverty rates, higher levels of unemployment and lower levels of educational attainment than other groups, including high dropout rates, and highly disparate health outcomes, among other relevant social conditions.

What accounts for these seemingly contradictory sets of facts, of low engagement in political activity despite increased political representation and persistent negative social and individual outcomes? Secularly, the increase of the Puerto Rican population over the past three decades and its dispersion throughout the country has both concentrated them in discrete jurisdictions and extended their presence beyond their initial settlement in the large urban centers of the Northeast and Midwest. Institutionally, Puerto Ricans have reaped tangible benefits from the reforms brought about by the Voting Rights Act, which led to increased participation of groups formerly barred from participating in the political process and the creation of legislative districts to provide easier electoral competition. Politically, the conservative revolution that started in the 1980s, whose policy aims and achievements rolled back the welfare state and prevented expansion of state involvement in socioeconomic policy, has thwarted examination of structural social problems. And structurally, the persistent and deep poverty of a substantial segment of the community overwhelms and obscures the improved economic position and advances of other segments of the Puerto Rican population observed through statistical analysis.

Puerto Ricans in the United States

Puerto Ricans in the United States have had a long-standing political presence. Their early presence, at the close of the nineteenth century, centered around activities in decolonizing Puerto Rico from Spain. The small Puerto Rican *colonia* that existed in New York included among its members advocates and activists in the fight against colonial rule from Spain. These highly active political operators aimed their efforts at lobbying the United States government towards the political future of the island in the context of exile politics (Sánchez-Korrol 1994; Haslip-Viera 1996). The island-centered focus tended to dominate the political efforts of these activists, even after Puerto Rico became a possession of the United States in 1898 and for decades thereafter; although its centrality has waned, it has not disappeared altogether from agenda of issues that concern Puerto Ricans in the United States (e.g., Vieques).

During the twenty-first century, the political agenda and mobilization efforts of Puerto Ricans in the United States have focused on conditions of Puerto Ricans living on the mainland. This orientation began to surface early on in the migration process of Puerto Ricans to the United States once the character of the migration stream shifted from one overrepresented with elites to one that was solidly working class spurred by a labor migration once Puerto Ricans were made United States citizens in 1917. The contentious incorporation of Puerto Ricans as citizens elicited affirming and self-organizing responses in reaction to opposition, at times violent, to their presence in the urban neighborhoods where they had settled (Falcón 1984; Sánchez-Korrol 1994). Incursions into electoral politics, including candidacies to elected office, began in the 1920s, even if the first Puerto Rican legislator was not elected until 1937. But it would take another fifteen years for a steady Puerto Rican presence in elected office to occur. It was in the 1960s, however, that the stage would be set for the present dynamics and structuration of Puerto Rican politics in the United States.

Puerto Rican Participatory Profile

Puerto Ricans are engaged in the political process in the United States, but their involvement is notably lower than it is for the population as a whole, particularly in the political activities that put the most pressure on and provide the most information to elected representatives—voting and contacting government officials. These are also the most common forms of political activities in which residents of the United States participate. Figure 1 and Table 1 show the degree of involvement in political activities of different segments of the population in the United States. It is readily apparent that the rates of participation across these different activities are much lower for Puerto Ricans than they are for the population of the country as a whole and for non-Hispanics in particular.

For instance, a smaller proportion of adult Puerto Ricans (60%) were registered to vote than were other adults of voting age (71%) in 2008 (Figure 1). In addition, only half of Puerto Ricans voted in the 2008 Presidential election, the latest election for which there are available data, compared with 64 percent of the population as a whole and 65 percent of non-Hispanics.[1] In contrast, Puerto Rican registration and voting rates, while lower than those of non-Hispanics, are commensurate with Hispanic turnout rates and voter registration levels. But in disaggregating the Hispanic vote, one can appreciate that Puerto Rican electoral participation, while exhibiting higher turnout rates than those of the largest Hispanic group—the Mexican-origin population—is lower than that of other Latino national-origin groups, most notably Cubans and South Americans. Cubans reported higher rates of voter registration and voter turnout in 2008 than any other Hispanic group, the population as a whole, and non-Hispanics in general.

Regarding citizen-initiated contacts with public officials, Puerto Rican engagement (5%) is about half that of the population as a whole and non-Hispanics in general. Among Hispanics, Puerto Rican rates of contacting public officials are higher than they are for any other Latino group with the exception of "other Hispanics," a residual category. Puerto Rican (and Hispanic) participation in other forms of political activity, such as campaigning for or contributing funds to a political party or candidate or attending meetings where political issues are discussed, is similarly half that of the population as a whole or non-Hispanics in general. The only form of political involvement in which Puerto Ricans exceed the national rate (and also the level of non-Hispanic participation) is engaging in protest activity, a political activity in which a relatively low proportion of the population engages.

FIGURE 1. Voted for President, 2008 (percent)

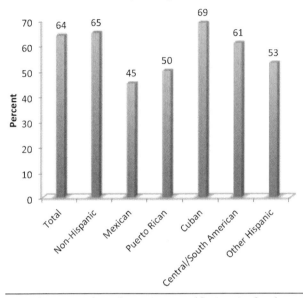

Source: Current Population Survey, Voting and Registration Supplement, November 2008.

TABLE 1. Political Activity in the Last 12 Months (2008) (percent)

	Total	Non-Hispanic	Mexican	Puerto Rican	Cuban	Central/ South American	Other Hispanic
Contacted Public Official	11	12	3	6	3	3	11
Attended Political Meetings	11	12	4	6	6	4	10
Taken part in march, rally, protest or demonstration	3	3	2	4	1	3	4
Campaigned for or Contributed to a political party or candidate	15	17	7	9	10	7	12

Source: Current Population Survey, Civic Engagement Supplement, November 2008.

These findings are consistent with current as well as long-standing research on the subject conducted over the last three decades (Mills et al. 1950; Falcón 1983; Nelson 1984; Jennings 1988; Arvizu and Garcia 1996; Vargas-Ramos 2003; DeSipio 2006; Garcia 2012). What accounts for this state of affairs? Among the factors that have contributed to lower levels of political involvement among Latinos in general, including Puerto Ricans, are language barriers, youthfulness of the population, lower levels of educational attainment, income, and membership in voluntary associations, shorter terms of residence, fewer prompts for participation, institutional barriers to participation, and systemic discrimination (Calvo and Rosenstone 1989; Hero 1992; Rosenstone and Hansen 1993; Verba et al. 1995; Diaz 1996; Garcia 1997; Nie et al. 1996; Vargas-Ramos 2003; DeSipio 2006; Cruz 2010; Garcia 2012).

Some of the most prevalent explanations for the lower levels of participation among Latinos in general and Puerto Ricans in particular have centered on the stock of resources available to devote to political engagement. These explanations have emphasized the advantages that some individuals have over others in the political arena in a political system that gives advantages to those

FIGURE 2. Turnout rate by education attainment, 2008 (percent)

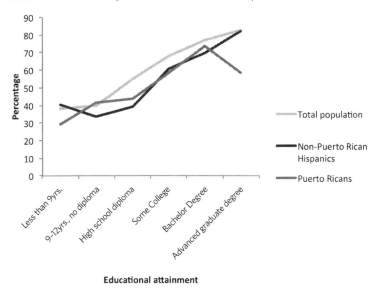

Educational attainment

Source: Current Population Survey, Voting and Registration Supplement, 2008.

with politically relevant resources, such as having a certain socioeconomic status because of educational attainment, occupational status and income, civic skills and motivation (Verba et al. 1995; Nie et al. 1996; Leighly and Vedlitz 1999; Jackson 2003). On this count, Puerto Ricans and other Latinos are not likely to fare as well as others as political actors in the United States because they tend to have lower levels of these resources. Figures 2 through 5 by and large illustrate these disparities.

Generally, those who have lower educational attainment will engage in political activity in lower proportions than those who have attended school longer and have earned higher academic degrees. Thus, 55 percent of individuals with a high school degree turned out to vote in 2008 compared with 77 percent of those who had a bachelor's degree (Figure 2). A somewhat similar pattern is observed among non-Puerto Rican Latinos and Puerto Ricans: those with less schooling turned out to vote at lower levels than those who had more schooling. An exception is noted, however, among those Puerto Ricans who had a graduate or professional degree, who turned out to vote at lower levels than those who had just a bachelor's degree or those who only had some years of college. Yet, the most notable finding is that, by and large, the turnout rate for Latinos generally and Puerto Ricans

FIGURE 3. Contact with public offical by educational attainment, 2008 (percent)

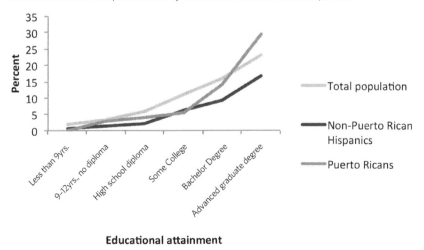

Educational attainment

Source: Current Population Survey, Civic Engagement Supplement, November 2008.

in particular never matched the turnout rates for the population as a whole. The turnout rate for Latinos with a high school or bachelor's degree was lower than it was for the population as a whole. In other words, despite similar educational attainment, Latinos generally and Puerto Ricans in particular have lower levels of voter participation than other groups and this is true for most levels of education attainment. In instances when turnout was greater among Latinos, including Puerto Ricans, it was among individuals with the very lowest levels of schooling.

The pattern for the levels of citizen-initiated contact with public officials by educational attainment categories is similar in that those who have lower levels of schooling were less likely to contact an official than those with more schooling (Figure 3). This effect is evident in the population as a whole, Latinos in general, and Puerto Ricans in particular. Moreover, Latinos in general and Puerto Ricans in particular have lower levels of contact with public officials at every category of educational attainment than does the population as a whole. (The exception is Puerto Ricans with advanced graduate degrees, who exceeded the population as a whole in the level of contacting.[2])

FIGURE 4. Turnout rate by income, 2008 (in percent)

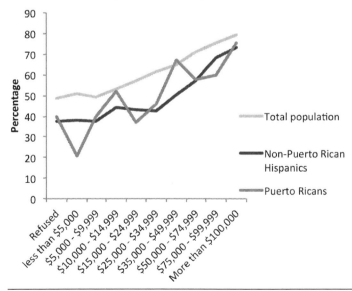

Source: Current Population Survey, Voting and Registration Supplement, 2008.

A similar pattern is observed when comparing turnout rates across income categories (Figure 4). Generally, those with lower incomes turned out to vote at lower levels than those with higher incomes. This was the case for the population as a whole as well as for non-Puerto Rican Latinos. Moreover, the turnout rate for the latter was lower across all income categories than it was for the population as a whole. Among Puerto Ricans, this linear pattern is not as smooth. As a general pattern, those with lower incomes turned out to vote in lower number than those with higher incomes. However, in some instances, those in the lower middle-income categories (e.g., $35,000 to $49,999) had a higher turnout rate than those in higher middle-income categories (e.g., $50,000 to $74,999 and $75,000 to $99,999). In fact, among this lower middle-income category, Puerto Ricans exceeded, if only slightly, the turnout rate for the population as a whole. But, by and large, Puerto Ricans of other income levels turned out at lower levels across income categories.

For contacting political offices, the linear effect of income is more prominent in the middle and higher categories for the population as a whole and for Hispanics as a whole, although it is noted that the levels of contacting among Latinos is consistently lower than for the population as a whole across the income spectrum (Figure 5). For Puerto Ricans, however, the pattern is

FIGURE 5. Contact with public offical by income, 2008 (percent)

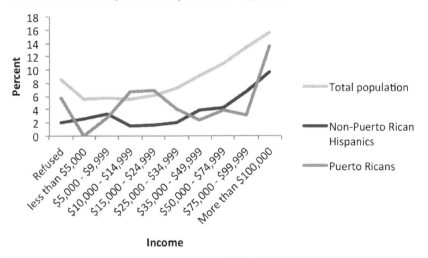

Income

Source: Current Population Survey, Civic Engagement Supplement, November 2008.

more divergent. For those in the lower income categories ($10,000 to $24,999 and $15,000 to $34,999), but not the lowest, the level of contacting was greater than it was among those in the middle and upper-middle income categories, exceeding even those of the population as a whole.

These observations are generally consistent with findings from other analyses, which likewise establish the positive impact of socioeconomic status variables on voting (Calvo and Rosenstone 1989; Arvizu and Garcia 1996; Leighly and Vedlitz 1999; Jackson 2003). These findings are also consistent with others that show the relation of educational attainment or income on voting among Latinos, while generally linear, is not monotonic (Arvizu and Garcia 1996).[3] When coupling the effect of socioeconomic status on participation with the fact that the effect of ethnicity or race on participation often disappears when it is held constant with other predictors of participation, many scholars conclude that race and ethnicity do not have an independent effect on participation, believing, in essence, that Latinos would not behave differently from others in the United States if their socioeconomic circumstances were different (Leighly and Vedlitz 1999; Garcia, Falcón and de la Garza 1996). Discounting the independent effect of ethnicity or race on participation because what underlies it is the effect of different socioeconomic status, fits with the tendency to rely on economic mobility (and assimilation) to bring marginal groups of society into the mainstream over time without trying to address the ways in which the present political and economic system perpetuates inequality in political engagement (Verba et al. 1995).

These results are also consistent with findings from other analyses which show that, while the resources provided by socioeconomic status promote political participation, the impact of these socioeconomic variables is different for Latinos in general and Puerto Ricans in particular than it is for the population as a whole and non-Hispanic whites in particular. Such analyses present evidence on how educational attainment and income have a greater effect on non-Latinos than they do on Latinos, and even within specific national-origin Latino groups (Calvo and Rosenstone 1989; Arvizu and Garcia 1996; Jackson 2003).

These inconsistencies do not necessarily challenge the validity of the models that rely on socioeconomic status to explain political participation, but they do highlight the skewed nature of the political system that not only gives advantages to those who are in a better position to mobilize material

TABLE 2. Membership in voluntary association in the last 12 months (2008) (in percentages)

Type of association	Total	Non-Hispanic	Mexican	Puerto Rican	Cuban	Central/South American	Other Hispanic
Community, neighborhood, school or PTA	15.2	16	10.1	9.9	8	10.3	13.1
Service or civic	6.6	7.3	1.6	2.3	1.9	1.3	5.6
Sports or recreation	11.4	12	7.4	8.2	5.1	5.9	9.3
Religious	17.5	18.6	10.2	12	8.5	13.4	14.6
Other type	5.5	6.1	2	2.3	2.5	2.5	6.8
Does not belong to any	66.7	64.9	78.2	76.6	82.6	76.8	70.9
Served as officer or in committee	9.8	10.8	2.9	5	2.2	3.6	7.7

Source: Current Population Survey, Civic Engagement Supplement, November 2008.

resources to engage in the political process (Verba et al. 1995), but also consistently favors some social groups over others and does so in such a way as to discount socioeconomic differences. Hero (1992) has persuasively argued that the United States has a political system divided into two tiers in which racial and/or ethnic minorities perform differently, indeed worse, in the political arena than does the population as a whole and non-Hispanic whites in particular.

Hero (2007) has further shown how resources, such as social capital, accentuate differences in this two-tier system of political participation. Thus, while some scholars have suggested the resources emanating from social institutions that build social capital and politically relevant skills and orientations, may attenuate or compensate for the inordinate impact that material resources have on the political system (Verba et al. 1995; Burns et al. 2001; Putnam 2000), they in fact do not. Rather, these social-capital-building institutions actually serve to magnify the gap of unequal political participation and representation, and neuter the purported attenuating

TABLE 3. Neighborliness in the past year (2008) (percent)

	Total	Non-Hispanic	Mexican	Puerto Rican	Cuban	Central/South American	Other Hispanic
Frequency of speaking with a neighbor during a typical month							
Basically every day	15.3	15.4	14.5	15.6	9.8	12.9	18.6
A few times a week	31.5	32.2	27.8	27.3	24.1	25.2	34.1
A few times a month	22.7	23.3	18.6	22	23.2	19.6	16.1
Once a month	12.3	12.4	11.1	11	13.1	13.5	10.2
Not at all	18.2	16.7	28	24.2	29.8	28.9	21
Frequency of doing favors for a neighbor during a typical month							
Basically every day	4	4.1	3.6	4.2	1.9	3.2	5.8
A few times a week	12.8	12.9	12.6	11.8	9.3	11.2	13.6
A few times a month	20.8	21.5	17.1	18.6	17.4	14.4	21.8
Once a month	20.4	21.1	16.4	16.6	14.1	16.3	15.6
Not at all	41.9	40.4	50.3	48.8	57.2	54.9	43.2

Source: Current Population Survey, Civic Engagement Supplement, November 2008.

or compensating effects that social-capital building institution have over socioeconomic inequities. Moreover, it appears as if higher social capital is strongly correlated with negative social outcomes for minorities across states and within states (Hero 2007), whereas lower social capital is associated with greater ethnic and racial diversity (Hero 2007; Putnam 2007).

On the question of social capital insofar as Puerto Ricans are concerned, one may expect them to exhibit lower levels of the norms of trust and reciprocity and social network linkages given the fact that they tend to live in locations (e.g., states, counties) that are fairly diverse in terms of race and ethnicity (even if the neighborhoods in which they reside are not), their level of geographical mobility is greater and they are of lower socioeconomic status. Indeed, Puerto Ricans in the United States exhibit lower levels of associational involvement than the population as a whole, and even relatively lower levels of social connectedness, which can serve as indicators of lower social capital (Table 2 and Table 3). Less than a quarter of Puerto Ricans belong to some type of civic association compared with a third for the population as a whole and 35 percent of non-Hispanics. Puerto Ricans, and other Latinos, not only have lower levels of associational involvement than the population as a whole and non-Hispanics in particular, but there is no singular associational category in which Puerto Ricans match or exceed the level of associational involvement of the population as a whole.

In terms of the social interactions of Puerto Ricans in particular and Latinos in general that not only exemplify social networks but also help sustain norms of trust and reciprocity (i.e., social capital), they tend to be overrepresented among those who do not speak with neighbors at all or never do a favor for a neighbor. Not only are Puerto Ricans overrepresented in these categories of interaction with neighbors relative to the population as a whole, but these categories of social connectedness that indicate lower social capital are the categories in which most Puerto Ricans fall.

These social-capital indicators might appear to be characteristics of the individuals surveyed; part of their individual stock of resources they may be able to mobilize and deploy in their social, political, economic, or cultural environment. By extension, this seems to be another area in which Puerto Ricans in particular and Latinos in general appear to be deficient compared with the population as a whole. In fact, the lack of associational involvement among Puerto Ricans has been noted as one of the reasons for their limited social mobility (Mills et al. 1950; Glazer and Moynihan 1963). If civic voluntarism is what has made the United States a nation of organizers (Skocpol et al. 2000), and is a feature that contributes to the exceptional place of the United States in the world (Lipset 1996), Puerto Ricans (and other Latinos) are then not becoming part of the social and political fabric of the United States in the same measure and to the same extent as others. By further extending this argument, it might be concluded that it is their fault if they continue to endure the negative social outcomes they exhibit as a group.

Yet, contextual analyses have shown how such features of decreased social capital may be less the result of a deficient individual stock of resources and more a feature of the environment in which Puerto Ricans and others find themselves (Putnam 2007). Greater diversity has been shown to turn people off socially. As Putnam, the leading proponent of social capital has noted:

..., inhabitants of diverse communities tend to withdraw from collective life, to distrust their neighbours, regardless of the colour of their skin, to withdraw even from close friends, to expect the worst from their community and its leaders, to volunteer less, give less to charity and work on community projects less often, to register to vote less, to agitate for social reform *more*, but have less faith that they can actually make a difference, and to huddle unhappily in front of the television. (2007:150-1)

It may turn out to be that Puerto Ricans (and others) are in fact suffering the effects of the environment they inhabit in the United States, rather than being the ones responsible for their own misfortunes. Yet, the benefit of such associationism, whether formal or informal, is evident (cf. Morris 1999). Particularly among ethnic and racial minorities as well as immigrants, such associational involvement provides crucial social functions including the adaptation process to new environments, community formation and development, and political representation (Cordero-Guzmán 2005; Cordero-Guzmán et al. 2008). Moreover, the myth that such associationist tendencies are independent from or an alternative to the state has been challenged empirically (Skocpol et al. 1999). Indeed, state sponsorship of organizations, such as funding their operations, has been shown to facilitate the incorporation of newcomers to the polity, with greater organizational capacity the more invested the state is in supporting the incorporation work of such associations (Bloemraad 2005).

Overall, then, Puerto Rican political and civic participation continues to be relatively lower than it is for the population as a whole. This relatively lower level of political and civic involvement is largely the result of Puerto Ricans' reduced stock of politically relevant resources in a system that assigns a premium to individuals and groups of individuals that are able to muster such resources as income, education, associational membership and the skills and capital that are associated with such membership, specific ethnic or racial membership, and the locale in which they reside. Yet, over the course of the past four decades, despite consistently turning out to vote at lower levels than the population as a whole, the proportion of Puerto Rican elected officials in many jurisdictions has approached parity in proportion to their numbers in the voting age population.

Puerto Rican Political Representation

Prior to the passage of the Voting Rights Act of 1965, there were no Puerto Rican federal legislators elected to office and only two legislators in the state of New

TABLE 4. Puerto Rican and Latino representation as percent of the adult population, 2013

	United States	Connecticut	Florida	New Jersey	New York
Population 18 years and over	235,186,182	2,759,274	14,854,381	6,733,978	15,075,404
Latinos 18 yrs. and over (percent)	14.3	11.6	21.1	16.3	16.3
Puerto Ricans 18 yrs. and over (percent)	1.4	6.2	4.1	4.4	5.2
Latino state senators (percent)		5.5	12.5	5	9.5
Puerto Rican state senator (percent)		2.8	5	5	6.3
Latino Assembly member (percent)		7.3	9.2	7.5	8
Puerto Rican Assembly member (percent)		6.6	1.6	3.8	4.6

Note: Population estimates based on results from the US Census Bureau, ACS, 3-year estimate, 2011. Data on state legislators are based on legislatures composition in 2013.

York, the state with historically the largest concentration of Puerto Ricans in the United States. Puerto Ricans were nevertheless critical electoral bases for some elected officials in that state (e.g., U.S. Representative Vito Marcantonio). Thirty-five years ago there were two New York state senators, five members of its assembly, one United States representative and three local members of the New York municipal legislature (Falcón 1983). Today, there are four United States representatives, four New York state senators, two New Jersey state senators, two Florida senators, one Connecticut state senator, ten members of the Connecticut House of Representatives, seven members of the New York State Assembly, three members of the New Jersey General Assembly, two Florida representatives, and several members of the Massachusetts House of Representatives and of the Illinois House of Representatives who are Puerto Rican. This is in addition to dozens of municipal legislators and mayors.

Thus, Puerto Rican political representation has increased in the intervening third of a century, which is in and of itself a positive development. Moreover, Puerto Ricans have achieved a measure of parity in representation in some legislatures. Table 4 shows the political representation of Puerto Ricans in Connecticut, Florida, New Jersey, and New York as a proportion of their adult populations; that is, the population that is allowed to register to vote in elections.[4] These results show that in the Connecticut House of Representatives, Puerto Ricans are represented at just above parity, with 6.6 percent of Puerto Rican representatives in the lower house of the legislature (cf. Cruz 2006). In the legislatures of Florida, New Jersey, and New York, Puerto Ricans are slightly underrepresented as a proportion of their adult populations. In New Jersey, Puerto Ricans represent 4.4 percent of the adult population but 3.8 percent of members of the state assembly. Similarly, Puerto Ricans represented 5.2 percent of the adult population, but only 4.6 percent of the New York State Assembly. The greatest legislative underrepresentation occurs in Florida, where Puerto Ricans represent 4.1 percent of the state's adult population, but only 1.6 percent of its House of Representatives. On the other hand, Puerto Ricans were represented above parity in the Florida, New Jersey, and New York state senates, but were underrepresented in the Connecticut senate. (Latinos as a group that also includes Puerto Ricans are notably underrepresented in both chambers of the legislature in all four states.)

The election of these Puerto Rican representatives to political offices in general is the result of several factors: the growth of the Puerto Rican population, which as a result of residential segregation aggregated Puerto Ricans in discrete jurisdictions; the political organization and mobilization of the population; and the institutional reforms of the Voting Rights Act, which contributed, on the one hand, to overturning obstacles to the effective participation of Puerto Ricans and other protected classes throughout the country (e.g., literacy tests, minority language ballots, pre-clearance) and, on the other hand, created awareness to facilitate the creation of districts from which historically underrepresented populations would be able to elect candidates of their choosing, usually of their own ethnic background.

The creation of districts that empower underrepresented minority groups has had positive outcomes for Latinos generally. Latino-majority districts appear to increase turnout in state legislative districts which increases the election of Latino elected officials (Barreto et al. 2004). But Latino turnout seems to increase not only in districts that elect Latino representatives, but also in districts not represented by Latinos as the total number of Latino elected representatives in legislative bodies increases (Rocha et al. 2010). Moreover, the type of representation offered by Latino-elected representatives to Latino constituents is distinct from that offered by non-Latino representatives of similar ideological positioning (Preuhs and Hero 2011). Furthermore, electing representatives from majority-minority districts has the added benefit of increasing the institutional position of those elected officials by creating seniority in the legislative body and turning potential outsiders into political insiders; a position that has the potential to increase the substantive representation of minority constituents (Preuhs and Gonzalez Juenke 2011).

However, the creation or maintenance of legislative districts in which minority elected representatives in general and Puerto Rican representatives in particularly are easily elected tend to have unintended consequences. For instance, these districts have contributed to assuring the continued election of representatives with less competition for votes—a perverse outcome. Candidates for office, particularly incumbents, have less need to appeal and mobilize untested voters to turnout at the polls on election day and therefore concentrate the electoral appeals and mobilization efforts on tried-and-true prime voters, who while self-motivated to vote, may also be receptive to electoral and policy-relevant messages that will affect their vote. The result is that Puerto Rican (and other minority) legislators then find themselves with fewer voters turning out at the polls. There are repercussions to this reduced turnout for Puerto Rican legislative representatives in the reduced capital the legislators may muster when interacting with elected officials in larger jurisdictions.

Votes are the currency in an elective system of government. Those who are able to garner the most votes win elected offices. Those who are able to muster votes and deliver them to candidates for office of larger jurisdictions are also able to gain influence with those elected officials in lower jurisdictions. Therefore, for example, a member of the city council may be able to secure enough votes to get elected, but the proportion of votes he or she may be able to deliver to a candidate for higher office may be insignificant, particularly in council districts with low turnout, reducing the influence over the elected official. Correspondingly, a member of the state assembly who is able to mobilize and turnout to the polls large segments of registered voters in his or her district in an election for the the Senate is likely to receive greater attention in the case of a win.

Moreover, turnout in a district is not simply a characteristic of a particular elected representative of the district but a characteristic of the district itself. Therefore, constituents of a district with low turnout pose less of a threat or advantage to an elected official than constituents in districts with high turnout. Therefore, an elected official is likely to pay greater attention to a district characterized by relatively higher voter turnout than to one with lower turnout. Puerto Ricans, and other Latinos with relatively lower voter registration and turnout rates, are at a disadvantage in this regard.

TABLE 5. Voter enrollment and turnout by legislative district in New Jersey and New York, 2011 and 2012

	NJ Assembly 2011	Percent difference	NJ Senate 2011	Percent Difference
Average total enrollment	129,818		129,818	
Puerto Rican	119,660	-0.078	104,575	-0.194
Latino	117,179	-0.097	*	*
NH Black	122,946	-0.053	120,478	-0.072
NH White	132,825	0.023	132,402	0.020
Average total turnout	35,356		35,356	
Puerto Rican	25,966	-0.266	16,513	-0.533
Latino	26,917	-0.239	*	*
NH Black	29,981	-0.152	24,071	-0.319
NH White	37,533	0.062	37,792	0.069
Average turnout rate	26.9		26.9	
Puerto Rican	21.4		15.8	
Latino	22.6		*	
NH Black	23.9		20	
NH White	28.1		28.4	

	NY Assembly 2012	Percent difference	NY Senate 2012	Percent Difference
Average total enrollment	79,794		189,988	
Puerto Rican	64,960	-0.186	171,696	-0.096
Latino	66,329	-0.169	170,510	-0.103
NH Black	76,173	-0.045	189,557	-0.002
NH White	82,283	0.031	192,504	0.013
Average total turnout	47,325		112,679	
Puerto Rican	31,927	-0.325	84,469	-0.250
Latino	33,613	-0.290	85,508	-0.241
NH Black	43,422	-0.082	107,099	-0.050
NH White	49,851	0.053	117,122	0.039
Average turnout rate	58.5		59	
Puerto Rican	49.1		49.2	
Latino	50.2		50.1	
NH Black	56.7		56.6	
NH White	59.9		60.6	

Note: Calculations based on published election results for New Jersey 2011, and for New York, 2012. * Latino senators are of Puerto Rican origin

TABLE 6. Correlates of Puerto Rican and Latino enrollment and turnout by legislative district

	Puerto Rican	Latino	Non-Hispanic Black	Non-Hispanic White
NJ Assembly District				
Enrollment 2011	-0.186	-0.241**	-.238**	.379***
Turnout 2011	-0.125	-.224**	-.188	.324***
Turnout rate 2011	-0.184	-.209	-.228**	.346***
NJ Senate District				
Enrollment 2011	-.36**	-.36**	-.194	.383**
Turnout 2011	-.434***	-.434***	-.378**	.582***
Turnout 2011	-.432***	-.432***	-.39**	.591***
NY Assembly District				
Enrollment 2012	-.25***	-.316***	-.114	.337***
Turnout 2012	-.29***	-.36***	-.138	.383***
Turnout rate 2012	-.293***	-.364***	-.107	.335***
NY Senate District				
Enrollment 2012	-.209	-.277**	-.008	.197
Turnout 2012	-.358***	-.43***	-.111	.388***
Turnout rate 2012	-.4***	-.452***	-.115	.439***

Note: Calculations based on published election results for New Jersey 2011, and for New York, 2012.

Puerto Ricans tend to live in districts of low turnout and Puerto Rican legislators represent constituents of low-turnout districts. This, in turn, undermines the influence of Puerto Ricans with elected officials, and it also undermines the influence of Puerto Rican elected representatives with elected officials in higher office.

As illustration, Table 5 shows the difference in average total enrollment (i.e., registration), total turnout as well as the proportion of registered voters who turned out to vote on election day (i.e., turnout rate) by legislative district in New Jersey and New York. The results show how the average total turnout and the average turnout rate are lower in districts represented by Puerto Rican legislators than they are in districts represented by non-Puerto Rican Latino legislators as well as non-Hispanic black and non-Hispanic white legislators. Table 6 presents the correlation analysis of enrollment and turnout by the ethnicity of the legislator representing a district. These correlation results also confirm that districts represented by Puerto Rican legislators had lower total turnout and lower turnout rates. In contrast, districts represented by non-Hispanic whites had higher enrollment and turnout. Moreover, these correlation results for Puerto Ricans were statistically significant in New Jersey state senate districts, New York state assembly districts and New York state senate districts.

Under these circumstances of low turnout and lower participation in other forms of political activity, what influence are Puerto Ricans (and other Latinos) likely to have in state political systems? Specifically, what is the influence of Puerto Ricans in heavily Puerto Rican (or Latino) districts that have low turnout and low involvement in political activities? What influence may Puerto Rican (and other Latino) elected representatives have in such state political systems? In fact, the influence they may have is likely circumscribed. Moreover, this influence in the political systems they occupy at the local, county, and state levels, to say nothing of the federal level, is likely to remain muted even if Puerto Ricans and other Latinos in general were to turnout and participate in the political process in proportions commensurate with their numbers in the voter-eligible population or if they elected representatives from within their ranks in proportion to their numbers. This will continue to be the case because, despite their population growth and the increased number of elected representatives, Puerto Ricans remain a numerical minority in the country and in the state and the municipalities they live in. Therefore Puerto Ricans are not going to be able to move a political agenda simply on the basis of this identification (cf. Pantoja 2006). But a Puerto Rican policy agenda is certainly undermined because of the reduced political participation of this population.

Puerto Ricans and other Latinos will not only need to increase their levels of political involvement, but actually exceed them to be able to realize their policy preferences. Moreover, they will need to resort to coalitions with other groups to advance those policy priorities. Maintaining the status quo will not result in improved chances to influence policy meaningfully. The political future of Puerto Ricans in the United States still hinges in their involvement in the political process. Unless the profile of lackluster engagement in politics changes to result in more robust participation, conditions are likely to remain the same. Factors working against Puerto Rican (and Latino) political participation continue to be their relatively lower socioeconomic status, their residence in jurisdictions with relatively uncompetitive elections, and their disengaged political and civic leadership.

In addition, aspects of the status quo that had prevailed for four decades no longer exists. The recent 2013 decision by the U.S. Supreme Court declaring unconstitutional the pre-clearance provision of the Voting Rights Act (i.e. Section 5) will have a deletirious impact on the fight against systemic barriers to participation for Puerto Ricans, other Latinos and other underrepresented ethnic groups.[5] It will no longer be a tool to which underrepresented groups can turn to address institutional discrimination in the political field. Even when Section 5 of the Voting Rights Act was in effect, and the federal government was able to preemptively question changes in electoral procedures that could have discriminatory outcomes, the process was never quick nor easy. The challenge to discriminatory political practices will grow more difficult. After all, as Puerto Ricans move out of traditional settlement sites in the Northeast and settle in new areas, particularly areas that had been subject to full or partial coverage of Section 5 of the Voting Rights Act, mostly in the South, their political presence has been stymied, even in the face of U.S. Department of Justice's scrutiny (Cruz 2010).

The answer to this is leadership, both from within the Puerto Rican political class as well as its civic elite. Political leaders then need to take the initiative and lead the community in this process of strategic mobilization.

In addition, in specific circumstances, the Puerto Rican electorate may nevertheless have an impact that exceeds its proportion of the electorate. These circumstances are bounded by close election contests in which even small segments of the electorate are important, particularly those that are vacant as can be the case for the more mobile segment of the Puerto Rican population. These contests are likely to take place in locations that are in flux as a result of geographical mobility of their populations, for instance, in areas of recent population growth as a result of migration (both internal and international). The tendency for Puerto Ricans (and other Latinos and the population as large) is to become more independent in their partisan allegiances, and independent voters and those who are willing to cross partisan lines in their voting become precious targets of candidates and parties seeking electoral advantages. Such was the case for Puerto Ricans in Florida in the role they played in the past presidential election.

Reliable national data on Puerto Rican turnout rates during the 2012 elections may not be available until 2014. However, presidential elections in the United States are not won nationally, but rather at the state level. Therefore, state-level analysis is likely to be more meaningful than national-level analysis. Of all the states with competitive races for president, the one in which Puerto Ricans may have played a decisive role was Florida. Reports from exit-poll data of voters in Florida lead to the conclusion that Puerto Ricans had a meaningful impact on those elections (Bendixen and Amandi International 2012). Analysis of exit-poll data revealed that Puerto Ricans represented 4.5 percent of the voters who turned out to the polls in Florida. In all, Puerto Ricans contributed 3.8 percent of the votes Barack Obama received in the state, and President Obama won Florida by less than one percent. Thus, Puerto Ricans were instrumental in that victory for the reelected president. By the same token, so were other Latino national-origin groups, including Cubans. Thus, as Puerto Ricans disperse throughout the country, they are also contributing to the electoral reconfiguration that is taking place.

NOTES

[1] Percentage based on voting age citizen participation.

[2] The percentages of the sample with advance graduate degrees are 8.7 percent for the population as a whole, 9.6 percent for non-Hispanics and 2.9 percent for Puerto Ricans and other Hispanics as a whole.

[3] These effects persist even when holding other factors constant in a regression analysis, whose findings are not shown.

[4] As U.S. citizens, adult Puerto Ricans are eligible to register to vote after a requisite period of residence in the jurisdiction in which they live.

[5] I thank Edgardo Meléndez for raising the point of the significance of this development.

REFERENCES

Arvizu, John and F. Chris Garcia. 1996. Latino voting participation: Explaining and differentiating Latino voter turnout. *Hispanic Journal of Behavioral Sciences* 18(2): 104-28.

Bendixen and Amandi International. 2012. Exit Poll of Hispanic Voters in Florida. 8 November. Accessed 13 December 2012. http://bendixenandamandi.com/wp-content/uploads/2011/05/ElectionResults-ExitPoll.pdf/.

Barreto, Matt A., Gary M. Segura and Nathan D. Woods. 2004. The mobilizing effect of majority-minority districts on Latino turnout. *American Political Science Review* 98(1): 65-75.

Bloemraad, Irene. 2005. The limits of de Tocqueville: How government facilitates organizational capacity in newcomer communities. *Journal of Ethnic and Migration Studies* 31(5): 865-87.

Calvo, Maria A. and Steven J. Rosenstone. 1989. *Hispanic Political Participation*. San Antonio, TX: Southwest Voter Research Institute, Inc.

Cordero-Guzmán, Héctor. 2005. Community-based organizations and migration in New York City. *Journal of Ethnic and Migration Studies* 31(5): 889-909.

Cordero-Guzmán, Héctor, Nina Martin, Victoria Quiroz-Becerra and Nik Theodore. 2008. Voting with their feet: Nonprofit organizations and immigrant mobilization. *American Behavioral Scientist* 52(4): 598-617.

Cruz, José E. 2006. Latino Politics in Connecticut: Between Political Representation and Policy Responsiveness. In *Latinos in New England*, ed. Andrés Torres. 237–52. Philadelphia: Temple University Press.

_____. 2010. Barriers to political participation of Puerto Ricans and Hispanics in Osceola County, Florida: 1991-2007. *CENTRO: Journal of the Center for Puerto Rican Studies* 22(1): 242–85.

De la Garza, Rodolfo O. and Louis DeSipio. 2005. *Muted Voices: Latino Politics in the 2000 Elections*. Lanham, MD: Rowman and Littlefield.

DeSipio, Louis. 2006. Latino Civic and Political Participation. In *Hispanics and the Future of America*, eds. Marta Tienda and Faith Mitchell. 447–79. Washington, DC: The National Academies Press.

Diaz, William A. 1996. Latino participation in America: Associational and political roles. *Hispanic Journal of Behavioral Sciences* 18(2): 154–74.

Falcón, Angelo. 1983. Puerto Rican Political Participation: New York City and Puerto Rico. In *Time for Decision: The United States and Puerto Rico*, ed. Jorge Henie. 27–54. Lanham, MD: The North-South Publishing Co.

_____. 1984. A History of Puerto Rican Politics in New York City: 1860s to 1945. In *Puerto Rican Politics in Urban America*, eds. James Jennings and Monte Rivera. Westport, CT: Greenwood Press.

Fiorina, Morris P. 1999. Extreme Voices: A Dark Side of Civic Engagement. In *Civic Engagement in American Democracy*, eds. Theda Skocpol and Morris P. Fiorina. 395–426. Washington, DC: Brookings Institution Press.

Garcia, F. Chris, Angelo Falcón and Rodolfo de la Garza. 1996. Introduction: Ethnicity and politics: Evidence from the Latino National Political Survey. *Hispanic Journal of Behavioral Sciences* 18(2): 91–103.

Garcia, John A. 1997. Political Participation: Resources and Involvement among Latinos in the American Political System. In *Latinos and the Political System*, ed. F. Chris Garcia. Notre Dame: Notre Dame University Press.

_____. 2012. *Latino Politics in America: Community, Culture, and Interests*. Lanham, MD: Rowman and Littlefield.

Glazer, Nathan and Daniel P. Moynihan. 1963. *Beyond the Melting Pot: The Negroes, Puerto Ricans, Jews, Italians, and Irish of New York City*. Cambridge, MA: MIT Press.

Haslip-Viera, Gabriel. 1996. The Evolution of the Latino Community in New York City: Early Nineteenth-century to the Present. In *Latinos in New York: Communities in Transition*, eds. Gabriel Haslip-Viera and Sherrie Baver. South Bend, IN: University of Notre Dame Press.

Hero, Rodney E. 2007. *Racial Diversity and Social Capital: Equality and Community in America*. New York: Cambridge University Press.

Jackson, Robert A. 2003. Differential influences on Latino electoral participation. *Political Behavior* 25(4): 339–66.

Jennings, James. 1988. The Puerto Rican Community: Its Political Background. In *Latinos and the Political System*, ed. F. Chris Garcia. 65–80. Notre Dame: Notre Dame University Press.

Leighly, Jan E. and Arnold Vedlitz. 1999. Race, ethnicity, and political participation: Competing models and contrasting explanations. *Journal of Politics* 61(4): 1092–114.

Lipset, Seymour M. 1996. *American Exceptionalism: A Double-Edged Sword*. New York: W. W. Norton and Company.

Meléndez, Edgardo. 2010. Vito Marcantonio, Puerto Rican migration, and the 1949 mayoral election in New York City. *CENTRO: Journal of the Center for Puerto Rican Studies* 22(2): 198–233.

Mills, C. Wright, Clarence Senior and Rose K. Goldsen. 1950. *The Puerto Rican Journey: New York's Newest Migrants*. New York: Russell and Russell.

Nelson, Dale C. 1984. The Political Behavior of New York Puerto Ricans: Assimilation or Survival? In *The Puerto Rican Struggle: Essays on Survival in the United States*, eds. Clara Rodríguez, Virgina Sánchez-Korrol and José O. Alers. 90-110. Maplewood, NJ: Waterfront Press.

Nie, Norman H., Jane Junn and Kenneth Stehlik-Barry. 1996. *Education and Democratic Citizenship in America*. Chicago: University of Chicago Press.

Pantoja, Adrian D. 2006. Descriptive Representation, Political Alienation, and Political Trust: The Case of Latinos in Connecticut. In *Latinos in New England*, ed. Andrés Torres. 225–36. Philadelphia: Temple University Press.

Putnam, Robert D. 2000. *Bowling Alone: The Collapse and Revival of American Community*. New York: Simon and Schuster.

_____. 2007. E Pluribus Unum: Diversity and community in the twenty-first century. The 2006 Johan Skytte Prize Lecture. *Scandinavian Political Studies* 30(2): 137–74.

Preuhs, Robert R. and Eric Gonzalez Juenke. 2011. Latino U.S. state legislators in the 1990s: Majority-minority districts, minority incorporation, and institutional position. *State Politics and Policy Quarterly* 11(1): 48–75.

Preuhs, Robert R. and Rodney E. Hero. 2011. A different kind of representation: Black and Latino descriptive representation and the role of ideological cuing. *Political Research Quarterly* 64(1): 157–71.

Rocha, Rene R. and Rodolfo Espino. 2010. Segregation, immigration and Latino participation in ethnic politics. *American Politics Research* 38(4): 614-635.

Rocha, Rene R., Caroline J. Tolbert, Daniel C. Bowen and Christopher J. Clark. 2010. Race and turnout: Does descriptive representation in state legislatures increase minority voting? *Political Research Quarterly* 63(4): 890–907.

Rosenstone, Steven J. and John M. Hansen. 1993. *Mobilization, Participation and Democracy in America*. New York: MacMillan Publishing Company.

Sánchez-Korrol, Virginia E. 1994. *From Colonia to Community: The History of Puerto Ricans in New York City*. Berkeley: University of California Press.

Skocpol, Theda and Ziad Munson. 2000. A nation of organizers: The institutional origins of civic voluntarism in the United States. *American Political Science Review* 94(3): 527–46.

Skocpol, Theda, Marshall Ganz, Ziad Munson, Bayliss Camp, Michele Swers and Jennifer Oser. 1999. How Americans Became Civic. In *Civic Engagement in American Democracy*, ed. Theda Skocpol and Morris P. Fiorina. 27-80. Washington, DC: Brookings Institution Press.

Vargas-Ramos, Carlos. 2003. The political participation of Puerto Ricans in New York City. *CENTRO: Journal of the Center for Puerto Rican Studies* 15(1): 40–71.

Verba, Sidney, Kay L. Schlozman and Henry E. Brady. 1995. *Voice and Equality: Civic Voluntarism in American Politics*. Cambridge, MA: Harvard University Press.

CONTRIBUTORS

KOFI AMPAABENG (sampaabeng@impaquint.com) is a research economist at IMPAQ International, LLC.

JUDITH APONTE (jap@hunter.cuny.edu) is associate professor at Hunter-Bellevue School of Nursing, Hunter College, CUNY.

RAMÓN BORGES-MÉNDEZ (rborgesmendez@clark.edu) is associate professor of Community Development and Planning at Clark University.

KURT BIRSON (kb315@hunter.cuny.edu)is a research assistant at the Center for Puerto Rican Studies, Hunter College, CUNY.

HARRY FRANQUI-RIVERA (hf14@hunter.cuny.edu) is a research associate at the Center for Puerto Rican Studies, Hunter College, CUNY.

JUAN C. GARCÍA-ELLÍN (jcgarcia@ucla.edu) is a former research associate at the Center for Puerto Rican Studies, Hunter College, CUNY.

ALEJANDRO MACARRÓN (alejandro@macarron.biz) is the founder and general manager of the Demographic Renaissance Foundation, Madrid, Spain.

EDWIN MELÉNDEZ (emele@hunter.cuny.edu) is the director of the Center for Puerto Rican Studies and a professor of Urban Affairs and Planning at Hunter College, CUNY.

LUIS O. REYES (luisoreyes@aol.com) is a research associate at the Center for Puerto Rican Studies, Hunter College, CUNY.

ANNA ROSOFSKY (anna.rosofsky@gmail.com) is a Ph.D. student at Boston University School of Public Health.

PATRICIA SILVER (patricia.silver@hunter.cuny.edu) is a research associate at the Center for Puerto Rican Studies, Hunter College, CUNY.

CARLOS VARGAS-RAMOS (cvargasr@hunter.cuny.edu) is a research associate at the Center for Puerto Rican Studies, Hunter College, CUNY.

M. ANNE VISSER (mavisser@ucdavis.edu) is assistant professor of Human and Community Development at University of California Davis.

INDEX

34789883R00179

Made in the USA
Charleston, SC
15 October 2014